T0301467

THE LABOR FORCE IN ECONOMIC DEVELOPMENT

JOHN D. DURAND

The Labor Force in Economic Development

A Comparison of
International Census Data,
1946-1966

PRINCETON UNIVERSITY PRESS · 1975

Library of Congress *Cataloging in Publication* Data
will be found on the last printed page of this book

Composed in Linotype Times Roman and printed
in the *United States of America* by Princeton
University Press, Princeton, New Jersey

ISBN 978-0-691-64463-9

Preface

This monograph presents a part of the results of a world-wide study of labor force dimensions and structure being conducted at the Population Studies Center, University of Pennsylvania, under the joint direction of the two undersigned research associates. The primary objective of the study is to explore factors and processes of growth and structural change in the labor force which accompany economic development. The present monograph sets out findings with regard to sex and age patterns of participation in economic activities, size of the labor force in proportion to population, and changes in these respects associated with the economic development of countries around the world during the first two decades following World War II. The variations of labor-force structure in terms of industry, occupation, and status groups are the subject of another monograph now in preparation. The research was made possible by a grant from the National Science Foundation.

The inspiration of this project came from discussions during 1965 and 1966 among a group of demographers and economists convened by the Social Science Research Council. The group consisted of Ansley J. Coale, Richard A. Easterlin, Milos Macura, George J. Stolnitz, Victor L. Urquidi, and the undersigned. Discussion focused on needs for information and avenues of research on interrelations of population, manpower, and economic development, with special reference to conditions of low income, predominance of agriculture, and rapid growth of population. Realization of the inadequacy of existing knowledge of these matters and their importance in relation to population policy and development strategy prompted us to undertake the research of which the present monograph reports some results. We are indebted to the members of the group named above for advice on initial drafts of the study plan.

We wish to express our gratitude also to the many others who have advised and assisted us in this work. We are indebted especially to Simon Kuznets, Pravin Visaria, Ester Boserup, and Richard Bilsborrow for advice on the design and execution of the research project as a whole and for critical review of drafts of the chapters of this monograph. Among those who have helped us by providing materials, we extend our thanks especially to Pravin Visaria, Zdenek Vavra, the Centro Latinoamericano de Demografia (CELADE), the United Nations Statistical Office, the Manpower Division of the International Labour Office, El Colegio de México, and the Office of Population Research, Princeton University. Last but not least, we are grateful for the hundreds of hours of devoted work by Phyllis Ryan and the team of research assistants under her direction in compiling and processing the statistical material, by Lydia Christaldi in preparing tables, drafting charts, and checking the manuscript, and by Miranda Reinis, Rebecca Brunswig, and Diana Kaneshige in typing the manuscript.

John D. Durand
Ann R. Miller

Contents

Contents

Appendices

List of Figures

List of Tables

Tables

xii

Tables

Appendix Tables

THE LABOR FORCE IN ECONOMIC DEVELOPMENT

ONE

Introduction

1.1. *Objectives and Scope of the Study*

A nation's economy has been described as a huge machine that devours natural resources, labor, and capital and turns out the multitude of goods and services that make up the gross national product.[1] But the economy is not an inanimate contraption of steel and concrete; it is primarily an organization of human beings, and it has some attributes of a living organism. It can grow and expand its capacity to consume inputs and produce outputs; and, like a tree, how well it grows depends very much on the environment in which it is planted. For the growth of the economy, while the wealth of the natural environment is relevant, it is the human environment that is crucial. The social and political institutions, the scales of values, and above all the qualities of the people are primary ingredients of the soil and atmosphere in which economic growth will flourish or languish.

The labor force plays a central role in the growth of the economy, directly as the supplier of the most important input into production, and indirectly as the dominant influence in the human environment. The qualities of this environment and the qualities of the labor input are inseparable. Many economists attribute more importance to these qualities than to any other cause of differences in the wealth of nations and their economic progress. Major importance is attached to the skills and aptitudes of the workers, their educational qualifications, the state of their health, their ambitions, their mobility, and their readiness to adopt new ideas and methods. The formation of such qualities is not exogenous to the economic system. It is fostered by the development of modern economic organization and nourished by consumption of the products, including not only such items as educational and medical services and essential food, clothing, and shelter, but also a wide range of other goods and services that may stretch the mind and whet the appetite for a better living.

Quantitative as well as qualitative aspects of development of the labor force are important: its growth in relation to the growth of

---

[1] Lance E. Davis and others, *American Economic Growth: An Economist's History of the United States* (New York, 1972), p. 2.

population and capital and to the advance of technology; its composition in terms of sex, age groups, and other characteristics of workers; its deployment among industry sectors, occupation groups, and status categories (employees, employers, self-employed, and unpaid family workers); its distribution between rural and urban sectors and among regions of a country. The formation of qualities of the labor force cannot be independent of these variables, and all are linked in mutual relationships with the productivity and dynamism of the economy. Efforts to manage economic and human development demand knowledge of these relationships—a fund of knowledge that the social sciences have only begun to accumulate.

Within the wide field of research relevant to these questions, the present study focuses on some basic demographic dimensions of the labor force and their changes in the process of economic development. The dimensions considered are the relative size of the labor force in proportion to the population, and measures of participation in the labor force by males and females and various age groups. The labor force/population ratio is one factor in the level of output per head that the economy is capable of producing. The labor force participation rates (or activity rates, as they will be called for convenience) relate to the demographic composition of the labor force as an aspect of its qualitative development as well as to the organization of the society and the style of life. Factors that influence these dimensions of the labor force and their changes will be examined, and an attempt will be made to define typical patterns of their changes in countries undergoing economic development and demographic transition.

The study is based on a world-wide compilation of labor force and population statistics of censuses taken during the two decades 1946–1966. This provides measures of labor force dimensions for a hundred countries in varied economic, demographic, and cultural circumstances. Associations between economic development and labor force characteristics can be studied both in a cross-sectional view of differences between countries and a longitudinal analysis of changes during the intervals between censuses.

Thanks to the progress of census taking in less-developed countries since World War II, the data base for such a comparative international study is much broader now than it was in the past. Before the war, limitations of data confined research on labor force characteristics largely to developed countries. Although the historical statistics of some of these countries provided some view of their experience in less advanced stages of development, this view was obscured by the defects of labor force classifications in the early censuses and the discontinuity caused by changes in the classification systems from one census to the next.[2] Progress since the war in modernizing census methods in less-developed countries, and the taking of censuses in many countries where this primary statistical source had been lacking, have opened a much wider and clearer view of labor force characteristics and changes under conditions of low income and little-developed technology and economic organization.

A path-breaking study undertaken during the 1950s by the United Nations Population Division, based on the data of early postwar censuses, produced a broad cross-sectional picture of patterns of participation in the labor force by sex-age groups of the population in countries at different levels of development.[3] This was supplemented by the Collver-Langlois study of economic activities of the female population in metropolitan areas of countries around the world, which also ranks as a classic in this field.[4] The present study goes farther along the paths marked out by those earlier studies, taking advantage of the wider coverage of countries and fuller classifications of labor force characteristics furnished by more recent censuses. Most important, a temporal dimension is added by the analysis of changes during the intervals between postwar censuses. The data from less-developed countries available to the authors of the earlier studies offered little scope for this.

A recent study by the International Labour Office,[5] undertaken to obtain a basis for a world-wide series of labor force projections,

[2] With reference to the United States, see Stanley Lebergott, *Manpower in Economic Growth: The American Record since 1800* (New York, 1964); John D. Durand, *The Labor Force in the United States, 1890–1960* (New York, 1948). For comparative historical studies of secular trends of labor force participation rates in developed countries, see Clarence E. Long, *The Labor Force under Changing Income and Employment* (Princeton, 1958); C. E. V. Leser, "Trends in Women's Work Participation," *Population Studies* 12 (1958), 100–10.

[3] United Nations, *Demographic Aspects of Manpower: Sex and Age Patterns of Participation in Economic Activities* (New York, 1958).

[4] Andrew Collver and Eleanor Langlois, "The Female Labor Force in Metropolitan Areas: An International Comparison," *Economic Development and Cultural Change* 10 (1962), 367–85.

[5] International Labour Office, *Labour Force Projections, 1965–1985. Part VI. Methodological Supplement, First Edition, 1971* (Geneva, 1973).

5

includes an analysis of variations of labor force participation rates and their changes during the decade of the 1950s in countries at different levels of economic development, which partly parallels the analysis in the present study. The patterns of variations found in the I.L.O. study are similar, on the whole, to those indicated by the present study, in spite of some important differences in the methods of analysis and the treatment of the problems of non-comparability in the census measures.

The monumental work of the United Nations, *The Determinants and Consequences of Population Trends*, recently published in a revised and updated edition, contains a chapter on "Demographic Aspects of Manpower," in which findings of many studies on the variations of labor force dimensions and factors influencing them are summarized, with extensive bibliographical references.[6]

No study of the kinds of questions addressed here can be expected to reach definitive conclusions. The findings are inevitably somewhat obsolete when the work is completed. As the results of new censuses become available, the scope for analysis widens. Especially for longitudinal study of changes in labor force dimensions in countries undergoing economic development, the material is being greatly enriched by tabulations of the returns of censuses taken around 1970, which could not be included in the data base for the present study. Its objectives have been achieved if it has charted useful directions for future research and if, in the meantime, its findings serve provisionally as useful contributions to knowledge of human factors in economic growth.

1.2. *Coverage of Data*

This study is based on a compilation of labor force statistics derived from national population censuses and demographic sample surveys taken in the years 1946 to 1966 inclusive, in countries which had 500,000 or more inhabitants in 1960. Sample survey data are included instead of comprehensive census data for some countries where the latter were lacking, but no attempt has been made to compile time series of sample survey data for countries where such surveys are conducted currently as supplements to

[6] United Nations, *The Determinants and Consequences of Population Trends. New Summary of Findings on Interaction of Demographic, Economic and Social Factors* I (New York, 1973), chapter IX.

census benchmarks. So far as possible, data were drawn from original publications of the national statistical agencies. Where the national publications could not be obtained, figures were taken from the United Nations *Demographic Yearbooks* and the International Labour Office *Year Books of Labour Statistics*.

Statistics of at least one census in the period 1946 to 1966 were obtained for 100 of the 136 countries listed in the United Nations *Demographic Yearbooks* with an estimated 1960 population of 500,000 or more. Statistics of two or more censuses, providing measures of labor force changes during intercensal periods, were obtained for 58 countries. Data of some censuses were not included in the compilation because they were obtained too late to be processed and tabulated, because large components of the population or areas of the country were not covered by the enumerations, because a comprehensive and consistent set of population and labor force tabulations was not found, because conditions of the economy and labor market at the time of the census were abnormal, or because the labor force enumerations were judged to be inconsistent with those of other censuses of the same country. The censuses that were excluded for various reasons are listed in Appendix B.1. Labor force estimates for some countries, shown in the I.L.O. *Year Books of Labour Statistics*, which appeared not to be based on national population censuses or demographic sample surveys, were not included.

This compilation of data provides comprehensive coverage as of at least one postwar census for countries in some regions, but relatively poorer coverage in others. Table 1.1 shows the extent of coverage of nine regional groups of countries that have been defined for the analysis of regional variations, as explained in chapter 3. It can be seen that there is serious underrepresentation of the less-developed regions, especially tropical Africa. The defects of coverage are greater when it comes to measures of changes between censuses. The regional distribution of the fifty-eight countries for which measures of intercensal changes were obtained is very uneven; tropical Africa is without any representation, and the representation of Moslem countries, South and East Asia, and Eastern Europe leaves much to be desired. In analyzing these data, we must be wary of distortions resulting from the defects of geographical coverage as well as those due to error and noncomparability in the labor force measures.

Introduction

Table 1.1. Coverage of data

Regional groups[a]	All countries of 500,000 or more population		Data of at least one census obtained			Data of two or more censuses obtained[b]		
	Number of countries	Total population in millions, 1960	Number of countries	Population in millions, 1960	Percent of total population	Number of countries	Population in millions, 1960	Percent total popul.
All regions	136	2,953	100	2,125	72.0	58	1,025	34
1. Tropical Africa	34	170	15	83	48.8	-	-	-
2. Arab countries	14	93	9	79	84.9	1	26	27
3. Other Moslem countries	14	271	7	241	88.9	3	50	18.
4. South and East Asia	26	1,559	16	835	53.6	9	148	9.
5. Latin America, Spain and Portugal	22	240	22	240	100.0	6	212	88.
6. Eastern Europe	9	332	9	332	100.0	7	100	30.
7. Middle Europe	7	176	7	176	100.0	6	165	93.
8. Northwestern Europe, Northern America, and Oceania	13	305	11	303	99.3	11	303	99.
9. Miscellaneous	9	30	9	30	100.0	6	23	76.

a
For definitions of regional groups, see Chapter 3, section 3.1. Sums of figures for regional groups exceed totals for all countries because some of the groups overlap.
b
Not including countries for which data of more than one census were found but only those of one census were included in the compilation for reasons noted in Appendix B.1.

1.3. Reliability and Comparability of Measures

According to internationally recommended standards for population censuses, the economically active population (labor force, in the terminology used for convenience in this study) is defined as those individuals who furnish the supply of labor for production of economic goods and services.[7] The concept of economic goods and services in this context corresponds to the concept of income in statistics of national accounts. Thus the members of the labor force are the producers of a nation's income, and the remainder of the population can be considered as dependents in the sense that they consume income without taking part in the work of producing it. Included in the labor force are paid employees, employers and self-employed persons who work for profit, and unpaid family workers (relatives who assist without pay in a family-operated income-producing enterprise such as a farm,

[7] United Nations, Statistical Office, *Principles and Methods for the 1970 Population Censuses* (ST/STAT/SER.M/44), pp. 61–63.

8

store, handicraft industry, etc.). Unemployed workers are included as well as those actually employed in income-producing jobs at any given time. Outside the labor force are housewives, students, retired and disabled workers, institutional inmates, young children, and others who do not work at income-producing jobs, although they may receive income in the form of rents, dividends, pensions, etc.

While this basic concept is fairly well established in census practices in most countries, there are important variations in details of the definitions and ways of formulating the census questions that detract greatly from international comparability of the measures. Comparability is impaired further by varying interpretations that field workers and respondents may give to similar questions and definitions, and by errors and biases in responses and coverage of the enumerations.

The most important point of divergence in definitions is in the classification of individuals who play a dual role, both as income producers and as housewives, students, etc. In some censuses, the questions refer to the individual's principal activity. Numerous part-time, seasonal, and other irregular workers may then be left out of the count of the labor force. In other censuses, it is provided in principle that all persons engaged to any extent in work for pay or profit or as unpaid family workers should be counted in the labor force, although it is unlikely that a complete enumeration would be achieved in any case. The latter basis of enumeration is the one specified in international standards for population census statistics, except that in the case of unpaid family workers some minimal amount or regularity of involvement in the work of the family-operated enterprise is recommended as a qualification for their inclusion in the labor force.

Another important point of divergence is the time reference of census questions about activities. Formerly, in most censuses, no particular time reference was specified; the questions referred more or less vaguely to the individual's usual occupation. The practice of asking about activities during a specified period of time has been gaining vogue in recent censuses, and this is recommended in the international standards, although some experts express doubts about the suitability of this procedure, especially for censuses in less-developed countries where measures of seasonal variations are lacking. The time references specified vary: sometimes it is the census day or a brief period such as one week, sometimes several months or a year, sometimes the "working season." These varia-

9

tions may have important effects on the enumeration of seasonal and casual workers and of persons having recently joined or withdrawn from the labor force. The longer the time reference, the larger will be the measure of the labor force if all persons involved in income-producing work to any extent during the specified period are included.

Definitions of unemployed workers also vary. When the concept of usual activity was the basis of labor force enumeration, the unemployed could be identified as persons having a usual gainful occupation who were out of a job at the time of enumeration, although the measures of unemployment obtained in this way were generally not very satisfactory. In recent censuses where a specific time reference has been adopted, the unemployed have been identified by various kinds of questions relevant to availability for employment: whether they were seeking work, wanted work, and so forth, during the specified period. Variations in the forms of such questions and in details of the definitions and instructions may greatly affect census measures of unemployment, and effects on the measures of the labor force may be substantial where there is much unemployment.

Although it is in keeping with the basic concept of the labor force to include armed forces, since they are paid employees (although their service may be involuntary), armed forces are classified in some censuses with the population not in the labor force, while in others they are excluded from the coverage of the census. Sometimes a distinction is drawn in these respects between regular members of the armed forces and temporary conscripts, or between those living in military quarters and those living outside. When armed forces are either counted as not in the labor force or excluded from the census, the effect is to understate both the absolute size of the labor force and its proportion to the population. Measures of the male labor force are affected proportionately more than those of the total of both sexes, and the effect may become very important when measures for military age groups of the male population are considered.

In addition to the formal definitions, census measures of the labor force are influenced by the phrasing of the questions and arrangement of the census questionnaires, details of the instructions, and the care taken by respondents and interviewers to provide complete and accurate information. Popular preconceptions and the level of literacy in the population are also influential factors. The same questions, definitions, and procedures for enumeration may produce different results in different cultural settings.

Varying definitions and other factors of noncomparability and error are likely, in general, to affect measures of the female labor force more than the male. Agricultural workers and unpaid family workers are groups that are most sensitive to these factors. Measures of the labor force in the rural population are likely to be affected more than measures in the urban population. Among age groups, those nearest the two extremes of the span of working life are most susceptible to such influences. International comparisons of the prevalence of child labor based on census statistics are especially dubious. On the whole, it is the statistics of little-developed countries that must be treated with the most cautious reserve. In such countries, where much of the work of income production is done in family enterprises, the distinction between breadwinners and others is generally less clear-cut than it is in industrialized countries, where most of the breadwinners work for wages outside the domain of the family.

The conditions that prevail in agriculture in many countries, both at low and high levels of economic development, are conducive to extreme variations in enumerations of the female labor force. It is usually the custom that women in farming families take some part, large or small, year-round or seasonal, in the production of field crops or in other farm work that is closer to the domestic sphere (such as milking, feeding livestock, and kitchen gardening), in addition to keeping house, preparing meals, and caring for children. The number of women counted as agricultural workers in such circumstances may be large or small, depending not only on how the census questions are worded, what is said in the instructions, and who is the respondent, but also on how the roles of women are regarded in the society and what values are placed on their contributions to agricultural production on the one hand and their domestic and maternal functions on the other. In some censuses, set rules have been adopted for classifying female members of farmers' families who do not report a nonagricultural gainful occupation—either considering them all to be employed in agriculture, or counting them all as housewives not in the labor force. Such rules may be viewed as reflecting evaluations of women's roles and status in the societies concerned.

Where very few of the agricultural workers recorded in the census are women, there is a strong presumption that women's share

11

in the agricultural labor force is understated by the statistics. In some countries, this is confirmed by information given in the census reports or by data from other sources. Some examples of evidence of such understatement in a number of countries are discussed in Appendix G.1. On the other hand, where many females are reported as active in agriculture, the statistics may give an exaggerated impression of the importance of their contribution to the labor supply, since many of them may be involved only to a small extent in agricultural work. In predominantly agricultural countries, the census measures of overall dimensions of the labor force are greatly affected by the extent to which women's participation in agriculture is reported.

Not only comparisons between countries but also measures of changes in labor force dimensions from census to census within the same country may be falsified by the factors of noncomparability, error, and bias. In many countries where the concept of usual activity was the basis of labor force enumerations in early postwar censuses, the basis has been shifted in more recent censuses to activities during a specified time period. In other respects, as well, there has been a widespread tendency to sharpen the questions and definitions with more exact specifications of criteria for reporting borderline groups. It is impossible to lay down any general rule with regard to effects of such changes upon the labor force measures. The labor force enumerations in the more recent censuses were probably inflated in some countries and deflated in others, in comparison with the measures provided by earlier censuses. In any country, the size of the effect, if not its direction, would be expected to vary in different sex-age groups, occupation, industry, and status categories, and in the rural and urban sectors. The uncertainty of trend measures is greatest where data of only two censuses are available. Series of data from three or more censuses showing a consistent pattern of trends merit more confidence.

For the purposes of this study, adjustments have been made in the data of some censuses to improve comparability between countries or in time series for the same country. For example, where the labor-force tabulations excluded groups such as armed forces, unemployed workers, or persons engaged only secondarily in economic activities, and the numbers of these groups were given or a satisfactory basis for estimating them could be found, the data were adjusted to include them in the labor force. Likewise, where groups such as women engaged only in domestic duties were included in the labor force, these were deducted if a satisfactory basis was available. Details of such adjustments are stated in Appendix B.2. But the feasible adjustments were far from adequate to put the data on a firm footing of comparability.

In view of what has been said, the reader may wonder how much meaning the results of a comparative study of these statistics could have. Actually, in spite of their faults, the data exhibit patterns of variations which are certainly significant and which afford valuable insights into economic and other factors affecting the levels and trends of participation in the labor force. But it is a matter of the first importance, in interpreting these variations, to bear in mind the limitations of reliability and comparability of the data as well as the defects of regional coverage. The risk of being deceived by distorted reflections of the true patterns of variations will be a constant preoccupation in our analysis.

In addition to the factors mentioned above, the comparability of the measures is impaired by differences in age limits of the labor force enumerations, but this difficulty has been largely overcome by adjustments of the statistics. As a rule, no upper age limit is imposed, but there is commonly a lower age limit, and this varies: as low as six years or as high as fifteen years among the censuses included in the present compilation. The understatement of size of the labor force due to the age limit is trivial in most cases because few children below the specified age would be much involved in income-producing work, but the understatement may be appreciable in some cases, where the age limit does not correspond closely to the prevailing conditions of child labor. For the purpose of the present study, the statistics have been adjusted to a standard age reference of ten years and over for the labor force, with estimates as necessary where a different age limit, or no limit, was imposed in the census enumerations. The methods used for this adjustment are stated in Appendix C.1. Errors in the estimates made for this purpose would seldom have appreciable effects upon the labor force totals for ten years and over.

Finally, comparative analysis of rates of participation in the labor force according to age groups in different countries is hampered by differences in the age classifications found in the census tabulations. For the present study, the classifications have been converted to a standard format of five-year age groups up to seventy-five years, with interpolations and estimates as required. The methods are described in Appendix C.2. Errors in the adjustments to the standard age classification are unlikely to be important in most instances for age groups under sixty-five years, but appreciable errors may occur in some instances for higher age groups.

TWO

Measures of Labor Force Dimensions

2.1. *The Ratio of Producers to Consumers*

The size of the labor force in proportion to the total population—
that is, the ratio of income-producers to consumers—is measured
by the crude activity rate (CAR). This is defined for the present
study as the number of labor force members ten years of age and
over per 100 of the total population. Crude activity rates and other
measures of labor force participation are listed in Table A.1,
Appendix A, for each of the hundred countries as of each census
year for which data were compiled.

For a cross-sectional view of levels of the rates, we consider the
data for the census year nearest 1961 in those countries where data
of two or more censuses were obtained, and whatever year is given
for other countries.[1] In this cross section, the crude activity rates
range from 21.6 percent in Algeria (1966) to 59.4 in Haiti
(1950),[2] with a mean level of 38.8. (This average, and all other
averages given in the text and tables, are unweighted means that
do not take into account the differences in size of population of
the countries.) The cross-sectional census dates for ninety-five of
the hundred countries are in the period 1956 to 1966, but the data
refer to 1953 for Cuba and 1950 for Bolivia, Mozambique, and
Portuguese Guinea, as well as Haiti. The distortion due to differences in the census dates is minor compared with the distorting
effects of unbalanced representation of countries and of the factors
of noncomparability and error in the labor force measures, discussed in the preceding chapter.

Table 2A gives a list of countries where the highest and lowest
crude activity rates were recorded as of the cross-sectional census
dates.

The trend of crude activity rates throughout the world has been
predominantly downward during the postwar years. In other words,

[1] In the cases of Iran and Rumania, where 1956 and 1966 data were obtained, those of 1966 were selected for the cross section.

[2] A factor of exaggeration in the rate for Haiti is understatement of the
denominator, due to faulty enumeration of young children in the census.
This error is present in varying degrees in the statistics of many other countries, but it appears to be unusually large in the case of Haiti.

Table 2A

Haiti (1950)	59.4	Iraq (1957)	28.2
Central African Rep. (1960)	55.7	Dominican Republic (1960)	28.1
Rumania (1966)	54.2	Morocco (1960)	28.0
Dahomey (1961)	53.3	Mauritius (1962)	27.4
Thailand (1960)	53.2	Syria (1960)	25.9
Turkey (1960)	52.5	Libya (1964)	25.8
U.S.S.R. (1959)	52.2	Puerto Rico (1960)	25.4
Bulgaria (1965)	51.9	Jordan (1961)	22.8
Guinea (1954/55)	51.7	Algeria (1966)	21.6
Zaire (1955/57)	51.4		

the labor force in most countries has been growing less rapidly than the population. Annual amounts of change in the recorded crude activity rates and other labor force measures during intercensal periods for fifty-eight countries are listed in Appendix A, Table A.2. In countries where data of more than one intercensal period were obtained, we select the period most closely approximating the decade of the 1950s for the purpose of comparisons with other countries.[3] In this way, decreases of crude activity rates by .10 or more per year are indicated for forty-five of the fifty-eight countries, increases by .10 or more for only four countries, and little change in nine countries. On the average of the fifty-eight countries, the CAR decreased by .28 per year. If the trend should continue at that pace, the average level of crude activity rates would be reduced from about 39 percent to nearly 30 percent in three decades. For reasons which will be brought out later, however, it appears likely that the pace of the decreasing trend may slacken in future decades.

Table 2B is a list of countries where increases of crude activity rates were recorded and those where the largest decreases were recorded. Because of changed definitions and procedures for enumeration of the labor force adopted in the more recent censuses of many countries, the measures of intercensal changes are likely to be falsified appreciably in some cases. The remarks in the preced-

[3] An exception was made in the case of Turkey, where the intercensal period of 1955–65 was selected instead of 1955–60, in order to deemphasize short-term variations. Data of the 1950 Turkish census are not included in the present compilation because the procedures for enumeration and classification of the labor force at that census were different from those of the later censuses. In the case of Hong Kong, measures for the period 1961–66 are included as the only available intercensal changes.

Table 2B

Annual change		Annual change	
Hungary, 1949–60	+.35	Guyana, 1946–60	−.62
Japan, 1950–60	+.32	Jamaica, 1953–60	−.64
West Germany, 1950–61	+.15	South Africa, 1946–60	−.69
Hong Kong, 1961–66	+.11	Rumania, 1956–66	−.74
		Turkey, 1955–65	−.74
		Sarawak, 1947–60	−.92
		Albania, 1955–60	−1.68

ing chapter about factors of error in intercensal change measures should be recalled here. A few countries where the labor force enumerations in successive censuses appeared to be grossly incomparable have been omitted (see Appendix B.1). Some others have been retained, although the credibility of the indicated changes looks doubtful on the face: for example, the decrease of Albania's crude activity rate from 53.4 at the 1955 census to 44.9 only five years later.

There is an apparent economic advantage in a high crude activity rate since, under given conditions of productivity and extent of employment of the labor force, the amount of income that could be produced per head would vary in proportion to this rate. Haiti would seem to have a great advantage in this respect over Algeria, with almost three times as large a labor force in proportion to the population in Haiti. The prevailing trend of decreasing crude activity rates would seem to be a factor of some inhibition to the growth of income per head in a majority of countries. Several reservations are in order, however, when the economic significance of the relative size of the labor force as enumerated in censuses is interpreted in this way.

First, the cautions stated in the preceding chapter with regard to factors of error and noncomparability in the census measures should be repeated. Caution is required, especially when measures for particular countries are compared. The meaning of the difference between the recorded crude activity rates for Haiti and Algeria is dubious when the measures for these two countries are considered in isolation. It takes on a more dependable significance if it is found to conform with a general pattern of variations among countries according to regional groupings, economic conditions, etc.

Second, not all producers of valuable goods and services are in-cluded in the measures of labor force, as not all such goods and services are considered as income. The most important group of producers not included is that of housewives who produce services and goods for home consumption only.[4] Although what they pro-duce is an important part of total production (more important in less-developed than in more-developed countries), its value is not included in national income measures. If the labor force is en-larged by movement of housewives and others from the domestic sector into the sphere of income production, national income is increased at the cost of some loss of production in the domestic sector. So the economic advantage or disadvantage of a large or a small labor force should be discounted to some extent, so far as it is a matter of the deployment of manpower (or rather, mainly, of womanpower) between the domestic and income sectors of pro-duction. This is, in fact, a primary factor of differences among countries in the levels of crude activity rates.

Third, the size of the labor force serves only as a crude measure of labor supply in the income-producing sectors, since it does not take account of the amounts of working time that members of the labor force are prepared to put in. At least in more developed countries, the prevailing secular trend of shortening hours of work means that the measure of growth of the labor force exaggerates the growth of labor supply, and there is a corresponding upward bias in the trend of the crude activity rate considered as a measure of changing relative size of labor supply. The same reservation ap-plies to the interpretation of differences between countries where the norms of working hours are not the same. How many workers are available for full-time, year-round employment is another im-portant question. In many little-developed agricultural countries, the labor force is inflated by the participation of great numbers of part-time, seasonal, and casual workers, mainly women and chil-dren in farm families, whose contributions to the labor supply may be relatively minor.

Fourth, even if the labor force were measured in units of man-days or man-hours per year (as, unfortunately, it is not possible to do with the data provided for most countries), it would not be

[4] Paradoxically, in a family that operates a subsistence farm and consumes the whole product at home, those members who take part in the farm work are included by definition in the labor force, while the housewife is excluded if she does only housework.

a strictly valid measure of labor supply, since conditions of demand interact with supply factors in determining the extent of participation in the labor force, especially by women, young people, and those who are handicapped by age, infirmity, lack of skill and education, etc. The results of studies in the United States and some other industrialized countries suggest that the labor force may expand considerably in response to growing demand for labor and rising wages, and contract when unemployment rises and wages fall.[5] Likewise, in less-developed countries it is possible that deficient opportunity for employment may depress rates of labor-force participation.

Finally, it is worth stressing the obvious fact that a large supply of labor is advantageous only to the extent that it can be productively employed. Under the conditions of chronically large unemployment and underemployment that are common among developing countries, if the labor force were enlarged by increasing rates of participation on the part of adults, the consequent increase in production of income would be likely to be less than proportionate. In the extreme case of an absolute glut of labor supply, the effect would be only to swell the ranks of the unemployed and underemployed. Even in such extreme circumstances, however, an increase in the crude activity rate due to reduction of the proportion of dependent children in the population—that is, reducing the denominator rather than increasing the numerator of the rate—would tend to raise the average income per head.

2.2. The Level of Participation by Males in the Labor Force

The size of a country's labor force in proportion to its population can be considered as determined by three components: (a) the level of participation in the labor force by males according to age groups, (b) the level of participation by females according to age groups, and (c) the sex-age structure of the population. In the present study, attention will be focused mainly on components (a) and (b) and their changes in the process of economic development. The role of population structure in variations of relative size of the labor force will, however, be examined in chapter 4.

The levels of participation in the labor force by males and females according to age are measured by standardized activity rates

[5] See, among others, William G. Bowen and T. Aldrich Finegan, *The Economics of Labor Force Participation* (Princeton, 1969).

in the male and female population ten years of age and over (Stand$_m$ and Stand$_f$). These are weighted averages of age-specific activity rates of each sex (that is, percentages of labor force among the male and female population in each five-year age group from ten years up), with standard weights according to the age-sex composition of a model population representing approximately the structure of the world population in 1960. They show what percentage of a country's population of each sex, ten years of age and over, would be in the labor force if the structure of the country's population were the same as that of the model, while the age-specific activity rates of each sex were those recorded in the country's census. It should be noted that different values of these measures would be obtained by using different models of population structure as the basis for the standardization. The importance of this point is illustrated by some examples in Appendix D.

In sixteen of the hundred countries covered by this study, age classifications of the labor force were lacking or inadequate for calculating standardized activity rates. In these cases, simple percentages of labor force among the population ten years of age and over of each sex, called "refined activity rates" (RAR$_m$ and RAR$_f$) are used as substitutes for the standardized rates. In the following text, these are marked with an asterisk. See Appendix D for discussion of the reliability of refined activity rates as approximations to standardized rates.

Among the hundred countries for which data were obtained, the standardized activity rates of males as of the cross-sectional censuses range from a minimum of 61.5 percent in Puerto Rico (1960) to a maximum of *92.9 percent in the Sudan (1956),[6] with a mean value of 76.8. Nearly two-thirds of the countries have rates between 70 and 80 (see Table 2.1). Table 2C is a list of countries with the highest and lowest rates.

The trend of male standardized activity rates was downward during the intervals between postwar censuses in almost all countries for which trend measures were obtained, as shown in the lower panel of Table 2.1. The rates decreased by .10 or more

[6] In the Sudan, the numbers of population ten years of age and over for each sex used as denominators for calculating the male and female refined activity rates are approximate estimates based on the census enumeration of vaguely defined functional age groups of the population. See United Nations, *Population Growth and Manpower in the Sudan* (New York, 1964). It is possible that the refined activity rates might be exaggerated because of underestimation of the denominators.

Table 2.1. Levels and intercensal changes of male standardized activity rates, in national total, rural and urban populations

	National totals, all countries	Countries for which rural and urban data were obtained	
		Rural	Urban

Levels of Stand$_m$ or RAR$_m$, cross-sectional censuses

Number of countries	100	41	41
Mean level	76.8	78.5	71.0
Frequency distribution:			
Under 70.0	10	5	15
70.0-74.9	28	8	18
75.0-79.9	35	9	8
80.0-84.9	20	12	-
85.0 and over	7	7	-

Intercensal changes of Stand$_m$ or RAR$_m$

Number of countries	58	16	16
Mean annual change	-.35	-.20	-.32
Frequency distribution:			
+.10 or more	2	-	3
+.09 to -.09	9	3	-
-.10 to -.49	34	13	8
-.50 or more	13	-	5

Table 2C

Sudan (1956)	*92.9	Czechoslovakia (1961)	69.7
Togo (1958/60)	*89.5	United States (1960)	69.2
Dahomey (1961)	*87.3	Belgium (1961)	69.1
Turkey (1960)	87.0	Mauritius (1962)	68.8
Haiti (1950)	86.6	Canada (1961)	68.6
Ecuador (1962)	85.2	South Korea (1960)	68.3
Honduras (1961)	85.1	Bulgaria (1965)	66.0
		Algeria (1966)	*65.7
		Israel (1961)	*65.6
		Puerto Rico (1960)	61.5

* Refined rates used as substitutes for standardized rates.

per year in forty-seven countries, changed by less than .10 per year in nine countries, and increased by .10 or more in only two countries (Portugal, with an increase from 80.3 at the 1950 census to 83.6 in 1960, and Ecuador, with an increase from 83.7 in 1950 to 85.2 in 1962). The increases in these two countries can be explained at least in part by changes in the census definitions.[7]

[7] In Ecuador, unemployed persons were excluded from the labor force enumeration in the 1950 census and included in 1962. Male refined activity rates excluding the unemployed at both census dates are 81.5 for 1950 and 78.5 for 1962. In Portugal, first-job seekers (persons without

Factors of error and noncomparability may also have affected the measures of intercensal changes in many other countries, possibly falsifying them considerably in some instances. But the fact of an almost universal trend of decreasing levels of participation by males in the labor force, in countries around the world, is beyond doubt.

2.3. *Age Patterns of Participation by Males in the Labor Force*

There are three principal phases in the typical cycle of working life for a cohort of male population: first, the ages of entry into the labor force, from the time when the first members of the cohort start working up to the age at which the activity rate in the cohort reaches its maximum; second, the prime working ages, when the activity rate remains on a high plateau; and third, the ages of retirement, when the rate drops off, gradually at first and more steeply as age advances. Retirement should be understood in this context as including forced withdrawal from the labor force on account of disability, superannuation, obsolescence of skill, or other causes, as well as voluntary retirement. Variations occur chiefly in the tempos of entry and retirement—in other words, the distributions of entries and retirements over the ages in the first and third phases of the cycle. It is mainly by these distributions that the overall level of participation by males in each country's labor force is governed, as measured by the standardized activity rate. Although the height of activity rates of men in the prime working ages may also vary, differences between countries in this respect are relatively slight in most cases.

In Figure 2.1, consider the curve of mean levels of age-specific activity rates of males according to the cross-sectional censuses of the eighty-four countries for which these measures were obtained. In this average pattern, the ages of entry into the labor force, defined as those younger age groups in which the activity rate has not yet reached its maximum, comprise the groups up to and including 25 to 29 years. The prime working ages comprise the groups between 30 and 45 years; and the ages of retirement,

---

previous work experience seeking work) were excluded in 1950 and included in 1960. Refined male activity rates excluding first-job seekers at both dates are 81.1 for 1950 and 82.2 for 1960.

Figure 2.I Age patterns of male activity rates

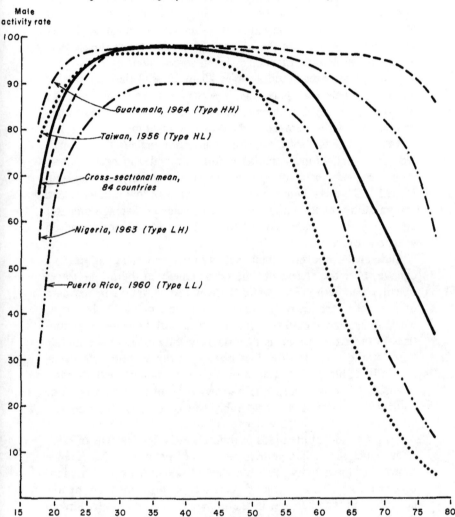

Male
activity rate

Guatemala, 1964 (Type HH)

Taiwan, 1956 (Type HL)

Cross-sectional mean,
84 countries

Nigeria, 1963 (Type LH)

Puerto Rico, 1960 (Type LL)

Age (years)

where the activity rate drops appreciably below its maximum, begin with the group of 45 to 49 years. (Strictly speaking, the curve
reaches its absolute maximum in the age group of 35 to 39, but
differences within the range of 30 to 44 years are insignificant.)
Since most of the entries into the labor force take place before the
age of 20 and most of the retirements after age 65, it is useful to
subdivide the entry and retirement ages, designating the ages under

23

20 as the primary ages of entry into the labor force, 20 to 29 as the ages of late entry, 45 to 64 as the ages of early retirement, and 65 and over as the primary ages of retirement. To be sure, the age limits of these phases of the working-life cycle are not the same in all countries; activity rates of males in some countries are already virtually at their maximum in ages 25 to 29, and they do not fall appreciably below the maximum in some countries before 50 to 54 or even 55 to 59. But in spite of such variations, the age ranges defined here with reference to the cross-sectional mean pattern will serve as a satisfactory frame for comparisons. Thus the age pattern of participation in the labor force by males in each country is represented succinctly by five figures: the activity rate for ages 15 to 19 (10 to 14 being omitted on account of low reliability and comparability of the measures), and unweighted average rates for age groups in the ranges of 20 to 29, 30 to 44, 45 to 64, and 65 years and over.[8]

Differences in levels of male activity rates between countries and changes over the course of time occur chiefly in the primary ages of entry and retirement, while there is less variation in the ages of late entry and early retirement, and least of all in the prime working ages. A measure of the extent of variations among countries in the cross section is furnished by the ranges of the middle third of the rates for the five phases of the working-life cycle, shown in Table 2.2. One-third of the countries have activity rates of males 30 to 44 within the narrow range of 97.1 to 98.0. The comparable ranges are considerably wider for ages 20 to 29 and 45 to 64, and very much wider for 15 to 19 and 65 and over.

To get a view of the kinds of differences in age patterns of these rates, we can classify countries by types of patterns with reference to levels of the activity rates in certain phases of the cycle. A country's rate for given ages may be classified as high, medium, or low according to whether it is in the upper, middle, or lower third of the distribution of all countries in the cross section. Denoting the combination of a high rate for ages 15 to 19 with a low rate for 65 and over as HL, low for 15 to 19 with high for 65 and over as LH, medium rates for both age groups as MM, and so forth, we

---

[8] A more sophisticated and detailed representation of the age pattern is obtained by constructing working life tables, which show, age by age, the rates of accession to the labor force and rates of separation by death and by retirement, as well as measures of average length of working life. See United Nations, *Methods of Analysing Census Data on Economic Activities of the Population* (New York, 1968).

Table 2.2. Levels of male age-specific activity rates in national total, rural
and urban populations, cross-sectional censuses

Age groups	National totals, all countries	Countries for which rural and urban data were obtained			
		Total	Rural	Urban	Urban-rural difference[a]
Number of countries	84	36	36	36	36
Mean levels of rates					
15-19 years	65.6	63.7	71.8	50.2	-21.6
20-29 years	93.4	92.2	94.2	88.8	-5.4
30-44 years	97.3	96.8	97.1	95.8	-1.3
45-64 years	90.5	90.8	92.8	87.3	-5.5
65 years and over	50.3	55.5	60.9	45.7	-15.2
20-24 years	90.5	89.1	92.3	84.0	-8.3
25-29 years	96.3	95.3	96.2	93.7	-2.5
30-34 years	97.4	96.7	97.1	95.8	-1.3
35-39 years	97.5	96.9	97.2	96.1	-1.1
40-44 years	97.0	96.6	97.0	95.6	-1.4
45-49 years	96.4	96.1	96.7	94.7	-2.0
50-54 years	94.4	94.0	95.2	91.9	-3.3
55-59 years	90.4	90.6	92.9	86.5	-6.4
60-64 years	80.5	82.6	86.3	76.0	-10.3
65-69 years	65.0	70.1	75.7	60.5	-15.2
70-74 years	50.7	56.3	61.9	46.6	-15.3
75 years and over	35.2	40.2	45.0	30.0	-15.0
Middle third ranges					
15-19 years	59.6-72.3	59.2-71.4	64.8-80.9	45.8-54.7	
20-29 years	92.8-95.1	92.6-94.3	92.5-97.0	89.9-91.2	
30-44 years	97.1-98.0	96.6-97.6	96.9-98.1	96.0-96.3	
45-64 years	89.4-93.5	89.5-92.5	91.3-95.4	86.1-90.2	
65 years and over	41.8-57.8	45.4-63.8	56.1-74.7	40.1-52.1	

[a] Urban minus rural rate.

obtain the frequency distribution of types in the cross section of eighty-four countries:

HH: Early entry, late retirement   14
MH: Medium entry, late retirement   10
LH: Late entry, late retirement   4
HM: Early entry, medium retirement   8
MM: Medium entry, medium retirement   11
LM: Late entry, medium retirement   9
HL: Early entry, early retirement   6
ML: Medium entry, early retirement   7
LL: Late entry, early retirement   15

Examples of types HH, LL, HL, and LH are charted in Figure 2.1. Type MM is represented, of course, by the curve of the mean rates for all countries in the cross section.

Types HH, MM, and LL constitute an ideal sequence in the transition from a regime of high participation by males in the labor force to one of low participation, which is presumed to be the typical experience of countries undergoing modern economic development. It is remarkable that these three regular patterns appear in less than half of the countries in the cross section and that the highly irregular patterns, LH and HL, are found in as many as ten out of the eighty-four countries. If the levels of activity rates in ages 20 to 29 and 45 to 64 as well as those in 15 to 19 and 65 and over are taken into account, the frequency of fully regular patterns is diminished further. Thus, denoting by HHHH the pattern of high rates in all four age groups of entry and retirement, by MMMM the pattern of medium rates in all four, and by LLLL the pattern of low rates in all four, we find these three patterns in fewer than one-fourth of the countries, namely:

HHHH: Ecuador, El Salvador, Guatemala, Haiti, Honduras, Mozambique, Namibia, Nicaragua, Paraguay, Turkey

MMMM: Central African Republic, Ireland, Panama

LLLL: Belgium, Bulgaria, Canada, South Korea, Mauritius, Puerto Rico, United States.

When the same scheme of classification is applied to a cross section of earlier postwar census data, from the censuses taken around 1950, most countries are assigned to the same type in the earlier and the more recent classification. In that sense, the age patterns of male activity rates in individual countries are stable in most cases. There has, however, been a general shift during the postwar years in the direction of lower activity rates of males in both entry and retirement ages, particularly below age twenty and above age sixty-five. This shift, which represents the age pattern of the decreasing trend of male standardized activity rates, is reflected in Table 2.3 by mean annual changes during intercensal periods in the rates for each age group.

2.4. Rural and Urban Patterns of Participation by Males in the Labor Force

Males in city populations typically enter the labor force later and retire earlier than they do in rural communities, and so urbaniza-

Table 2.3. Levels and intercensal changes of male and female age-specific
activity rates, national total populations

Age groups	Males		Females	
	Mean level	Mean annual change	Mean level	Mean annual change
15-19 years	65.6	-1.05	36.4	-.50
20-29 years	93.4	-.06	37.6	+.11
30-44 years	97.3	+.01	34.0	+.11
45-64 years	90.5	-.16	29.3	-.03
65 years and over	50.3	-1.00	11.8	-.37
20-24 years	90.5	-.16	40.8	+.11
25-29 years	96.3	+.03	34.4	+.11
30-34 years	97.4	+.04	33.2	+.10
35-39 years	97.5	+.01	33.9	+.11
40-44 years	97.0	-.03	34.8	+.12
45-49 years	96.4	-.03	34.5	+.09
50-54 years	94.4	-.06	32.5	+.07
55-59 years	90.4	-.13	28.2	-.06
60-64 years	80.5	-.43	21.8	-.21
65-69 years	65.0	-.98	16.4	-.37
70-74 years	50.7	-1.08	11.7	-.38
75 years and over	35.2	-.95	7.2	-.35

Mean levels refer to cross-sectional censuses of 84 countries.
Mean annual changes refer to intercensal periods in 45 countries.

tion is a factor in the levels and trends of national activity rates of males. While urbanization and economic development are, of course, not the same thing, they are akin to each other and related in similar ways to the patterns of labor force participation.

Data on the labor force in rural and urban sectors were obtained for forty-one countries, thirty-six of them with data by age groups, only sixteen with measures of intercensal changes in standardized or refined activity rates, and only twelve countries with measures of intercensal changes in rural and urban age-specific activity rates. The data are tabulated for each country in the Appendix, Tables A.2, A.4, A.9, and A.10.[9]

Several shortcomings of the rural and urban data should be noted, in addition to their relatively narrow coverage of countries. First, their regional distribution is badly unbalanced. Fourteen of the forty-one countries for which any rural and urban data were obtained are in the regional group of Latin America, Spain, and Portugal, while Africa and Eastern and Middle Europe are very scantily represented. The small number of countries and the un-balanced distribution restrict especially the analysis of time trends

[9] The following analysis corroborates and in some respects amplifies the findings of Ettore Denti, "Sex-age Patterns of Labour Force Participation by Urban and Rural Populations," *International Labour Review* (December 1968).

Labor force dimensions

in rural and urban labor force dimensions. Second, the census definitions of rural and urban population are far from being standardized, and variations in this respect may affect considerably the rural and urban activity rates. Finally, the distribution of the urban population by size of cities is left out of account, and variations in this respect also may influence the levels of urban activity rates. In view of these defects, it is advisable to focus attention on the broad outlines of patterns that appear in the data, without attaching undue significance to details and irregularities.

As measured in the censuses, activity rates of males are almost universally lower in the urban than in the rural sector. Higher urban than rural male standardized activity rates appear in the cross-sectional censuses of only three of the forty-one countries, namely, Canada, Israel, and the United States.[10] The size of the urban-rural difference is quite substantial in most countries, as indicated by the mean levels of 78.5 for the rural and 71.0 for the urban standardized rates. More than three-fourths of the countries in the cross section have urban rates below 75 and none exceeds 80, while less than one-third have rural rates below 75 and nearly one-half are above 80 (Table 2.1). We can infer that the advance of urbanization makes for diminishing differences among countries as well as a generally decreasing trend of participation by males in the labor force.

In every age group, the average level of activity rates of males is lower in the urban than in the rural sectors of the thirty-six countries for which rural and urban age-specific rates were obtained (Figure 2.2 and Table 2.2). In each of the five age ranges representing phases of the working-life cycle, moreover, the middle third of the distribution of urban activity rates is wholly below that of the rural rates. The urban-rural difference is greatest in the frequency of early entry into the labor force, before age twenty; quite large also in the tempo of retirement after age sixty-five; and

[10] In the United States, the level of male activity rates in the rural population is depressed by the location of a disproportionately large fraction of the institutional population in rural areas as well as by the presence of a large suburban population, including many commuters employed in the cities. At the 1960 census, male activity rates were highest in the rural-farm population, lowest in the rural-nonfarm, and intermediate in the urban population. See *United States Census of Population, 1960, United States Summary, Detailed Characteristics*, table 194. The measures for Israel are refined activity rates and it is possible that differences in age structure between the urban and the rural population might account for the anomaly in this case.

28

Figure 2.2 Age-specific activity rates of males in rural and urban sectors: cross-sectional mean patterns for 36 countries

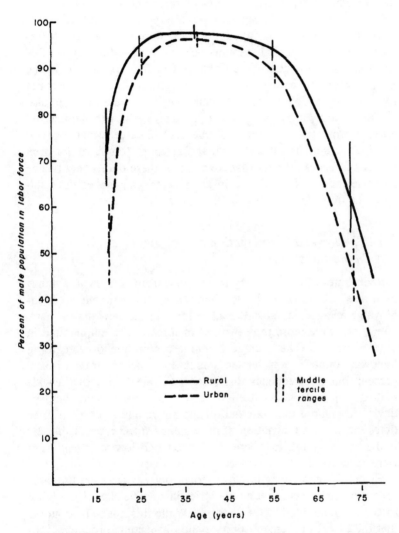

smaller but still quite substantial in the frequency of earlier retirement and the tempo of entry after age twenty. A slight urban-rural difference appears also in the height of the activity rates of men in prime working ages. Although the difference in average levels of the rates for ages 30 to 44 is small, it is remarkably consistent; thirty of the thirty-six countries have lower urban than rural activity rates of men in this age group.

29

The decreasing trend of participation by males in the labor force was almost universal both in rural and urban populations during the postwar years, if the measures of rural and urban intercensal changes obtained for sixteen countries are representative. Decreases of rural male standardized activity rates were recorded in all sixteen countries, in annual amounts ranging from —.08 in Argentina to —.43 in Puerto Rico (see Table A.4 in the Appendix). In the urban sector, the annual changes ranged from —.65 in Nicaragua to +.19 in the United States. Smaller increases were recorded also in Japan and Puerto Rico. On the average, the urban rates decreased more than the rural (Table 2.1). Intercensal changes of age-specific activity rates in rural and urban sectors have not been tabulated because the narrow coverage of these data (only twelve countries, eight of which are in Latin America) makes their significance doubtful.

2.5. The Level of Participation by Females in the Labor Force

Activity rates of females vary much more from country to country than those of males do. Fewer than one out of ten females of employable age is counted in the labor force in the censuses of many countries, while more than two out of three are so enumerated in other countries. The average in our cross section of data for a hundred countries is a female standardized activity rate of 32.0 percent, but the frequency distribution (Table 2.4) shows a wide scatter with little concentration around the mean. The standard deviation is more than one-half of the mean, and more than three times the standard deviation of male standardized rates. Table 2D is the list of countries where the highest and lowest female rates were recorded in the cross-sectional censuses.

Evidently the varying levels of female activity rates are the main source of differences among countries in relative size of the labor force, as enumerated in the censuses. While it is not to be doubted that the extent of women's participation in income-producing jobs does differ significantly from country to country, the statistics almost certainly exaggerate the amount of variation. For the reasons noted in chapter 1, census enumerations are likely to understate the numbers of women who take some part in the labor force, especially on family farms and in other family-operated enterprises. (See Appendix G.1, where examples of evidence of such under-

Table 2.4. Levels and intercensal changes of female standardized activity rates in national total, rural, and urban populations

	National totals, all countries	Countries for which rural and urban data were obtained	
		Rural	Urban
Levels of $Stand_f$ or RAR_f, cross-sectional censuses			
Number of countries	100	41	41
Mean level	32.0	26.2	25.0
Frequency distribution:			
Under 10.0	11	8	5
10.0-19.9	21	14	8
20.0-29.9	23	7	16
30.0-39.9	14	1	9
40.0-49.9	12	6	1
50.0-59.9	9	1	1
60.0-69.9	4	1	1
70.0 and over	6	3	1
Intercensal changes of $Stand_f$ or RAR_f			
Number of countries	58	16	16
Mean annual change	-.10	-.07	+.05
Frequency distribution:			
+.50 or more	3	1	2
+.10 to +.49	17	3	5
+.09 to -.09	16	5	5
-.10 to -.49	13	5	2
-.50 or more	9	2	2

Table 2D

	$Stand_f$		$Stand_f$
Dahomey, 1961	*81.0	Syria, 1960	7.8
Haiti, 1950	75.2	Angola, 1960	*6.9
Thailand, 1960	74.7	Mozambique, 1950	6.5
Central African Rep., 1960	73.5	United Arab Rep., 1960	5.9
Zaire, 1955/57	*73.3	Libya, 1964	4.5
Guinea, 1954/55	70.8	Jordan, 1961	3.8
Botswana, 1964	*66.7	Iraq, 1957	3.1
Turkey, 1960	62.8	Algeria, 1966	*2.6
Togo, 1958/60	*61.7	Portuguese Guinea, 1950	1.0

* Refined rates used as substitutes for standardized rates.

statement are given.) The degree of understatement varies widely, affecting especially the measures of female labor force in the rural and agricultural sectors. The resulting distortion of the measures of female participation in the labor force as a whole is generally greater in less-developed than in more-developed countries.

31

There is as much diversity in the picture of postwar trends of female activity rates recorded in the censuses as there is in the picture of their levels. No prevailing direction of changes, either upward or downward, is apparent. Increases of female standardized activity rates by .10 or more per year during intercensal periods were recorded in twenty of the fifty-eight countries for which these measures were obtained, decreases by .10 or more per year in twenty-two countries, and smaller changes in either direction in sixteen countries. The average was an annual decrease of .10, but this does not have much significance in view of the limited coverage of countries. If measures were available for all countries, it is not sure whether the average change would be found to have been positive or negative.

Countries where the largest positive and negative annual changes in the standardized rates for females were recorded are listed in Table 2E.

Table 2E

Hungary, 1949–60	+.88	South Africa, 1946–60	−.85
Hong Kong, 1961–66	*+.79	Rumania, 1956–66	−.93
Nicaragua, 1950–63	+.52	Sarawak, 1947–60	*−1.10
United States, 1950–60	+.50	Ecuador, 1950–62	−1.37
		Turkey, 1955–65	−1.42
		Albania, 1955–60	*−2.03

* Refined rates used as substitutes for standardized rates.

The activity rates of females were more volatile than those of males in the sense that the average size of their changes, without regard for sign, was proportionately larger. As the measure of relative volatility, we may take the average annual amount of change in the rates, irrespective of sign, as a percentage of the average level (mean level of rates both at the beginning and ending dates of the intercensal periods considered). This works out to 0.5 percent for the intercensal changes in male standardized activity rates and 1.2 percent for the females. These observations are consistent with the findings of a number of studies to the effect that activity rates of females are more sensitive than those of males to changes in the structure of labor demand, varying levels of wages and income, rates of unemployment, and other conditioning factors.[11]

[11] For example, Bowen and Finegan, *The Economics of Labor Force Participation*, p. 482.

32

Probably, however, the relatively high volatility of the female standardized rates is due in part to errors and noncomparability in the measures.

2.6. Participation by Females in Rural and Urban, Agricultural and Nonagricultural Sectors

Sectoral disaggregation is particularly needed in studying the variations of participation by females in the labor force. This is helpful not only for separating categories most affected by noncomparability and error factors, but also for gaining insight into the determinants of levels and trends of female activity rates. Women's participation is influenced more than that of men by the kinds of employment opportunities that are open to them. In addition to the rural-urban dichotomy, it is highly valuable to consider measures of women's participation in the agricultural and nonagricultural sectors of employment. Further disaggregation according to industry groups of women's employment within the nonagricultural sector, occupational groups, and status (as employee, self-employed, unpaid family worker, etc.) would also be useful, but analysis of the data at this level of detail is beyond the scope of the present study.

In the case of females, there is no such general rule of lower activity rates in urban than in rural populations as is observed in the case of males. Among the forty-one countries for which rural and urban data were obtained, female standardized activity rates are higher in the urban population in twenty-five countries and higher in the rural in sixteen countries, but it is not warranted to infer that higher urban than rural rates would be found in a majority of all countries if comprehensive data were available. Average levels of rural and urban female rates in the cross section of forty-one countries are not very different (Table 2.4), but there is more variation of levels on the rural than on the urban side. So urbanization appears as a factor that tends to diminish differences among countries in the levels of female as well as male activity rates.

Measures of participation by females in agricultural and nonagricultural employment are much more widely available than rural and urban activity rates. Numbers of employed workers or labor force of each sex in the agricultural sector (including forestry and fishing as well as agriculture) and the nonagricultural sector (comprising all other fields of employment) were obtained for ninety-one of the hundred countries as of the cross-sectional censuses. To measure participation by females in the two sectors, we calculate percent shares of female workers among all workers in each sector, denoted as FS_{ag} and FS_{nonag}. Each country's female standardized activity rate is determined principally by the levels of FS_{ag} and FS_{nonag} together with the proportionate shares of the two sectors in total employment, although this relationship is modified somewhat by varying levels of male activity rates and sex ratios in the population of working ages (see Appendix F). The levels of FS_{ag} and FS_{nonag} vary, on the whole, roughly in proportion to the levels of female activity rates in the rural and urban population, respectively, although they are influenced also by the extent of employment of rural women in nonagricultural industries and urban women in agriculture. Among thirty-eight countries for which cross-sectional measures of both FS_{ag} and FS_{nonag} and $Stand_f$ for rural and urban sectors were obtained, Spearman rank correlation coefficients are .89 between FS_{ag} and $Stand_f$ rural, and .82 between FS_{nonag} and $Stand_f$ urban.

Countries having the highest and lowest levels of FS_{ag} and FS_{nonag} in the cross section are listed in Table 2F.

Higher female shares in agriculture than in nonagriculture are indicated by the censuses of thirty-six countries in the cross section, and higher shares in nonagriculture in fifty-five countries. Although high female shares in both sectors are found in some countries (USSR, for example) and low shares in both sectors in some other countries (Algeria, for example), there is on the whole little correlation between the levels of FS_{ag} and FS_{nonag} in the cross section $(r = .11)$. The position of Zaire is extraordinary, at the head of the list for the female share in agricultural employment and at the foot of the list for nonagriculture. The reliability of the measures for this country is suspect.

Cross-sectional mean levels and frequency distributions of female shares in the two sectors are shown in Table 2.5. Although both FS_{ag} and FS_{nonag} vary over extremely wide ranges, the distribution of levels of FS_{nonag} is more compact. FS_{ag} tends to be very high or very low; only eighteen of the ninety-one countries are in the medium range of 20 to 40 percent, while fifty-eight countries have FS_{nonag} in this medium range. So it is apparent that the decreasing proportionate share of agriculture in total employment that typically goes with economic development tends to reduce the

Table 2F

Agricultural sector (FS_{ag})		Nonagricultural sector (FS_{nonag})	
Zaire (1955/57)	59.4	Haiti (1950)	59.6
Rumania (1966)	57.3	Jamaica (1960)	49.3
Poland (1960)	54.7	U.S.S.R. (1959)	44.2
West Germany (1961)	54.7	Nigeria (1963)	43.4
Bulgaria (1965)	54.7	Philippines (1960)	42.7
U.S.S.R. (1959)	54.0		
Dominican Republic (1960)	1.8	Turkey (1960)	8.1
Cuba (1953)	1.8	Libya (1964)	7.8
Algeria (1966)	1.8	Algeria (1966)	7.7
Iraq (1957)	1.8	Pakistan (1961)	7.3
Puerto Rico (1960)	1.7	Jordan (1961)	6.3
Costa Rica (1963)	1.7	Iraq (1957)	6.0
Honduras (1961)	1.0	Mozambique (1950)	2.1
Portuguese Guinea (1950)	0.0 [a]	Zaire (1955/57)	0.9

[a] The occupational classification of the returns of the Portuguese Guinea census shows no females in the category of agricultural workers. There is a large number of females classified as "domesticas rurais"; these have been excluded from the labor force in calculating the measures for the present study. No doubt many of the "domesticas rurais" were farmers' wives who took some part in the farm work in addition to their domestic duties. If they were all counted as agricultural workers, the female share in agriculture would be 52.8 percent and the female refined activity rate would jump from *.9 to *83.0—that is, from the lowest to the highest rank in the cross section.

frequency of very high and very low levels of female activity rates in countries undergoing development.

The caution with regard to reliability and comparability of the census measures of female labor force, particularly in agriculture, deserves repeating. In many countries where very low levels of FS_{ag} are recorded, a traveller in the rural districts might see many women at work in the fields, at least during some seasons.[12] While it may well be true that the extent of women's participation in agriculture varies more from country to country than does their participation in nonagricultural industries, the variations are almost certainly exaggerated in the statistics because of the error and noncomparability factors, which affect the enumerations of female la-

[12] The reader is referred again to the examples of census underreporting of female agricultural workers in some countries (Appendix G.1).

35

Labor force dimensions

Table 2.5. Levels and intercensal changes of female shares in agricultural and nonagricultural employment

	Female share in agricultural employment (FS_{ag})	Female share in nonagricultural employment (FS_{nonag})
Levels of female shares, cross-sectional censuses		
Number of countries	91	91
Mean level	22.4	26.8
Frequency distribution:		
Under 10.0	36	10
10.0-19.9	15	13
20.0-29.9	7	31
30.0-39.9	11	27
40.0-49.9	9	9
50.0 and over	13	1
Intercensal changes of female shares		
Number of countries	54	54
Mean annual change	-.13	+.10
Frequency distribution:		
+.50 or more	3	5
+.10 to +.49	14	21
+.09 to -.09	14	14
-.10 to -.49	13	11
-.50 or more	10	3

bor force more in the agricultural than in the nonagricultural sector. That the census statistics present a distorted picture does not mean, however, that the picture is wholly false. There is some reassurance in the observation that differences between the recorded levels of FS_{ag} and FS_{nonag} are consistent, in most countries, with the sex ratios of migrants between rural and urban areas (see Appendix Table G.1).

The intercensal changes (Table 2.5) show a mixture of increasing and decreasing female shares in both employment sectors. There is a predominance of decreases in FS_{ag} and of increases in FS_{nonag}, but the difference in this respect might easily be due to chance in the representation of countries in the sample. In a majority of countries, in fact, the trends of the female shares in the two sectors moved upward or downward in unison, but the movements of FS_{ag} were larger on the average. The relative volatility of FS_{ag} was half again greater than that of FS_{nonag} among the countries for which intercensal change measures were obtained. In many countries, the time series of census enumerations of the female labor force in agriculture is highly unstable, influenced strongly by varying definitions, enumeration procedures, and quality of reporting.

2.7. Age Patterns of Participation by Females in the Labor Force

The life cycles of participation by females in the labor force take different forms in different societies, varying much more than those of males do. In the case of females, the phases of the cycle are commonly much less clearly defined in terms of age groups. Many women may enter the labor force when many others in the same age group retire, and many may enter and retire repeatedly during their lives. The age at which the female activity rate reaches a maximum and its level at the peak age vary widely from country to country. In the cross-sectional averages of age-specific female activity rates (Table 2.3), the peak is in ages 20 to 24, but the average rates are not a great deal lower in other ages between 15 and 55. The peak in some countries is in ages 15 to 19, or even younger, while in other countries the highest rates are recorded in ages over 50 years. The age curves of female activity rates in many countries have two peaks separated by a trough of lower rates in the central age groups. The number of women in the labor force at the age of the peak rate may be much less than the number who enter at some time during their lives.

The ages under 20 are primarily labor-force entry ages for females as well as males; but in many countries, girls frequently drop out of the labor force before age 20 as they marry and begin having children while, on the other hand, a majority of female workers in many countries enter at later ages. For both sexes, likewise, the ages over 65 are primarily ages of retirement; but a majority of women workers in many countries retire much younger. In the cross-sectional averages, the activity rate of females in ages 60 to 64 is slightly more than half of the peak level in ages 20 to 24.

The life cycle of women's participation in the labor force is related, in different ways in different countries, to the life cycle of marriage and the family. In some societies, it is almost exclusively the single and exmarried women who work for income; marriage is the occasion for retirement from the labor force, and widowhood may be the occasion for reentry. In other societies, women frequently continue working after marriage until they have children, and they may return to the labor force when the children are old enough no longer to need the mother's constant care; while in still other societies, motherhood is frequently combined with work for income.

37

Differences in the phases of the life cycle of marriage and the family contribute to the variations in age patterns of female activity rates. Where marriage is relatively late, there is an interval of early adult years in which females have little useful alternative to paid jobs or participation as unpaid helpers in family enterprises; but there is little of this in such countries as India, where girls are married very young. The span of ages in which maternal responsibilities are at a maximum varies with the level and age-pattern of fertility. In the United States and other highly developed countries at present, this period is typically between the ages of 20 to 25 and 35 to 40, while it is prolonged considerably in high fertility countries. The level of mortality conditions the span of ages in which many marriages are broken by widowhood, which may impose on the widow the necessity of joining the labor force, or give her an opportunity to do so in the capacity of heir to the family enterprise.

For the purpose of the following analysis, types of age patterns of participation by females in the labor force are defined with regard for the shape of the curve of age-specific activity rates in each country, irrespective of the level. Four principal types and four subtypes, represented by examples in Figure 2.3, are defined as follows. Type A (central peak or plateau), represented in the chart by the examples of India and Thailand, resembles the typical pattern of male activity rates in that participation is at a maximum in the central adult ages, between 30 and 44. In Type B (late peak), the curve of the female activity rates rises to a maximum at an age above 45 years, as in the examples of Ghana and Nigeria.[13] In Type C (early peak), the maximum is reached at an age below 30 and the activity rate declines thereafter, continuously, as in the example of Costa Rica, or with some interruption of the decline, as in Switzerland. The Costa Rican pattern is identified as subtype C–1, while the Swiss pattern, which may be described as a "peak-and-shoulder" curve, is identified as subtype C–2. In Type D (double peak), the curve has two definite peaks separated by a trough, which usually reaches its lowest level at an age between 25 and 34. If the earlier peak is the higher of the two, as in the example of Mexico, the pattern is identified as subtype D–1. Subtype D–2 is the pattern exemplified by the United States, where the later peak of the double-peak curve is the higher.

---

[13] This feature may be explained by the high proportions of Ghanaian and Nigerian women engaged in trade, an activity in which female workers tend generally to be of mature age.

Some arbitrary rules for classification of borderline cases have to be used in the application of this scheme of types. We define as a central plateau pattern one in which all age groups between 25 and 54 have activity rates at least nine-tenths as high as the highest rate for any age group. Otherwise the curve is considered as having a peak or peaks. The "peak-and-shoulder" pattern (subtype C–2) is defined as one in which, after declining from the early peak, the activity rate levels off or rises by less than one-tenth in two or more consecutive age groups. The double-peak pattern (Type D) is defined as one in which the activity rate declines by more than one-tenth from an early peak, then rises by more than one-tenth to a later peak. In a few instances, only slight differences distinguish between Type D patterns and those of subtype C–2 or the central plateau pattern of Type A.

Applying this scheme to the data of the cross-sectional census of each country, we find the distribution of types and subtypes shown in Table 2G.

Table 2G

	Number of countries
A. Central peak or plateau	14
B. Late peak	8
C. Early peak:	
C–1. Without shoulder	21
C–2. Peak and shoulder	14
D. Double peak:	
D–1. Early peak higher	19
D–2. Late peak higher	8
All types	84

The curve of average female activity rates for the eighty-four countries in the cross section is of the C–2 type, but this is not a predominant pattern; it is the result of averaging different types. The most frequent patterns are C–1 and D–1; C–2 and A also occur frequently, while B and D–2 are less common.

These different patterns imply different relationships between labor-force participation and the life cycle of marriage and family. The early-peak pattern implies that the female labor force is composed largely of single or young married women without children, most of whom drop out of the labor force when they marry or when they become mothers. The peak-and-shoulder pattern (C–2) sug-

39

Labor force dimensions

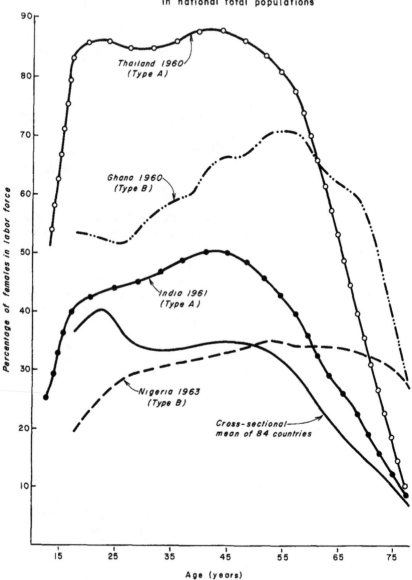

Figure 2.3 (continued)

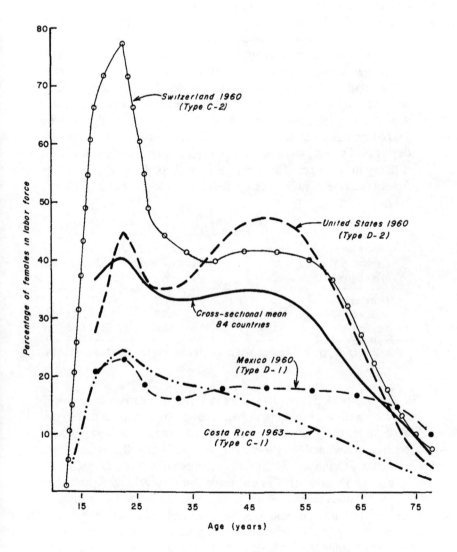

gests that some of the dropouts reenter the labor force when their children have grown old enough no longer to need incessant care. Widowhood also may force some women to go to work in later adult ages. This reflux of older women into the labor force, after the ages in which the responsibilities of motherhood are heaviest, is stronger in the double-peaked patterns, especially D–2. A relatively small average number of children and high concentration of child-bearing in the early years of married life, as in the United States, are conditions favorable to development of the double-peaked patterns and heightening of the later peak. Where the pattern is of Type D, the share of married women in the labor force is likely to be larger than where it is of Type C, as illustrated by the comparison between the United States and Switzerland (Table 2H).

Table 2H

Percent of female labor force	United States 1960	Switzerland 1960
Married	60.7	25.3
Widowed, divorced, and separated	15.7	12.1
Single	23.6	62.5

Source: Data from United Nations, *Demographic Yearbook* (1964), Table 14.

The late-peak pattern (Type B) suggests that early marriage and early motherhood inhibit high participation by young women in the labor force; it is more the older married women and widows who feel free or compelled to work for income. Where the average age of women at marriage is higher, conditions are more favorable to Type C or D patterns. Central peak and central plateau patterns (Type A) suggest that women's participation in the labor force is less closely related to marriage and motherhood. Type A patterns appear chiefly in countries where most of the women in the labor force are family farm workers or employed in cottage industries, etc., where it is relatively easy for them to function at the same time as housewives and mothers. But other patterns are also often found in such circumstances.

How urbanization relates to the age patterns of women's participation in the labor force is indicated by the distributions of types of patterns in rural and urban sectors of thirty-six countries, shown in Table 2.6. On the whole, the simple early-peak pattern (Type C–1) appears to be more characteristic of urban than of rural populations. Types A, C–2, and D–2 appear more frequently in rural than in urban populations, while the frequency of Type B and D–1 is about the same in rural and urban.

Table 2.6. Types of age patterns of female activity rates in rural and urban populations, cross-sectional censuses

	Rural patterns	Urban patterns
Total number of countries	36	36
A. Central peak or plateau	10	4
B. Late peak	4	4
C. Early peak		
C-1. Without shoulder	5	15
C-2. Peak and shoulder	5	2
D. Double peak		
D-1. Early peak higher	6	8
D-2. Late peak higher	6	3

During the postwar years, the age patterns of female activity rates in countries around the world shifted generally in the direction of increasing concentration of activity in the ages between 20 and 65 (although not necessarily toward rising absolute levels of the rates for women in these ages). In ages under 20 and over 60, the trends of the rates for females, as for males, were predominantly downward (Table 2.3). In proportion to the mean levels of the rates, the average annual decreases in ages 15 to 19 and 65 and over were about the same for both sexes. In the age groups between 20 and 60, female activity rates increased in some countries and decreased in others, with relatively small net changes in the averages. The relative volatility (average amount of changes irrespective of sign, in proportion to the mean level) was noticeably greater in the rates for women in the older than in the younger age group.

In spite of the ups and downs in different age groups, the types of age patterns of female activity rates did not change in a majority of countries during the intercensal periods (Table 2.7). The shift from the peak-and-shoulder to a double-peaked pattern, which took place during the 1940s in the United States, was repeated in a few other countries during the postwar intercensal periods, but it does not appear as a very widespread trend. Shifts from peak-and-shoulder to simple early peak, central peak, central plateau,

43

Labor force dimensions

Pattern of earlier census	Pattern of more recent census						
	All types	A	B	C-1	C-2	D-1	D-2
Total number of countries	45	4	3	12	8	15	3
A. Central peak or plateau	4	2	-	1	1	-	-
B. Late peak	3	-	2	-	1	-	-
C. Early peak							
C-1. Without shoulder	12	1	-	10	-	1	-
C-2. Peak and shoulder	11	1	1	1	5	3	-
D. Double peak							
D-1. Early peak higher	13	-	-	-	1	10	2
D-2. Late peak higher	2	-	-	-	-	1	1

or late peak patterns seem to have taken place in about as many countries.

On the whole, the picture of women's changing roles in income production is a mixed one. Women have been moving into the labor force in some countries and out in others. The mixture of increasing and decreasing trends in women's participation appears equally in the agricultural and nonagricultural, rural and urban sectors. Women in some countries show a growing disposition to combine motherhood with a career by joining or rejoining the labor force in later years of their married life when the children are older, but this trend was not very widespread around the world during the postwar periods referred to in the census statistics analyzed here. For men, on the other hand, the trend that appears in almost every country is one of shortening years of working life, both by longer schooling and later entry into the labor force, and by earlier retirement. Mainly as a result of this trend, together with the changes in population structure analyzed in chapter 4 below, the ratio of income producers to consumers was decreasing in the population of almost all countries during the early postwar period.

THREE

Regional Patterns

3.1. *Definition of Regions*

Labor-force participation rates can be viewed as products of demand and supply factors interacting within a framework of culture
and social institutions that govern the functional roles of individuals according to sex, age, and other attributes. Since this framework is not the same in different societies, it is to be expected that
the levels of the participation rates may differ between countries in
similar economic circumstances, and that similar economic developments may have different effects on the trends of the rates over
time.[1] The extent to which participation is reported in the censuses
may also be affected by cultural and institutional factors.

All relevant features of each country's culture and social institutions should ideally be taken into account, along with economic
and demographic variables, in a comprehensive analysis of factors
affecting the levels and trends of labor force participation rates.
Such an analysis is not feasible here, but by classifying countries
in regional groups which have some degree of homogeneity of culture and institutions, we can partly control the influences of these
factors. The classification that will be used for this purpose is that
of the nine regional groups set forth in the tables of Appendix A.

This regional classification was formed empirically in the following way. First, various groupings of countries according to linguistic, religious, ethnic, and political criteria were tried, with the aim
of identifying groups that differed considerably from world average
distributions of male or female labor force participation measures,
in ways which were not explained by the economic levels of the
countries. Four regional groups defined by such criteria were
retained, namely the Arab countries, other Moslem countries (having a majority of Moslem population), Spanish and Portuguese-

---

[1] Several authors have stressed this point as regards participation by females in the labor force. See Andrew Collver and Eleanor Langlois, "The
Female Labor Force in Metropolitan Areas: An International Comparison,"
Economic Development and Cultural Change 10 (1962), 367–85; Nadia
Youssef, "Social Structure and the Female Labor Force: The Case of Wom-
en Workers in Muslim Middle Eastern Countries," *Demography* 8 (1971),
427–39; Ester Boserup, *Woman's Role in Economic Development* (London, 1970).

45

language countries (Spain, Portugal, Brazil, and the Spanish-speaking countries in America), and the Eastern European socialist countries. Next, three major geographical regions were considered, namely tropical Africa (comprising all Africa south of the Sahara except South Africa), South and East Asia, and Europe (except Spain, Portugal, and the Eastern countries). Various ways of subdividing these three regions were tried, but the only subdivision found to be useful in distinguishing the labor force participation measures was the difference between northwestern Europe (Sweden, Norway, Denmark, Netherlands, Belgium, United Kingdom, and Ireland) and "middle Europe" (France, Switzerland, Austria, West Germany, Finland, Italy, and Greece). The United States, Canada, Australia, and New Zealand were added to the northwest European group, as their measures of labor force participation were found to be similar. Finally, a miscellaneous group was formed of nine countries that did not fit well into any regional rubric: Jamaica, Trinidad and Tobago, Guyana, Haiti, South Africa, Cyprus, Israel, Hong Kong, and Singapore.

The list of countries in each regional group will be found in Table A.1, Appendix A. The number of countries in each group and the ranking in ascending order of levels of economic development of the constituent countries are shown in Table 3A.[2] It should be noted that some of the groups overlap and, as a result, the sums of figures for regional groups exceed the totals of all countries. The

[2] The rank order of economic level is based on mean values, for each regional group, of the index of relative development level described in Appendix H. Quintile groups of individual countries ranked by this index are shown in the last column of Table A.1 (Group I comprising the least developed and Group V the most developed countries). The "miscellaneous" group (9) is disregarded in this ranking of the regional averages.

Jamaica, Trinidad and Tobago, and Guyana could be regarded as a regional group having some similarity of labor force participation measures as well as linguistic and ethnic affinities, but it was considered doubtfully warranted to make a separate group of only three countries. South Africa was separated from the regional group of tropical Africa in view of the large and influential minority of European population in South Africa, which exhibits labor force characteristics similar to those of "Northwestern Europe, Northern America, and Oceania." The pattern of labor-force participation measures for the latter group would not be changed much if South Africa were added. Hong Kong and Singapore were separated from the regional group of South and East Asian countries in view of the peculiarities of labor force structure in Hong Kong and Singapore associated with the fact that their population is almost entirely urban. Mauritius, which is conventionally considered as belonging to Africa (although the island is not much closer geographically to that continent than to Asia), is included in the regional group of South and East Asian countries in view of its large minority of population of Asian origin.

Table 3A

	Number of countries	Rank order of economic level
1. Tropical Africa	15	1
2. Arab countries	9	4
3. Other Moslem countries	7	2
4. South and East Asia	16	3
5. Latin America, Spain, Portugal	22	5
6. Eastern Europe	9	6
7. Middle Europe	7	7
8. Northwestern Europe, Northern America, and Oceania	11	8
9. Miscellaneous	9	—

group of "Other Moslem" countries overlaps three other groups, including Guinea and Senegal in tropical Africa, Pakistan and Indonesia in South and East Asia, and Albania in Eastern Europe.

The coverage of regional groups is uneven in the data compiled for this study, as shown in chapter 1, Table 1.1. Coverage is complete for countries of 500,000 or more population in Latin America (with Spain and Portugal), Eastern Europe, and middle Europe, and virtually complete for northwestern Europe, northern America, and Oceania, where only Papua and New Guinea are missing. There are important gaps in the data for South and East Asia (where the omission of China brings the population coverage down to only a little more than half of the regional total) and for the Arab and other Moslem countries. Coverage is poorest in tropical Africa, where data were obtained for less than half of the countries of 500,000 or more.

3.2. Overview of Regional Patterns

For each regional group, Table 3.1 shows the cross-sectional mean levels of crude and standardized activity rates, age-sex indices,[3] and female shares in agricultural and nonagricultural employment. Regional patterns of levels and postwar changes in male and female activity rates and female shares in the two employment sectors are tabulated in Tables 3.2–3.12. The most important regional differences appear in the measures of participation by females in the labor force, and in the following discussion attention is focused

[3] For explanation of the meaning of age-sex indices and the method of calculating them, see chapter 4, section 4.2, and Appendix E.

47

primarily on these. Some significant regional variations in the measures of participation by males are also noted. The discussion is concerned mainly, but not exclusively, with cross-sectional levels of the measures, because regional patterns are marked more distinctly in the levels than in the changes during intercensal periods.

The regional differences in the levels of female activity rates and female shares, especially in agricultural employment, that are indicated by the census statistics are likely to reflect, in part, effects of varying definitions, enumeration procedures, and reporting errors and biases. On this account, the measures of regional differences must be treated with reserve, but there is little doubt about the presence of significant real differences related to traits of culture and social institutions that are common to countries within each regional group.

In the interpretation of regional differences in levels of male activity rates, it is important to take account of the levels of development of the countries. This is a less important consideration in the case of females, since the levels of participation by females in the labor force are not related so consistently to levels of economic development. For males, the regional tabulations are concerned not only with the absolute levels of the rates, but also with deviations from mean levels of the rates for countries at similar levels of development (shown in Table 5.1). Thus in Table 3.2, where the cross-sectional picture of regional levels of male standardized rates is shown, panel B gives the numbers of countries within each regional group where the rate deviates positively and negatively from the mean for countries at the corresponding level of development, and the average amount of the deviations with due regard for sign.[4] One can tell l these figures to what extent the male rates for coun-

---

[4] For example, the calculations for countries in region 3 ("Other Moslem Countries") are as follows:

Level of development (1)	Mean Stand$_m$ for this level (2)	Stand$_m$ for this country (3)	Deviation (3) − (2) (4)
Guinea 1954/55	I	81.0	80.7	−0.3
Pakistan 1961	I	81.0	84.5	+3.5
Senegal 1960/61	II	80.1	*80.7	+0.6
Turkey 1960	II	80.1	87.0	+6.9
Indonesia 1961	II	80.1	78.3	−1.8
Iran 1966	III	76.0	79.2	+3.2
Albania 1960	III	76.0	*77.8	+1.8
Mean deviation				+2.0

tries in each region are above or below the levels expected in view of the economic conditions of the countries. While the average deviation from the expected levels is not very large in any region, it is significant that in several regions there is a distinct predominance of either positive or negative deviations.

The nine regional groups are classified in Table 3B, according to the frequency distributions of levels of the female and male

Table 3B

	Predominantly high male rates	Predominantly low male rates	Medium, mixed, or indefinite patterns of male rates
Predominantly high female rates	—	6. Eastern Europe	—
Predominantly low female rates	5. Latin America, etc.	2. Arab countries	—
Predominantly medium female rates	—	—	7. Middle Europe 8. N.W. Europe, etc.
Mixed or indefinite patterns of female rates	3. Other Moslem countries	—	1. Tropical Africa 4. South & East Asia

standardized activity rates in their component countries (Tables 3.2, 3.7), taking into account the economic levels of the countries for the assessment of levels of the male rates, as explained in the preceding paragraph.

Main features of the patterns displayed by the data for each regional group will now be described, approximately in the order of levels of the female standardized rates as listed in Table 3B.

3.3. Eastern Europe (region 6)

The cross-sectional levels of female standardized activity rates for Eastern European socialist countries range from *39.0 in Yugoslavia to *61.5 in the Soviet Union. Although higher rates are recorded for some countries in other regions, no other regional group exhibits such a consistently high level. This, combined with favorable age structure of the population in most of the Eastern European countries, produces a higher average level of crude activity rates than is found in any other region, yet the levels of male standardized activity rates in a majority of the Eastern European countries are below average for their levels of development.

High participation by women in the labor force is in harmony with the emphasis in Marxist ideology on equality of the sexes in employment as well as in other spheres, but it is actually only in the agricultural sector that women's participation as recorded in the censuses is consistently very high in this region. Among the seven countries in Eastern Europe for which measures of female shares in agricultural and nonagricultural employment were found, the mean level of female shares in agriculture (50.0 percent) is far higher than the mean for any other regional group. Women outnumber men in the agricultural labor force in Rumania, Poland, Bulgaria, and the Soviet Union. The lowest FS_{ag} recorded in Eastern Europe is Hungary's 37.5 percent (1960), and even this is well above the average of other regions.

In the nonagricultural sector, while it is true that the average level of female shares (34.7 percent) is higher than the average for any other region, it is only a little above the averages for Latin America, middle Europe, and northwestern Europe, northern America, and Oceania. The Soviet Union is the only Eastern European country where the census shows a very high value of FS_{nonag}: 44.2 percent as of 1959, which is exceeded only by Haiti and Jamaica among other countries in the cross section. Other Eastern European countries have FS_{nonag} in the medium range of 20 to 40 percent. The deficit of males in the adult population of the Soviet Union, due to war losses, is one factor which contributes to the high female shares in both agricultural and nonagricultural employment in that country. With a balanced sex ratio in the population ten years of age and over, given the rates of participation by males and by females in agricultural and in nonagricultural employment as recorded in the 1959 census, FS_{ag} for the USSR would be reduced to 47.4 percent and FS_{nonag} to 37.8, which still exceeds the 33.6 percent for the United States in 1960.

The relatively low average level of male standardized activity rates in Eastern Europe is due both to early retirement and late entry of males into the labor force. In the ages of 15 to 19 and 45 to 64, the average level of male activity rates in the four Eastern European countries for which data were obtained is below the average for any other regional group (Table 3.4). For men over age sixty-five, while the Eastern European average is higher than that of middle Europe or northwestern Europe, northern America, and Oceania, it is lower than it might be expected to be in view of the levels of development of the countries.

The data on intercensal changes indicate a general trend of increasing shares of females in both agricultural and nonagricultural sectors in Eastern European countries during the postwar years (Table 3.9). In spite of this, female standardized activity rates have decreased in some of the countries as a result of the counteracting effect of the expansion of the nonagricultural share in total employment. This tends to depress female activity rates in this region because female shares in nonagricultural employment are smaller than in agriculture.

In those Eastern European countries where the socialist regimes have become established since World War II, it is interesting to compare the labor force measures provided by the postwar censuses with those of earlier censuses. Data for such a comparison have been found for six countries (Table 3C).

It seems that the pattern of high female participation in agriculture already existed, except in Hungary, before the People's Republics were established, but female shares in the agricultural labor force have increased further under the socialist regimes. In the nonagricultural sector, the postwar increases in employment of women continue an earlier trend, again with the exception of Hungary, where FS_{nonag} at the 1949 census was at approximately the same level recorded in 1930. The greatest increases in the female shares during the period of socialist development have taken place in areas where their shares were relatively low before: in agriculture in Hungary and nonagricultural employment in Bulgaria and Czechoslovakia.

In the case of males, the relatively low level of activity rates in a majority of Eastern European countries appears to be mainly a result of recent trends. Eastern Europe stands out as one of the regions where the largest decreases of male rates were recorded, on the average, in intervals between postwar censuses (Table 3.3). In Bulgaria, Czechoslovakia, Rumania, and Yugoslavia, sharp decreases of the male rates between the postwar censuses appear as acceleration of earlier trends, doubtless related to accelerated progress in industrialization, urbanization, provisions for education, and retirement pensions for aging workers under the socialist governments.

Table 3C

		Labor force per 100 population 15–64		Female shares in employment or labor force	
		Males	Females	Agriculture	Non-agriculture
Bulgaria	1934	104.2	83.1	51.0	17.1
	1956	95.3	69.4	50.5	31.0
	1965	85.6	67.9	54.7	35.5
Czechoslo-					
vakia	1930	104	48	—	—
	1947	95	48	49.1	26.7
	1961	88.7	59.2	49.5	38.2
Hungary	1930	105.6	35.9	23.2	30.3
	1949	99.9	36.9	29.7	28.2
	1960	100.8	50.3	37.5	33.6
Poland	1931	95.0	55.3	44.3	30.3
	1950	94.1	64.1	—	—
	1960	93.7	66.2	54.7	34.8
Rumania	1930	105.7	80.7	50.9	23.9
	1956	102.2	79.3	53.6	26.4
	1966	91.7	72.6	57.3	29.2
Yugoslavia	1931	106.7	49.7	—	—
	1953	100.4	47.7	41.2	20.6
	1961	95.9	49.2	42.5	26.0

Sources of prewar figures: United States Bureau of the Census, International Population Statistics Reports, Series P–90, Washington, D.C.: No. 4 (1954), *The Population of Poland*, by W. Parker Mauldin and Donald S. Akers, p. 165; No. 13 (1960), *The Labor Force of Czechoslovakia*, by James N. Ypsilantis, pp. 6, 8; No. 14 (1961), *The Labor Force of Rumania*, by Samuel Baum, pp. 6, 28; No. 16 (1962), *The Labor Force of Bulgaria*, by Zora Prochazka, pp. 8, 32; No. 20 (1964), *The Labor Force of Poland*, by Zora Prochazka and Jerry W. Combs, Jr., p. 9; No. 22 (1965), *The Labor Force of Yugoslavia*, by Andrew Elias, p. 8.
Hungary, Central Statistical Office, Census of Hungary, 1960, historical resume of data from censuses since 1900.

3.4. *Arab and Other Moslem Countries (regions 2 and 3)*

The Arab countries are at the opposite extreme from the Eastern European group in levels of participation by females in the labor force. Female standardized activity rates below 10 percent are indicated by the censuses of seven of the nine Arab countries for which data were obtained, and the regional average level of this measure is below that of any other region. Women take little part either in agriculture or nonagricultural employment, according to the censuses of most of the Arab countries. Sudan and Morocco are the only countries in the group where recorded shares of females exceed 10 percent in either sector (FS_{ag} of 28.5 percent and FS_{nonag} of 37.4 percent for the Sudan, 1956; FS_{ag} of 7.8 percent, FS_{nonag} of 17.5 percent for Morocco, 1960).[5] In the Sudan, there are large non-Arab minorities. Moreover, the unusually efficient design of the Sudanese census enquiry about occupations (each individual being asked to state his secondary occupation, if any, as well as his primary activity) probably resulted in a fuller reporting of the female labor force than was obtained in the censuses of many other countries.[6] Evidence of large underenumeration of female agricultural workers in the censuses of Algeria and Morocco is noted in Appendix G, and it is quite likely that a similar underenumeration may have occurred in recent censuses of other Arab countries.

The standardized activity rates of males recorded in the censuses of the Arab countries are also relatively low in most cases, being below average for the levels of development in all except Sudan and Iraq. This feature is due mainly to a rather retarded tempo of entry of young males into the labor force, as the regional average level of male activity rates is most noticeably low in the age group of 15 to 19 years, especially in the urban sector (Tables 3.4, 3.6). An additional factor that tends to minimize the size of the labor force in Arab countries is a high percentage of children in the population, due to the high birth rates. So low participation by females in the labor force, as well as rather low participation by males and an adverse population structure, all conspire to put the Arab countries at the foot of the list of regional groups for average level of the crude activity rates.

The factors responsible for low recorded levels of participation by both females and males in the labor force seem to be associated with Arabic culture rather than with Islamic religion. Among Moslem countries outside the Arab group, the levels of female activity

[5] Tunisia would be a third exception if proper measures of FS_{ag} and FS_{nonag} could be obtained from the 1966 census tabulations, which do not include unpaid family workers in the industry classifications of the labor force. The data without unpaid family workers show FS_{ag} of 1.8 percent and FS_{nonag} of 8.9 percent. Including unpaid family workers, it is estimated that FS_{ag} might be about 35 percent and FS_{nonag} between 10 and 15 percent.

[6] If only those who reported a gainful occupation as their primary activity are considered, the female refined activity rate for the Sudan drops from 39.7 to 9.6 percent.

rates recorded in the censuses vary widely, some being very high and others rather low, but none as low as the average for the Arab countries. Iran follows the Arabic pattern, with a very low female share in agricultural employment, but Iranian women take a larger part in the nonagricultural sector, where many are employed in carpet-making. In Pakistan, FS_{nonag} is as low as in Arab countries, but FS_{ag} as reported in the census is somewhat higher. Turkey has low FS_{nonag} but very high FS_{ag}, with the result that the Turkish female standardized activity rate is one of the world's highest. Very high female activity rates are recorded also in Albania, Senegal, and Guinea, and a medium level in Indonesia. Activity rates of males in the non-Arab Moslem countries are generally high, the regional average of male standardized activity rates being higher than that of any other group.

Nadia Youssef, analyzing the statistics of females in the labor force in Arab countries, Iran, Pakistan, and Turkey, attributes the low participation by women in nonagricultural employment to the combined effects of the traditions of seclusion (voluntary abstention of women from public activities) and exclusion (prohibitions and limitations imposed by men). Youssef writes:

An important consideration in understanding female seclusion and exclusion from participation in public life is the criterion of family honor and esteem. In Middle Eastern societies, family standing depends largely, if not exclusively, upon conformity to behavioral norms that are conceived as having to do with "male" honor. This honor is determined above all by the sexual conduct of a man's womenfolk: premarital chastity of the daughter and sister, fidelity of the wife, continence of the widowed and divorced daughter or sister, these are basic principles upon which a family's reputation and status in the community depend. . . . It is because the male honor is so intimately tied up with a woman's sexual conduct that Middle Easterners look with suspicion and mistrust upon the social intermingling of the sexes. Under these conditions the great fear that the employment of women outside the home represents is understandable. The most fundamental change that women's participation in the occupational sphere will have to bring about is a reconsideration of the relationship between men and women both within and outside of the family.[7]

[7] "Social Structure and the Female Labor Force," pp. 431–32.

54

This explanation does not account for the even lower rates of participation by females in agriculture as recorded in the censuses of most Arab countries. Without much doubt, these are explained at least in part by underreporting, and it is possible that accurate measures might show female shares in agriculture in the Arab countries to be no lower than the average of developing countries in several other regions of the world. But if this is so, the question arises why women's participation in agricultural work should go to such a large extent unreported in the censuses of Arab countries. Possibly a strong feeling that women's proper role is motherhood and homemaking inhibits both their actual participation in the labor force and the reporting of their participation when it occurs, to a greater extent in Arab societies than in others.

The difference between the Arab and other Moslem countries in levels of male activity rates is no less remarkable and puzzling. Age group by age group, in both rural and urban sectors, the mean levels of male activity rates are almost always lower in the Arab than in the other Moslem countries, and the former are consistently below the averages for corresponding levels of economic development, even in the prime working ages of middle adulthood. That the rates of participation by Arab males in the labor force should be relatively low appears all the more remarkable in view of the strong male dominance that is characteristic of Arab societies, and the minimal participation by women in paid employment—traits that might be expected to favor high participation by males. The statistics suggest that some other trait or traits of Arabic culture and institutions tend especially to discourage early entrance of males into the labor force and, to a lesser extent, to encourage early retirement, in spite of opposite influences apparently associated with Islam that make for relatively high male activity rates in non-Arab Moslem societies scattered widely around the world. It may be significant that the two exceptions to the prevailing Arab pattern, namely Iraq and the Sudan, are on the periphery of the Arabic cultural zone and that there are large non-Arab minorities in the Sudan.

Available data on intercensal changes in labor force participation measures in Arab and other Moslem countries are not adequate to furnish a basis for generalizations as regards the trends in either group. Among the Arab countries, only the United Arab Republic is represented in these data.[8] For the other Moslem group,

[8] Indications of intercensal changes were obtained also for Algeria,

the significance of the large average annual decreases in standardized activity rates of both males and females is doubtful in view of the fact that only three countries are represented. One of these is Albania, with recorded annual decreases of *1.37 for males and *2.03 for females (in refined activity rates). Without Albania, the mean annual intercensal changes of the rates in other Moslem and Eastern European countries would be as shown in Table 3D.

Table 3D

	Males	Females
Other Moslem	—.45	—.56
Eastern Europe	—.60	+.04

3.5. The Spanish-Portuguese Language Group (region 5)

Recorded activity rates of females in the Latin American and Iberian countries are generally somewhat above the levels of the Arab countries, but distinctly lower than the average of other regions. Of the twenty-two countries that make up the regional group of Latin America, Spain, and Portugal, sixteen have female standardized activity rates between 10 and 20 as of the cross-sectional censuses, and the only one exceeding 25 is Bolivia, at the wholly nonconforming level of 58.4, according to the 1950 census. The activity rates of males, on the other hand, are generally high. All

Libya, Morocco, and Tunisia, but their reliability is dubious. The clearly spurious decreases in female agricultural labor force indicated by the Algerian and Moroccan censuses are discussed in Appendix G. The measures of changes in male activity rates are less questionable. These indicate a general trend of relatively rapid decrease in the North African region:

	Annual changes of male refined activity rates
Algeria, 1954–66	—.83
Libya, 1954–64	—1.21
Morocco, 1952–60, Moslem population	—.19
Tunisia, 1956–66	—.39
United Arab Republic, 1947–60	—.69

Rates for Algeria 1954, Libya 1954, Morocco 1952, and Tunisia 1956 were taken from: United Nations, Cairo Demographic Center, "Demographic Patterns of Labour Force in Arab Countries" (Document SMP/71/P4), 1971, by Zdenek Vavra, Table 1, pp. 34–35.

countries in the regional group except Puerto Rico and Uruguay have male standardized activity rates above the mean levels for the corresponding quintile groups of relative development level.

Low participation by women in agricultural employment accounts for the generally low level of female activity rates as recorded in the censuses of Latin American countries, Spain, and Portugal. Female shares in agricultural employment, according to the censuses, are below 15 percent in all countries in this regional group except Bolivia. In the nonagricultural sector, the female shares are consistently at medium levels, ranging from 21 percent in Cuba (1953) to 42 percent in Nicaragua (1963). The regional mean level of FS_{nonag} is higher than the mean of the world-wide cross section. This feature is partly due to the relatively large numbers of women and girls employed as domestic servants in many Latin American countries; and this, in turn, may be related to the high prevalence of consensual marriages, which afford little economic security for women.[9]

The higher female shares in nonagricultural than in agricultural employment imply that in this region, unlike Eastern Europe, the increasing relative share of nonagriculture in employment favors an increasing trend in the total participation by females in income-producing jobs. In spite of this, there were only five countries in the region where postwar censuses showed female standardized activity rates increasing by .10 or more annually, and the regional average was an annual decrease of .26. Decreases of the already low female shares in agricultural employment in a majority of the countries were mainly responsible for this; in addition, large decreases of female shares in the nonagricultural sector were recorded in several countries. In Ecuador FS_{nonag} dropped from 40.7 percent at the 1950 census to 30.5 in 1962, and in Puerto Rico from 36.5 in 1950 to 31.3 in 1960. The reliability of the measure for Ecuador is, however, doubtful.

Women's participation in agriculture in the Latin American countries, Spain, and Portugal is not really as low, on the whole, as the census statistics make it appear. Some evidence of underreporting of female agricultural workers in the censuses is noted in Appendix G. The indication given by the statistics that agriculture

[9] This was suggested by Youssef, "Social Structure and the Female Labor Force," p. 435. Collver and Langlois, "The Female Labor Force in Metropolitan Areas," p. 375, offered a similar explanation for high rates of participation by females in the labor force in metropolitan areas of Caribbean countries.

offers relatively little economic opportunity for women in this region is supported, however, by the observation that, almost without
exception, females outnumber males in net migration from rural
to urban areas (see Appendix G.2).

Early-peaked age patterns of female activity rates (Type C)
are characteristic of this region; sixteen of the twenty-two countries exhibit such patterns (Table 3.11). The pattern of the regional
mean age-specific female activity rates, tabulated in Table 3.10
and charted in Figure 3.1,[10] is of the peak-and-shoulder type
(C–2), but simple early-peaked patterns without the shoulder

Figure 3.1 Mean age-specific activity rates of females in regional
groups of countries, cross-sectional censuses

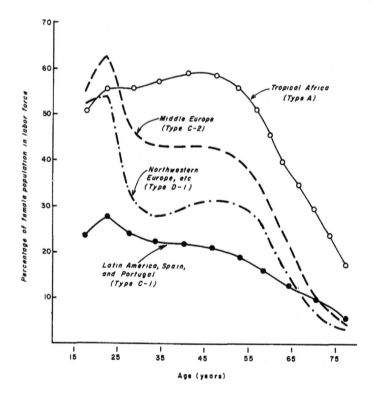

[10] These patterns are charted only for the four regions where there is
enough homogeneity of patterns among the constituent countries to give
some representative meaning to the regional averages.

(C–1) are predominant among countries within the region. The early peak implies that females take part in the labor force mainly while they are single, and that most of them drop out when they marry or when they start having children. Marital status classifications confirm that a majority of females in the labor force are single in most Latin American countries.[11] Particularly in the cities, early-peaked patterns are characteristic of participation by Latin American women in income-producing jobs (see Table 3.11).

The high level of male standardized activity rates in Latin America, Spain, and Portugal stems both from early entry of males into the labor force and late retirement. The HH pattern of male age-specific activity rates is more prevalent in this region than in any other (Table 3.5). Eight of the fourteen countries in the worldwide cross section that exhibit the HH pattern are in this region. Only Puerto Rico, Argentina, and Uruguay have early retirement patterns, and late entry is recorded only in the censuses of Peru and Puerto Rico. This is the only region where cross-sectional mean levels of male activity rates are consistently higher both in the entry and retirement ages than would be expected in view of the levels of development of the countries. This pattern is especially pronounced in the rural sectors.

There might be a causal link between high participation by males and low participation by females in rural-agricultural employment. But why should it be so in the countries of Spanish and Portuguese language and not elsewhere, in the Arab countries for example? And how can Puerto Rico's conspicuously exceptional pattern be explained? This study can only pose such questions without attempting to find the answers.

3.6. Middle and Northwestern Europe, Northern America, and Oceania (regions 7 and 8)

In the two regional groups that constitute the so-called "Western" industrialized countries—middle Europe on the one hand, northwestern Europe, northern America, and Oceania on the other—male standardized activity rates are relatively low, in keeping with the generally high level of economic development, while the female rates are consistently in the medium range, from 20 to 50. Thus

---

[11] See the compilation of data on female labor force classified by marital status, in United Nations, *Demographic Yearbook* (1968), Table 9.

Regional patterns

the patterns of the two groups are similar, but differences in certain respects warrant their treatment as separate groups.

With regard to the female shares in agricultural and nonagricultural employment, the prevailing pattern in northwestern Europe, etc., is similar to that of the Latin American countries, Spain, and Portugal, with the FS_{ag} low and FS_{nonag} at medium levels. It is the preponderance of the nonagricultural sector in the countries of northwestern Europe, etc., which brings their female activity rates to a much higher level than that of the Latin American countries. The levels of FS_{nonag} are also similar in the middle European countries, but here FS_{ag} levels are higher, with the result that the average level of female standardized activity rates is somewhat higher than in northwestern Europe, etc.

On the map of Europe showing the levels of female shares in agricultural employment as recorded in the censuses (Figure 3.2), one can see a general pattern of downward gradations horizontally from east to west and vertically from the center to the north and south. A zone of FS_{ag} exceeding 40 percent embraces the Slavic countries, Rumania, Germany, and Austria, while there are two zones where this index is below 20 percent: one in the northwest and the other in the Iberian peninsula. Medium-level FS_{ag}, between 20 and 40 percent, is found on the borders of the high and low zones and in between: in France, Switzerland, Italy, Greece, and Finland; also in Hungary, although in this case the level is high in all the surrounding countries. It is as if cultural influences tending to minimize participation by women in agricultural work had diffused from two poles in the northwest and southwest, while an opposite influence diffused from a pole in the east center. The Iberian zone of low FS_{ag} is projected overseas to Latin America, while the northwest European zone is projected to the United States, Canada, Australia, and New Zealand. In South Africa, the European, Asiatic, and "Coloured" minorities follow the northwest European pattern, while Bantu women take a larger part in agriculture: FS_{ag} of 4.9 percent for Europeans, 10.2 for Asiatics, 6.7 for Coloured, and 31.3 for Bantu, according to the 1946 census.[12]

[12] Smaller differences between ethnic groups are recorded in the United States: FS_{ag} of 8.6 percent for whites, 15.9 for blacks, and 14.1 for others at the 1960 census. (*United States Census of Population, 1960, United States Summary, Detailed Characteristics*, Table 213.) One might expect to find medium-level FS_{ag} projected from France to the French-speaking region of Canada, but the Canadian statistics do not show this. For example, FS_{ag}

Figure 3.2. Female shares in agricultural employment (FS$_{ag}$) in countries of Europe, cross-sectional censuses

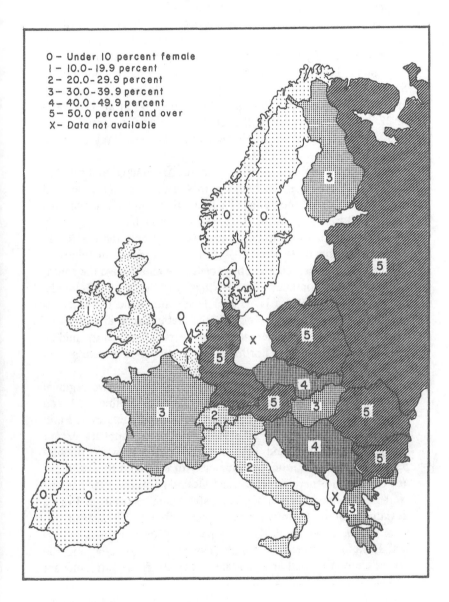

0 – Under 10 percent female
1 – 10.0-19.9 percent
2 – 20.0-29.9 percent
3 – 30.0-39.9 percent
4 – 40.0-49.9 percent
5 – 50.0 percent and over
X – Data not available

Regional patterns

Evidence of underreporting of female agricultural workers in the censuses of Sweden, Denmark, and the United States is noted in Appendix G. No doubt such underreporting occurs also in the censuses of other countries in northwestern Europe, northern America, and Oceania, but there is little reason for thinking that the true levels of participation by females in agricultural work are as high in these countries as in central and Eastern Europe. In Sweden, a careful effort in the 1965 census to get a correct enumeration of women active in agriculture resulted in an FS_{ag} ratio of 22.7 percent, which is well over twice the level recorded in the 1960 Swedish census, but still less than half the level recorded in West Germany in 1961.

The European map of female shares in nonagricultural employment (Figure 3.3) exhibits a narrower range of variations and less consistency of geographical pattern than appears in the map for agriculture. None of the European countries has FS_{nonag} below 20 percent at the cross-sectional censuses, and only the USSR and Finland are above 40 percent. A belt of countries with relatively low FS_{nonag}, between 20 and 30 percent, stretches across the southern part of the continent from Portugal to Greece and Rumania, but not including Bulgaria. Higher levels are found in the countries farther north, except Belgium, the Netherlands, and Norway. There is no consistent difference in this respect between the middle European group and the northwestern group, as both have a mixture of relatively high and low levels of FS_{nonag}.

There is a more consistent difference between the two regional groups in age patterns of female activity rates (Table 3.11 and Figure 3.4). The early-peaked pattern that predominates in Latin America is found also in all middle European countries except Finland (late peak) and France (double peak), while double-peaked patterns are found in a majority of countries in northwestern Europe, northern America, and Oceania (except Belgium, the Netherlands, and Sweden). Curiously, Spain as well as France deviates from the Latin norm by displaying the double-peaked pattern. On the other hand, the early-peaked pattern appears in several Eastern European countries (Hungary, Yugoslavia, and the Soviet Union) as well as in middle Europe.[13] These variations are

---

was recorded as 9.2 percent in Quebec Province, 13.2 in Ontario, and 8.7 in British Columbia at the 1961 census (*1961 Census of Canada, Bulletin 3.2–1*, Table 1A).

[13] Age patterns of female activity rates in Poland and the Soviet Union

Figure 3.3. Female shares in nonagricultural employment (FS_{nonag}) in countries of Europe, cross-sectional censuses

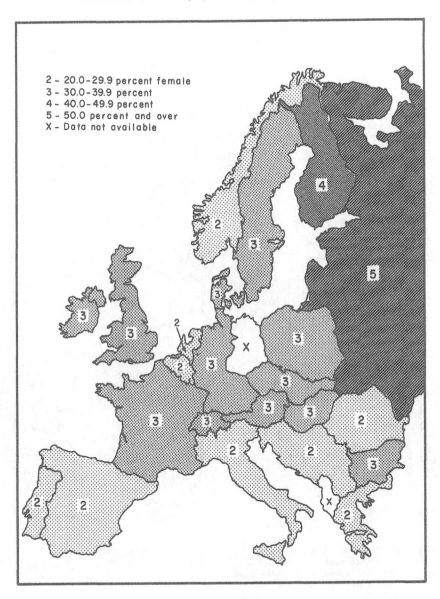

2 - 20.0-29.9 percent female
3 - 30.0-39.9 percent
4 - 40.0-49.9 percent
5 - 50.0 percent and over
X - Data not available

Figure 3.4. Age patterns of female activity rates in European countries, cross-sectional censuses

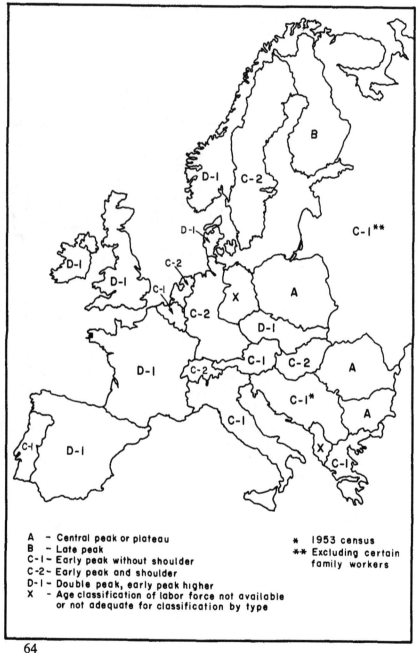

A – Central peak or plateau
B – Late peak
C-1– Early peak without shoulder
C-2– Early peak and shoulder
D-1– Double peak, early peak higher
X – Age classification of labor force not available
    or not adequate for classification by type

* 1953 census
** Excluding certain
    family workers

not readily explainable in terms of either economic or demographic conditions of the countries. The problem of identifying cultural and institutional factors that could explain them is beyond the scope of this study.

The same remark applies to the age patterns of male activity rates, which are mapped for countries in Europe in Figure 3.5 according to the classification scheme described in chapter 2. The variations in tempo of entry of males into the labor force among the European countries are especially remarkable. The late entry pattern, expected to be associated with a well developed industrial economy and a high degree of urbanization, appears in only one country in the middle European group (Finland), while it is found in five of the eleven countries in northwestern Europe, northern America, and Oceania, and in three of the five Eastern European countries for which data are available. As a result, the average level of male activity rates in the entry ages is noticeably higher in the middle European countries than in both Eastern Europe and northwestern Europe, etc. Early entry patterns (HL or HM) occur in a group of European countries centered in West Germany and Austria that also includes Hungary, Yugoslavia, Denmark, and the United Kingdom, as well as in the Iberian countries (HH for Portugal, HM for Spain). The contrast between the HL pattern in such highly developed countries as the United Kingdom, Denmark, and West Germany on the one hand, and the LL pattern in Belgium, Norway, Sweden, and Finland, on the other, is not to be explained in terms of such factors as economic structure and levels of wages and incomes. A factor in such differences may be the system of apprenticeship related to secondary school education, or the procedure followed in the census for classifying young people who work as apprentices while attending school.

3.7. Tropical Africa (region 1)

A high average level of female standardized activity rates is recorded in the fifteen tropical African countries for which data

and of female and male rates in Yugoslavia are indicated in Figures 3.4 and 3.5, although these countries are not included in the cross-sectional tabulations of age-specific rates (in Poland's case because the labor force statistics by age groups do not include the armed forces, in the case of the Soviet Union because they do not include certain unpaid family workers, and in the case of Yugoslavia because the age classification was not found in the 1961 census tabulations but only in those of the 1953 census).

Regional patterns

Figure 3.5. Age patterns of male activity rates in European countries, cross-sectional censuses

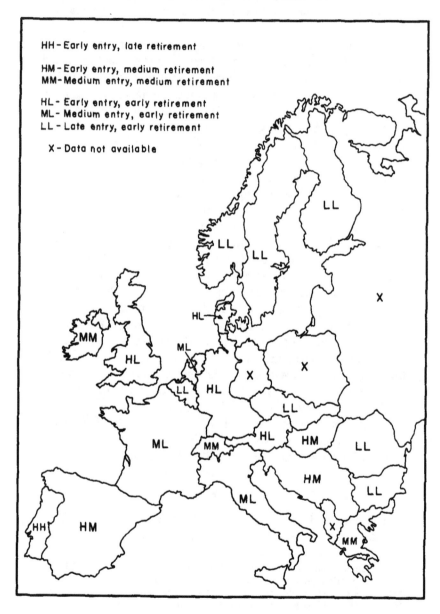

HH – Early entry, late retirement

HM – Early entry, medium retirement
MM – Medium entry, medium retirement

HL – Early entry, early retirement
ML – Medium entry, early retirement
LL – Late entry, early retirement

X – Data not available

were obtained, but the consistently high level of these rates that distinguishes the Eastern European countries is not found in tropical Africa. Here the rates range from only 1.0 in Portuguese Guinea to *81.0 in Dahomey. Since agriculture accounts for a large majority of the labor force in all countries in this region, it is mainly the female share in agricultural employment that determines the level of each country's female activity rates. Recorded levels of FS_{ag} range from zero in Portuguese Guinea to 52.3 percent in Botswana and 59.4 in Zaire.[14] Female shares in nonagricultural employment are equally varied, with Zaire at one extreme, reporting FS_{nonag} of less than 1 percent, and Ghana and Nigeria at the opposite extreme, with 42.2 and 43.4 percent, respectively. Nigerian and Ghanaian women are especially noted for their role in commerce.

Levels of participation by males in the labor force also are uneven in tropical Africa. Although no extremely low male standardized activity rates are found in this region, the measures range from modest levels of *71.6 in Botswana and 71.9 in Liberia to extremely high *87.3 in Dahomey and *89.5 in Togo. (Recall that asterisks denote the use of refined activity rates as substitutes for standardized rates where the data were insufficient for calculating the latter.) In a majority of cases, the male rates are below average for the low levels of development of the countries.

If the eight tropical African countries for which we have measures of age-specific activity rates are representative, the most frequent age patterns of the rates for females in this region are those of the central peak or plateau (Type A) and the late peak (Type B). The early-peaked pattern that predominates in Latin America is not found in any of the tropical African countries for which we have data.

The three Portuguese territories (Angola, Mozambique, and Portuguese Guinea), designated in the tables as subregion 1a, stand apart from the rest of the tropical African region with conspicuously low activity rates of females as recorded in the census, and high rates for males. Female shares are low in both agricul-

[14] In several tropical African countries, female shares in the agricultural labor force are heightened by the absence of many men who have gone to seek work outside the country. This is true especially of Botswana among the countries represented in the cross-section, and it may be for this reason that Botswana's male standardized activity rate is relatively low. In Lesotho, the proportion of absent male workers is so high that it was considered advisable to omit Lesotho's statistics from the cross section.

tural and nonagricultural employment, and female standardized activity rates rival those of the Arab countries for the distinction of the world's lowest, while the standardized activity rates of males are on a higher average level than those of any other region. The low levels of FS_{ag} contrast especially with those of most other countries in Africa south of the Sahara. What these three territories have in common, of course, is a Portuguese colonial administration, which may be inclined to cast the census definitions and procedures for enumeration and classification of the returns in a Portuguese mold. But the recorded female shares, especially in agriculture, are lower than those indicated by the census for Portugal. The extreme case is that of the 1950 census of Portuguese Guinea, where the occupational category of agricultural workers was apparently confined by definition to males.

On the whole, the statistics of the tropical African countries serve better to dispel any preconceptions about typical patterns of labor force participation in African societies than to identify features that are characteristic of the region. In this connection, it is pertinent also to consider the contrast between the patterns shown by the census of Haiti and those of Jamaica, Guyana, and Trinidad and Tobago. In Haiti, according to the 1950 census, both the male and the female standardized activity rates and female shares in both agricultural and nonagricultural employment are among the highest in the world. Jamaica, Trinidad and Tobago, and Guyana, on the other hand, have medium levels of female standardized activity rates and female shares in agricultural employment, and male standardized activity rates also in the medium range (74.0 to 76.6). It is only the female share in nonagricultural employment in Jamaica that can be regarded as high (49.3 percent); the corresponding figures for Guyana and Trinidad and Tobago are at medium levels.

3.8 South and East Asia (region 4)

The statistics of the South and East Asian countries present a picture of levels of participation by males and females in the labor force which is hardly less varied than that of the tropical African region, yet it is distinctive in some respects. No extremely low female standardized activity rates are found in South and East Asia, but several countries have very high rates, Thailand, Khmer Republic (Cambodia), Nepal, and Ryukyu Islands being above 50 percent. The regional average of the female activity rates is some-what higher than the average of the world-wide cross section. For males, on the other hand, a majority of the South and East Asian countries have standardized activity rates below the average levels for countries at corresponding levels of economic development. No country in this region exhibits a male standardized rate above 85 and the rates for two countries are very low: South Korea and Mauritius, both below 70 percent.

In South and East Asia, as in Eastern Europe, women generally have larger shares in the agricultural than in the nonagricultural labor force. This pattern is the opposite of the pattern found in the Arab countries, Latin America, Spain, Portugal, northwestern Europe, northern America, and Oceania (Table 3.8). The two exceptions in South and East Asia are Indonesia, where FS_{nonag} is a little higher than FS_{ag} (30.0 compared with 26.1 percent at the 1961 census) and the Philippines, where there is a much larger difference in favor of FS_{nonag} (42.7 compared with 14.8, according to the census of 1960). It is a curious and possibly significant fact that the Filipino pattern, so exceptional in South and East Asia, resembles the pattern found both in Spain and the United States. Japanese, Thai, and Cambodian women seem to be outstanding for their large shares in nonagricultural as well as agricultural em-ployment, although their participation in agriculture is greater. On the other hand, the women of Pakistan, Taiwan, and Mauritius are distinguished for low shares in both sectors.

The censuses of South and East Asian countries show mixed trends in participation by women in both the agricultural and the nonagricultural labor force, increasing in some countries and de-creasing in others, although increases predominate in the nonagri-cultural sector. There seems to be a slight decrease in average level of female participation in the labor force as a whole. This can be attributed partly to the negative effect of the increasing share of nonagricultural industries in employment in this region, where the female shares are generally smaller in the nonagricultural than in the agricultural sector.

3.9. Data from Local Studies of Agricultural Labor in Tropical Africa and South and East Asia

In conclusion, it should be noted once again that the census statis-tics provide a blurred and distorted picture of differences between

69

and within regions, especially with respect to the participation of women in agriculture. Other data confirm, however, the existence of wide differences in this respect, related to the cultural traditions of different societies. As an illustration, it is pertinent to cite some data compiled by Ester Boserup from local studies of agricultural labor inputs in various countries in tropical Africa and South and East Asia. The estimates shown in Table 3E, extracted from Boserup's compilation,[15] refer to: (A) percentages of females

Table 3E

Areas in which villages studied are located	A	B	C
Western India	36	18	17
Central India	24	16	6
Southern India	40	20	25
Philippines	21	30	13
Northern China	27	—	9
Southern China	31	—	16
of which, subregion with multiple cropping of paddy	42	—	30
Senegal	53	8	29
Gambia	52	20	67
Nigeria	57	3	9
Central African Republic	58	15	60
Cameroon	62	13	56
Congo (Brazzaville)	57	24	68
Uganda	57	17	55

[15] *Woman's Role in Economic Development*, data extracted from Tables 1 and 2, pages 21 and 25. Figures for western India are averages of data from three samples and for central India from two samples, shown separately in Boserup's table. Data for China are from studies made during 1929–1933. Figures for Gambia are averages of data from studies carried out in the same village in two years, those for Central African Republic are averages of data from three samples, and those for Uganda are averages from seven samples, shown separately in Boserup's table. Boserup's note, referring to the figures for Africa, is important for the interpretation of these estimates:

Some of the sources from which the information was collected failed to specify the length of the work day, or the type of activities classified as agricultural (for instance, it was sometimes not clear whether threshing and transport to and from the field were included). In cases where workdays per year were given without specification of their length, the total number of hours worked per year was calculated on the assumption of a six-hour day, and this figure was then divided by 52 to give average number of hours worked per week. The assumption of a six-hours day among family workers in agriculture, (B) average hours of work per week on own farm by female family workers, (C) percentages of all work on farms performed by female family workers, for certain villages in the countries listed.

Although such local data cannot be taken to represent conditions in any country as a whole, they do confirm the existence of large differences in women's contributions to agricultural labor supply among communities in these parts of the world. They support the indication given by the census statistics that this contribution is greater, on the average, in tropical Africa than in South and East Asia, although wide variations within both regions are indicated. It is evidently not uncommon among the peoples of tropical Africa for agriculture to be mainly a female occupation. Boserup observes that "female farming" tends to be associated with nonintensive systems of shifting cultivation without the use of the plow, such as are practiced throughout much of tropical Africa and some parts of Latin America and South and East Asia. Men commonly take a larger part in agricultural work where the plow is used.[16]

---

may well be on the high side, since shorter hours were recorded in many of the samples, and days of more than six hours were recorded only in a few cases and then in the busiest seasons only. For these reasons, the figures in the table can convey only a broad picture of the input of work in African farming, and it must not be assumed that the table gives a satisfactory picture of differences in work input among the localities mentioned.

[16] *Ibid.*, chapter 1.

Regional patterns

Table 3.1. Mean levels of principal measures of labor force dimensions for regional groups of countries, cross-sectional censuses

Regional groups	Number of countries	Crude activity rate (CAR)	Age-sex index (ASI or ASI')	Standardized activity rates Both sexes, all ages (Stand'$_t$)	Males 10+ (Stand$_m$ or RAR$_m$)	Females 10+ (Stand$_f$ or RAR$_f$)	Female shares in employment[a] Agri-cultural (FS$_{ag}$)	Nonagri-culture (FS$_{nonag}$)
All regions	100	38.8	-1.6	40.4	76.8	32.0	22.4	26.8
1. Tropical Africa	15	42.2	-4.0	46.2	79.3	45.1	27.9	19.7
1a. Portuguese Africa	3	29.4	-2.5	31.9	81.4	4.8	5.6	10.0
2. Arab countries	9	28.5	-4.0	32.5	76.5	11.1	7.6	12.5
3. Other Moslem countries	7	41.8	-4.0	45.8	81.2	42.3	24.6	16.1
4. South and East Asia	16	38.4	-3.0	41.4	77.0	36.0	33.5	23.5
5. Latin America, Spain, and Portugal	22	32.9	-3.1	36.0	79.0	19.2	6.9	31.6
6. Eastern Europe	9	49.1	+3.1	46.0	73.8	50.0	50.0	34.7
7. Middle Europe	7	45.5	+3.6	41.9	74.2	38.6	38.3	32.3
8. Northwestern Europe, Northern America, and Oceania	11	40.3	+2.2	38.1	72.9	29.6	9.5	30.4
9. Miscellaneous	9	38.5	-1.9	40.4	75.5	33.2	28.2	31.3

a
Excluding 9 countries for which industry classifications of employed workers or labor force by sex were not found (5 in region 1, 1 in region 2, 3 in region 3, 1 in region 5, 2 in region 6).

Table 3.2. Levels of male standardized activity rates in regional groups of countries, cross-sectional censuses

	All regions	Region 1	Region 1a	Region 2	Region 3	Region 4	Region 5	Region 6	Region 7	Region 8	Region 9
A. Levels of national total rates (Stand$_m$ or RAR$_m$)											
Number of countries	100	15	3	9	7	16	22	9	7	11	9
Mean level	76.8	79.3	81.4	76.5	81.2	77.0	79.0	73.8	74.2	72.9	75.5
Frequency distribution:											
Under 70.0	10	-	-	1	-	2	1	2	-	3	1
70.0-74.9	28	3	-	4	-	3	3	3	4	5	3
75.0-79.9	35	5	1	2	3	5	8	4	3	3	4
80.0-84.9	20	5	2	1	3	6	8	-	-	-	-
85.0 and over	7	2	-	1	1	-	2	-	-	-	1
B. Deviations from mean rates for countries at corresponding levels of development											
Mean deviation	0.0	-1.5	+0.4	-1.0	+2.0	-2.2	+2.2	-0.2	+0.5	-0.3	+1.1
Positive deviations	58	6	2	2	5	6	20	3	4	6	6
Negative deviations	42	9	1	7	2	10	2	6	3	5	3
C. Levels of rural and urban rates											
Number of countries	41	4	-	4	5	6	14	1	2	5	3
Mean levels:											
Rural	78.5	77.0	-	75.5	84.9	78.0	82.8	76.6	77.5	71.2	73.2
Urban	71.0	71.1	-	68.3	73.5	69.3	72.8	66.2	69.5	69.9	71.7

Table 3.3. Intercensal changes of male standardized activity rates in regional groups of countries

Regional groups	Number of countries	Mean annual change	+.10 or more	+.09 to -.09	-.10 to -.49	-.50 or more
All regions	58	-.35	2	9	34	13
1. Tropical Africa	-	-	-	-	-	-
2. Arab countries	1	-.66	-	-	-	1
3. Other Moslem countries	3	-.75	-	-	2	1
4. South and East Asia	9	-.26	-	3	5	1
5. Latin America, Spain and Portugal	16	-.24	2	1	11	2
6. Eastern Europe	7	-.72	-	1	1	5
7. Middle Europe	6	-.29	-	2	3	1
8. Northwestern Europe, Northern America, and Oceania	11	-.26	-	2	9	-
9. Miscellaneous	6	-.49	-	-	3	3

The columns +.10 or more, +.09 to -.09, -.10 to -.49, -.50 or more fall under the heading: Frequency distribution

Table 3.4. Levels of male age-specific activity rates in regional groups of countries, cross-sectional censuses

Regional groups	Number of countries	Mean levels of male activity rates 15-19 years	20-29 years[a]	30-44 years[a]	45-64 years[a]	65 years & over[a]	Average deviations from mean rates for countries at corresponding levels of development 15-19 years	20-29 years[a]	30-44 years[a]	45-64 years[a]	65 years & over[a]
All regions	84	65.6	93.4	97.3	90.4	50.3	-	-	-	-	-
Region 1	8	73.6	93.8	97.4	94.0	66.6	-0.5	-0.1	-0.1	+0.5	+2.0
Region 2	7	58.5	91.4	96.2	89.0	55.3	-6.3	-1.8	-0.8	-1.0	-1.4
Region 3	5	74.7	93.7	97.1	92.2	65.9	+4.1	0.0	-0.3	-0.4	+3.0
Region 4	16	63.2	92.2	97.1	89.5	52.0	-6.5	-1.4	-0.3	-2.7	-9.7
Region 5	22	71.1	94.3	97.2	91.4	61.3	+6.2	+1.1	0.0	+1.4	+7.9
Region 6	4	52.5	93.4	98.2	84.9	34.4	-8.3	+0.4	+0.9	-2.8	-3.3
Region 7	7	69.4	93.0	97.0	87.3	29.6	+7.9	-0.3	-0.3	-1.7	-6.2
Region 8	11	59.8	92.7	97.4	91.0	27.7	-1.6	-0.8	-0.1	+1.1	-2.8
Region 9	7	62.3	96.0	98.4	91.7	49.6	-0.4	+2.8	+1.1	+3.4	+7.5

a
Unweighted average rates for 5-year age groups.

Regional patterns

Table 3.5. Types of age patterns of male activity rates in regional groups of countries, cross-sectional censuses

	All regions	Region 1	Region 2	Region 3	Region 4	Region 5	Region 6	Region 7	Region 8	Region 9
Total, all types	84	8	7	5	16	22	4	7	11	7
HH: Early entry, late retirement	14	2	1	2	1	8	-	-	-	1
MH: Medium entry, late retirement	10	1	2	1	3	4	-	-	-	-
LH: Late entry, late retirement	4	2	-	-	1	1	-	-	-	-
HM: Early entry, medium retirement	8	2	-	1	2	3	1	-	-	-
MM: Medium entry, medium retirement	11	1	1	1	2	3	-	2	1	-
LM: Late entry, medium retirement	9	-	3	-	4	-	-	-	-	2
HL: Early entry, early retirement	6	-	-	-	1	-	-	2	2	1
ML: Medium entry, early retirement	7	-	-	-	-	2	-	2	3	-
LL: Late entry, early retirement	15	-	-	-	2	1	3	1	5	3
All early entry patterns	28	4	1	3	4	11	1	2	2	2
All medium entry patterns	28	2	3	2	5	9	-	4	4	-
All late entry patterns	28	2	3	-	7	2	3	1	5	5
All late retirement patterns	28	5	3	3	5	13	-	-	-	1
All medium retirement patterns	28	3	4	2	8	6	1	2	1	2
All early retirement patterns	28	-	-	-	3	3	3	5	10	4

Table 3.6. Levels of rural and urban male age-specific activity rates in regional groups of countries, cross-sectional censuses

Age groups	All regions	Region 1	Region 2	Region 3	Region 4	Region 5	Region 6	Region 7	Region 8	Region 9
Number of countries	36	4	2	5	6	14	1	2	4	1
Mean rural rates:										
15-19 years	71.8	66.4	67.8	82.3	63.5	80.8	68.8	70.8	52.0	80.9
20-29 years	94.2	92.0	93.2	95.4	93.0	96.2	92.5	94.3	89.6	98.2
30-44 years	97.1	96.8	96.3	97.5	97.0	97.5	98.4	97.5	95.2	98.2
45-64 years	92.8	91.4	91.3	93.5	92.6	94.4	95.2	92.1	89.2	90.4
65 years and over	60.9	59.4	61.8	69.3	62.4	70.1	63.3	49.1	32.4	41.9
Mean urban rates:										
15-19 years	50.2	52.5	39.9	56.1	45.8	53.8	31.8	50.6	45.7	71.5
20-29 years	88.8	87.5	90.7	89.4	85.2	90.4	82.5	88.9	88.5	93.5
30-44 years	95.8	93.6	95.3	95.4	95.6	96.2	96.2	96.3	96.4	96.2
45-64 years	87.3	87.7	86.4	87.0	84.4	88.3	86.6	83.6	90.3	86.1
65 years and over	45.7	54.3	40.1	52.5	45.1	52.4	45.5	24.4	27.4	37.2
Mean urban-rural differences:[a]										
15-19 years	-21.6	-13.9	-27.9	-26.2	-17.7	-27.0	-37.0	-20.2	-6.3	-9.4
20-29 years	-5.4	-4.5	-2.5	-6.0	-7.8	-5.8	-10.0	-5.4	-1.1	-4.7
30-44 years	-1.3	-3.2	-1.0	-2.1	-1.4	-1.3	-2.3	-1.2	+1.2	-2.0
45-64 years	-5.5	-3.7	-4.9	-6.5	-8.2	-6.1	-8.6	-8.5	+1.1	-4.3
65 years and over	-15.2	-5.1	-21.7	-16.8	-17.3	-17.7	-17.8	-24.7	-5.0	-4.7

a
Urban minus rural rates.

Table 3.7. Levels of female standardized activity rates in regional groups of countries, cross-sectional censuses

	All regions	Region 1	Region 1a	Region 2	Region 3	Region 4	Region 5	Region 6	Region 7	Region 8	Region 9
National total rates ($Stand_f$ or RAR_f)											
Number of countries	100	15	3	9	7	16	22	9	7	11	9
Mean level	32.0	45.1	4.8	11.1	42.3	36.0	19.2	50.0	38.6	29.6	33.2
Frequency distribution:											
Under 10.0	11	3	3	7	-	-	1	-	-	-	1
10.0-19.9	21	-	-	-	2	3	16	-	-	-	-
20.0-29.9	23	2	-	1	1	5	4	-	1	6	4
30.0-39.9	14	1	-	1	-	1	-	1	2	5	3
40.0-49.9	12	2	-	-	-	3	-	3	4	-	-
50.0-59.9	9	1	-	-	2	3	1	4	-	-	-
60.0 and over	10	6	-	-	2	1	-	1	-	-	1
Rural and urban patterns											
Number of countries:											
Total	41	4	-	4	5	6	14	1	2	5	3
Rural exceeds urban rate	16	3	-	1	5	6	-	1	1	-	2
Urban exceeds rural rate	25	1	-	3	-	-	14	-	1	5	1
Mean level of rural rates	26.2	59.8	-	10.2	43.1	32.2	10.8	64.3	43.3	21.5	30.6
Mean level of urban rates	25.0	42.7	-	9.6	17.1	19.0	24.7	33.7	34.0	32.3	24.7

Table 3.8. Levels of female shares in agricultural and nonagricultural employment in regional groups of countries, cross-sectional censuses

	All regions	Region 1	Region 1a	Region 2	Region 3	Region 4	Region 5	Region 6	Region 7	Region 8	Region 9
Number of countries	91	10	3	8	4	16	21	7	7	11	9
Female shares in agricultural employment (FS_{ag})											
Mean level	22.4	27.8	5.6	7.6	24.6	33.5	6.9	50.0	38.3	9.5	28.2
Frequency distribution:											
Under 10.0	36	3	2	7	1	-	17	-	-	8	-
10.0-19.9	15	2	1	-	1	3	3	-	-	3	4
20.0-29.9	7	-	-	1	1	3	-	-	2	-	1
30.0-39.9	11	1	-	-	-	4	-	1	3	-	2
40.0-49.9	9	2	-	-	-	3	1	2	-	-	1
50.0 and over	13	2	-	-	1	3	-	4	2	-	1
Female shares in nonagricultural employment (FS_{nonag})											
Mean level	26.8	19.7	10.0	12.5	16.1	23.5	31.6	34.7	32.3	30.4	31.3
Frequency distribution:											
Under 10.0	10	2	1	6	2	1	-	-	-	-	-
10.0-19.9	13	4	2	1	1	6	-	-	-	-	1
20.0-29.9	31	2	-	-	-	4	9	2	2	6	6
30.0-39.9	27	-	-	1	1	3	10	4	4	5	-
40.0-49.9	9	2	-	-	-	2	2	1	1	-	1
50.0 and over	1	-	-	-	-	-	-	-	-	-	1
FS_{ag} exceeds FS_{nonag}		4	1	1	2	14	1	7	4	-	3
FS_{nonag} exceeds FS_{ag}		3	2	7	2	2	20	-	3	11	6

Regional patterns

Table 3.9. Intercensal changes of female standardized activity rates and female shares in agricultural nonagricultural employment in regional groups of countries

	All regions	Region 1	Region 2	Region 3	Region 4	Region 5	Region 6	Region 7	Region 8	Region 9
	Female standardized activity rates ($Stand_f$ or RAR_f)									
Number of countries	58	-	1	3	9	16	7	6	11	6
Mean annual change	-.10	-	-.29	-1.05	-.17	-.26	-.26	-.05	+.06	-.1
Frequency distribution:										
+.50 or more	3	-	-	-	-	1	1	-	-	1
+.10 to +.49	17	-	-	1	1	4	1	2	7	1
+.09 to -.09	16	-	-	-	3	8	2	2	-	1
-.10 to -.49	13	-	1	-	4	1	1	2	3	1
-.50 or more	9	-	-	2	1	2	2	-	1	2
	Female shares in agricultural employment (FS_{ag})									
Number of countries	54	-	1	2	9	14	5	6	11	6
Mean annual change	-.13	-	-.45	-.08	0.0	-.14	+.35	-.20	-.16	-.5
Frequency distribution:										
+.50 or more	3	-	-	-	-	-	1	-	1	1
+.10 to +.49	14	-	-	1	3	2	3	1	3	1
+.09 to -.09	14	-	-	-	3	6	1	2	2	-
-.10 to -.49	13	-	1	1	3	4	-	1	3	-
-.50 or more	10	-	-	-	-	2	-	2	2	4
	Female shares in nonagricultural employment (FS_{nonag})									
Number of countries	54	-	1	2	9	14	5	6	11	6
Mean annual change	+.10	-	+.26	+.10	+.07	-.07	+.55	+.11	+.09	+.14
Frequency distribution:										
+.50 or more	5	-	-	-	-	-	3	-	-	2
+.10 to +.49	21	-	1	1	4	4	2	2	7	-
+.09 to -.09	14	-	-	1	3	5	-	3	1	1
-.10 to -.49	11	-	-	-	1	3	-	1	3	3
-.50 or more	3	-	-	-	1	2	-	-	-	-

Table 3.10. Mean levels of female age-specific activity rates in regional groups of countries, cross-sectional censuses

	All regions	Region 1	Region 2	Region 3	Region 4	Region 5	Region 6	Region 7	Region 8	Region 9
Number of countries	84	8	7	5	16	22	4	7	11	7
Mean levels of rates:										
15-19 years	36.4	38.9	10.5	40.4	41.7	23.4	47.8	54.9	52.0	36.9
20-29 years[a]	37.6	42.8	8.9	42.0	42.2	26.0	67.5	55.1	43.4	42.0
30-44 years[a]	34.0	44.8	8.7	43.4	42.6	22.0	70.1	43.3	29.0	41.1
45-64 years[a]	29.3	39.4	8.1	38.8	37.4	17.7	50.2	36.0	26.9	39.1
65 years and over[a]	11.8	19.6	4.0	22.8	15.2	8.6	13.3	9.4	6.5	16.8
20-24 years	40.8	42.9	9.7	41.9	44.2	27.8	67.8	62.8	54.0	44.2
25-29 years	34.4	42.7	8.1	42.1	40.3	24.2	67.2	47.4	32.7	39.8
30-34 years	33.2	43.8	8.2	42.5	40.9	22.6	68.4	43.2	27.6	39.4
35-39 years	33.9	44.7	8.7	43.0	43.0	21.8	70.8	43.3	28.7	40.7
40-44 years	34.8	45.9	9.3	44.8	44.0	21.8	71.2	43.4	30.5	43.0
45-49 years	34.5	45.4	9.4	43.8	43.9	20.9	68.1	42.9	31.4	44.2
50-54 years	32.5	43.2	8.8	41.8	40.9	19.4	61.6	40.5	30.6	42.2
55-59 years	28.2	38.7	7.7	37.0	36.6	16.6	42.0	35.6	27.2	38.3
60-64 years	21.8	30.4	6.7	32.4	28.0	13.7	29.1	25.2	18.5	31.9
65-69 years	16.4	25.4	5.6	27.1	21.7	11.1	19.4	15.2	10.8	24.5
70-74 years	11.7	19.8	3.8	23.5	15.1	8.8	13.0	8.6	5.7	17.5
75 years and over	7.2	13.5	2.6	17.9	8.9	5.8	7.6	4.3	2.9	8.3

a
Unweighted average rates for 5-year age groups.

able 3.11. Age patterns of female activity rates in regional groups of countries, cross-sectional censuses

Regional groups	Total number of countries	Type A. Central peak or plateau	Type B. Late peak	Type C. Early peak		Type D. Double peak	
				C-1. Without shoulder	C-2. Peak and shoulder	D-1. Early peak higher	D-2. Late peak higher
			National totals				
All regions	84	14	8	21	14	19	8
. Tropical Africa	8	4	2	-	-	1	1
. Arab countries	7	-	-	2	1	3	1
. Other Moslem countries	5	2	1	-	1	-	1
. South and East Asia	16	4	3	2	2	2	3
. Latin America, etc.	22	2	1	11	5	3	-
. Eastern Europe	4	2	-	-	1	1	-
. Middle Europe	7	-	1	3	2	1	-
. Northwestern Europe, etc.	11	-	-	1	2	7	1
. Miscellaneous	7	1	1	2	-	1	-
			Rural				
All regions	36	10	4	5	5	6	6
. Tropical Africa	4	3	1	-	-	-	-
. Arab countries	2	-	-	-	-	1	1
. Other Moslem countries	5	2	1	1	-	-	1
. South and East Asia	6	3	1	-	1	-	1
. Latin America, etc.	14	1	2	3	3	3	2
. Eastern Europe	1	1	-	-	-	-	-
. Middle Europe	2	1	-	-	1	-	-
. Northwestern Europe, etc.	4	-	-	1	-	2	1
. Miscellaneous	1	-	-	-	-	-	1
			Urban				
All regions	36	4	4	15	2	8	3
1. Tropical Africa	4	1	3	-	-	-	-
2. Arab countries	2	-	-	-	-	1	1
3. Other Moslem countries	5	1	2	-	-	1	1
4. South and East Asia	6	2	1	1	-	2	-
5. Latin America, etc.	14	-	-	13	-	1	-
6. Eastern Europe	1	1	-	-	-	-	-
7. Middle Europe	2	-	-	1	1	-	-
8. Northwestern Europe, etc.	4	-	-	-	1	?	1
9. Miscellaneous	1	-	-	-	-	/	-

ble 3.12. Mean levels of rural and urban female age-specific activity rates in regional groups of countries, cross-sectional censuses

Age groups	All regions	Region 1	Region 2	Region 3	Region 4	Region 5	Region 6	Region 7	Region 8	Region 9
mber of countries	36	4	2	5	6	14	-	2	-	-
an levels of rural rates:										
15-19 years	30.8	65.3	22.2	46.8	31.7	14.2	-	48.3	32.1	-
20-29 years	32.5	72.0	17.6	47.5	37.7	13.2	-	55.4	32.0	-
30-44 years	32.2	76.0	20.8	48.7	40.2	11.2	-	53.7	23.6	-
45-64 years	29.0	63.2	21.7	43.7	36.3	10.9	-	46.4	23.1	-
65 years and over	14.1	25.2	12.8	27.8	17.0	7.6	-	14.0	5.7	-
an levels of urban rates:										
15-19 years	29.5	39.3	16.8	15.8	21.4	29.8	-	39.0	41.4	-
20-29 years	35.5	47.7	14.0	18.0	24.1	36.0	-	50.8	48.6	-
30-44 years	31.9	57.7	14.2	21.9	22.8	29.1	-	41.3	37.3	-
45-64 years	26.8	52.6	13.8	20.2	20.9	21.6	-	32.2	37.6	-
65 years and over	9.9	21.9	6.2	8.2	9.0	9.4	-	5.6	8.2	-

FOUR

Economic Development and Relative Size of the Labor Force

4.1. Levels and Trends of Crude Activity Rates in Countries at Different Levels of Development

Let us turn now to the question, how labor force dimensions and patterns of participation in income-producing work may change in the processes of economic development. Beginning with the measures of crude activity rates and their components as defined in chapter 2, let us see how their levels and their changes between censuses differ among countries at different levels of development.

To classify countries by relative levels of economic development, we will use an index composed of two indicators: energy consumption per head and the percent share of the nonagricultural sector in total employment or labor force. The two are combined by ranking the hundred countries in ascending order of each indicator as of the cross-sectional census year (or the nearest year for which data are available in the case of energy consumption), and adding together the two rank numbers for each country. The sum of the rank numbers is the index of relative development level (RDL). The hundred countries are divided into quintile groups by rank order of this index, and the groups are numbered I to V in ascending order, so that Level I comprises the twenty least developed countries and Level V the twenty most developed countries in the cross section. See Appendix H for technical details.

In the cross-sectional tabulation of crude activity rates for countries at the five levels of development (Table 4.1), the mean level of the rates describes a U-shaped curve moving up the scale of development levels. Relatively high crude activity rates, on the average, are found both in the least developed and the most developed countries, and a considerably lower average in those at the middle level of development. However, the association between levels of the rates and levels of development of the countries is not as clear cut as this pattern makes it seem. A glance at the wide-ranging frequency distributions of the rates among countries at each development level is enough to make it plain that other factors play a large part in determining the relative size of the labor force in each country.

Development and size of labor force

Table 4.1. Levels and trends of crude activity rates in countries at different
levels of development

	Total	Level I	Level II	Level III	Level IV	Level V
Cross-sectional levels of crude activity rates						
Number of countries	100	20	20	20	20	20
Mean level	38.8	44.2	35.2	32.3	40.1	42.0
Frequency distribution:						
Under 25.0	2	-	-	2	-	-
25.0-29.9	13	3	3	6	1	-
30.0-34.9	25	2	10	7	4	2
35.0-39.9	18	-	2	1	8	7
40.0-44.9	17	5	4	4	1	3
45.0-49.9	15	4	-	-	4	7
50.0-54.9	8	4	1	-	2	1
55.0 and over	2	2	-	-	-	-
Intercensal changes						
Number of countries	58	3	10	11	17	17
Mean annual change	-.28	-.20	-.44	-.35	-.28	-.17
Frequency distribution:						
+.10 or more	4	-	-	-	3	1
+.09 to -.09	9	1	-	1	1	6
-.10 to -.29	21	1	4	6	3	7
-.30 to -.49	14	1	2	2	7	2
-.50 or more	10	-	4	2	3	1

On the face of it, the cross-sectional pattern suggests that a typical secular trend in countries undergoing economic development might be one of a diminishing relative size of the labor force during early stages of development, and an increasing relative size during later stages. It is well known, though, that there is uncertainty in such inferences about changes over time drawn from associations between variables observed in a cross section. In the present case, a very different pattern appears in the changes of crude activity rates during intervals between censuses. (See the lower panel of Table 4.1. Here, as in the upper panel, the classification of countries by levels of development refers to the date of the cross-sectional census, which, in most instances, is the terminal date of the intercensal period.) It is unfortunate that measures of intercensal changes were obtained for only three countries in Level I, obviously too few to make a firm basis for generalization as regards the trend in countries at the lowest level of development. Subject to this reservation, the trend of crude activity rates during the postwar years appears to have been downward, with few exceptions, in countries at all development levels. There is, however,

79

an apparent association between the level of development and the speed of decline of the rate. The amounts of annual decreases are much smaller, on the average, for Level v countries than for those in Levels II, III, and IV. If the measures for the three countries in Level I could be trusted to be representative, the speed of the declining trend in countries at that level also would appear to be relatively slow. Thus a trend in the form of an inverted S, or logistic curve, is tentatively suggested as typical of changes in relative size of the labor force during the course of economic development: a trend that gets under way slowly in early stages of development, picks up speed in middle stages, and slackens speed again in later stages, possibly terminating eventually in a stable, low level of the crude activity rate. Again, however, the wide variations in amounts of decreases in the rates recorded during the intercensal periods in countries at each level of development should be emphasized. Clearly it is not the level of development alone that governs the speed of this trend.

To gain insight into the mechanism of relationships between economic development and the levels and trends of crude activity rates, and reasons for the discrepancy between the apparent patterns in the cross section and the intercensal change data, let us examine the components of variations of these rates.

4.2. Components of Crude Activity Rates and Their Changes in Countries at Different Levels of Development

As stated in chapter 2, each country's crude activity rate can be considered as determined by three components: (a) the level of participation of males in the labor force according to age, (b) the level of participation by females according to age, and (c) the sex-age composition of the population.

Components a and b are represented by the standardized activity rates of males and females ($Stand_m$ and $Stand_f$). To measure effects of their variations upon the levels and trends of crude activity rates, however, these standardized rates have to be reduced to a common denominator with the crude rates. This is done by multiplying the standardized rate for each sex by the ratio of the population ten years of age and over of the corresponding sex to the total (both sexes, all ages) of the model population on which the standardized rates are based, namely, .37035 for males and .37280 for females. The standardized rates deflated in this way

Development and size of labor force

are denoted $Stand'_m$ and $Stand'_f$. For example, in Bulgaria (1965), with $Stand_m = 66.0$ and $Stand_f = 53.7$, we obtain $Stand'_m = 24.5$ and $Stand'_f = 20.0$ percent.

The effect on the crude activity rate of the difference between the age-sex structure of a country's population and that of the model (component c in the above scheme) is measured by the difference between the crude activity rate as recorded and the sum of $Stand'_m$ and $Stand'_f$, which is denoted as $Stand'_t$. This difference will be called the age-sex index (ASI). Thus:

$$Stand'_t = Stand'_m + Stand'_f$$
$$ASI = CAR - Stand'_t$$

For example, in Bulgaria (1965), with a recorded crude activity rate of 51.9, we have $Stand'_t = 24.5 + 20.0 = 44.5$ and $ASI = 51.9 - 44.5 = +7.4$. This signifies that Bulgaria's crude activity rate is 7.4 points higher than it would be if the population structure were the same as that of the model, with the age-specific activity rates of males and females as recorded in the Bulgarian census. This is the highest positive value of the age-sex index found in any country in the cross section. At the opposite extreme, Nicaragua (1963) has $CAR = 30.9$, $Stand'_t = 37.9$, and $ASI = -7.0$. Values of ASI for each country and census year are listed in Appendix A, Table A.5 for national totals, and Table A.6 for rural and urban sectors.

In the sixteen countries in the cross section where the age classification of the labor force was lacking or not in suitable form for calculating standardized activity rates, an approximation (ASI') to the age-sex index was calculated. This approximate measure takes account of the proportions of population under and over ten years of age and the sex ratio in the population ten and over, but not the age structure of the population ten and over. Values of ASI' used as substitutes for ASI are marked by an asterisk in the following text. See Appendix E for the method of calculating ASI', discussion of its reliability as a substitute for ASI, and other technical details.

A device commonly adopted for simplicity in assessing economic implications of variations in population structure is to treat an age group such as 15 to 59 or 15 to 64 years as "workers," and the remainder of the population as "dependents," irrespective of their actual activities. This has the advantage of avoiding the pitfalls of noncomparability and error in census measures of the labor

81

force, but the price is a serious loss of realism. How the proportion of a country's population in a particular age-sex category affects the relative size of the labor force depends, evidently, on the extent to which persons in that sex-age group participate in the labor force. The wide differences among countries in levels and age-patterns of participation by males and females in the labor force are taken into account by the age-sex index calculated as described above.

It should be noted that the age-sex index is not determined by the population structure alone; it may be different between two countries having the same population structure if their specific activity rates are different. The higher the level of the specific activity rates, other things being equal, the larger will be the value (positive or negative) of the index. A measure that does not depend on the level of the specific rates is obtained by expressing the index as a percentage of the crude activity rate. This is called the relative age-sex index. Its values are $+14.2$ percent for Bulgaria (1965) and -22.6 percent for Nicaragua (1963). Sweden's relative age-sex index as of 1965 ($+14.1$) percent is nearly the same as Bulgaria's, although the absolute index for Sweden ($+6.4$) is smaller. This is because the overall level of the specific activity rates is higher in Bulgaria than in Sweden.

For countries at different levels of economic development, Table 4.2 shows cross-sectional mean values of the three components of crude activity rates: (a) participation by males in the labor force (Stand'$_m$), (b) participation by females (Stand'$_f$), and (c) effects of population structure (ASI). It can be seen that participation by males decreases on the average as the level of development rises, while participation by females follows the pattern of the U-curve of mean levels of crude activity rates, being highest on average in the least developed countries, falling to a minimum in countries in the middle of the development scale, and rising again at higher levels of development. The effect of population structure is strongly negative in countries at the three lowest levels of development, slightly positive in Level IV countries on the average, and strongly positive in Level V.

We can now see how the U-curve of mean levels of crude activity rates in relation to economic development levels of countries is formed. The downswing on the left arm of the U is caused mainly by the decrease in average level of participation by females

Development and size of labor force

	Total	Level I	Level II	Level III	Level IV	Level V
Cross-sectional levels						
Number of countries	100	20	20	20	20	20
Mean level of crude activity rates	38.8	44.2	35.2	32.3	40.1	42.0
Components of mean level:						
Participation by males (Stand'$_m$)	28.4	30.0	29.7	28.1	27.3	27.1
Participation by females (Stand'$_f$)	11.9	17.8	9.8	7.3	11.9	12.7
Population structure (ASI)	-1.6	-3.6	-4.3	-3.1	+0.9	+2.2
Deviation from mean level of CAR in total cross-section	-	+5.5	-3.5	-6.4	+1.4	+3.3
Components of deviation:						
Participation by males	-	+1.6	+1.3	-0.3	-1.1	-1.3
Participation by females	-	+5.8	-2.1	-4.6	0	+0.8
Population structure	-	-2.0	-2.7	-1.5	+2.5	+3.8
Intercensal changes						
Number of countries	58	3	10	11	17	17
Mean annual change of crude activity rates	-.28	-.20	-.44	-.35	-.28	-.17
Components of mean annual change:						
Participation by males	-.13	.00	-.11	-.16	-.17	-.10
Participation by females	-.04	+.02	-.16	-.06	-.02	+.01
Population structure	-.11	-.22	-.17	-.15	-.09	-.08

from Level I to Level III, and partly also by the smaller decrease in participation by males. Population structure changes tending in the opposite direction dampen the downswing to some extent. The upswing on the right arm of the U is due equally to the upturn of female participation and to the shift from negative to positive population structure effects. The continuing decrease of male participation dampens the upswing somewhat.

Components of changes in crude activity rates during the intervals between postwar censuses are analyzed in the lower panel of Table 4.2. On the average, for the fifty-eight countries for which these measures were obtained, about one-half of the decrease in crude activity rates was due to diminishing participation by males, and most of the remainder of the decrease was due to changes in population structure. Effects of changes in participation by males and changes in population structure were negative, on the average, among countries at all development levels, but the importance of both was relatively small in the most developed countries. These two components were mainly responsible for the slower pace of the declining trend of crude activity rates in Level v countries than in

83

countries at medium and lower levels of development. Average effects of changes in participation by females were minor except in the ten countries in Level II for which data were obtained.

Where is the explanation for the discrepancy between the U-shaped curve of mean levels of crude activity rates and the logistic pattern of their mean intercensal changes? It has to be sought in the behavior of the female participation and population structure components in Level IV and Level V countries. Why the mean level of female participation turns upward here in the cross-section, while intercensal changes are neutral on the average is one of the questions to be pursued in chapter 6. The next section of the present chapter will explain why, during the postwar years, effects of population structure changes in Level IV and V countries were negative on the average, although the cross-sectional mean value of this component shifts from negative to positive in the progression from Level III to Levels IV and V of development.

4.3. Components of Population Structure Effects in Countries at Different Levels of Development

The facet of population structure that is most important in connection with the size of the labor force is the proportion of adults to children, and this depends mainly on the level of the birth rate. It is chiefly because the birth rate is generally much lower in highly developed countries than in little-developed countries that the former generally have positive age-sex indices and the latter generally negative indices. The level of infant and child mortality, which is generally higher in less-developed countries, is a partially counteracting factor. The age structure and sex ratio in the adult population also affect the level of the crude activity rate, but the influence of variations in these aspects is of secondary importance in most countries. Variations in age structure of the adult population tend on the whole to be parallel to the variations in proportions of children and adults; that is, the adult population is younger, on the whole, in less-developed than in more-developed countries mainly on account of the difference in levels of the birth rates. The adult population structure is affected appreciably in some countries by immigration, which tends to inflate the proportion of young adults, or emigration, which has an opposite effect. The sex ratio in the adult population is unbalanced in some countries as a result of migration or excess of mortality among males in recent wars.

By the methods explained in Appendix E, the age-sex index can be factored into components that measure the effects of different aspects of the population structure upon the level of the crude activity rate. Four component indices are considered here:

AI_c: effect of difference in the proportion of children under ten years of age in the total population;

AI_m: effect of differences in composition by five-year age groups of the male population ten years of age and over

AI_f: effect of differences in composition by five-year age groups of the female population ten years of age and over

SI: effect of difference in the sex ratio in the population ten years of age and over.

The sum of these four partial indices ordinarily differs slightly from the age-sex index (ASI) as a result of interactions. In the cases considered in the present study, the amount of the residual due to interactions ranges from virtually zero to -0.04.

In the examples of Bulgaria and Nicaragua, the values of these components of the age-sex index are shown in Table 4A.

Table 4A

	Bulgaria 1965	Nicaragua 1963
ASI	+7.4	−7.0
AI_c	+6.0	−5.0
AI_m	+1.3	−1.3
AI_f	+0.1	−0.2
SI	−0.01	−0.5
Residual	−0.02	−0.01

Values of the component indices for each country and census year are listed in the Appendix Tables A.5 and A.6. Where an adequate age classification of the labor force was lacking, AI_m and AI_f could not be calculated, but approximate values of AI_c and SI could be calculated even without the age classification of the labor force. In such cases, the value of ASI', used as a substitute for ASI, is the sum of AI_c and SI.

Table 4.3 gives a cross-sectional view of the age-sex indices and the four component indices for countries at different levels of development.

85

Development and size of labor force

Table 4.3. Indices of effects of population structure on levels of crude activity
rates in countries at different levels of development,
cross-sectional censuses

	Total	Level I	Level II	Level III	Level IV	Level V
Age-sex index (ASI or ASI')						
Number of countries	100	20	20	20	20	20
With positive index	33	1	-	3	12	17
With negative index	67	19	20	17	8	3
Mean absolute index	-1.6	-3.6[a]	-4.3	-3.1	+0.9	+2.2
Mean relative index (percent of CAR)	-5.3	-8.4	-12.8	-10.9	+0.9	+4.6
Effect of proportion of population under age 10 (AI_c)						
Number of countries	100	20	20	20	20	20
With positive index	35	1	-	3	13	18
With negative index	65	19	20	17	7	2
Mean absolute index	-1.0	-3.8[a]	-3.7	-2.3	+1.3	+3.4
Mean relative index (percent of CAR)	-3.6	-8.7	-10.6	-8.2	+2.2	+7.4
Effect of age structure of male population 10+ (AI_m)						
Number of countries	84[b]	13	19	17	18	17[b]
With positive index	24	3	1	3	9	8
With negative index	58	9	18	14	9	8
Mean absolute index	-0.3	-0.1[a]	-0.7	-0.8	+0.1	0.0
Mean relative index (percent of CAR)	-1.2	-0.4	-2.2	-2.9	-0.2	0.0
Effect of age structure of female population 10+ (AI_f)						
Number of countries[b]	84[b]	13	19	17	18	17[b]
With positive index	25	10	6	5	4	-
With negative index	58	3	13	11	14	17
Mean absolute index	-0.2	+0.6[a]	0.0	-0.1	-0.3	-1.1
Mean relative index (percent of CAR)	-0.6	+1.1	-0.1	-0.3	-0.7	-2.5
Effect of sex ratio in population 10+ (SI)						
Number of countries[b]	100	20	20	20	20	20
With positive index	35	5	10	9	5	6
With negative index	63	13	10	11	15	14
Mean absolute index	-0.1	-0.1	0.0	0.0	-0.2	-0.3
Mean relative index (percent of CAR)	-0.2	-0.1	0.0	0.0	-0.4	-0.6

a
Mean values excluding erratic figures for Central African Republic and Guinea are
-3.8 for ASI, -3.8 for AI_c, -0.3 for AI_m, +0.1 for AI_f.
b
Including one country with an index of zero.

There are not many exceptions to the rule that little-developed countries have negative age-sex indices (that is, their population structure is such as to depress the crude activity rate), and well-developed countries have positive indices. Negative values of ASI or ASI' are found in all but four of the sixty countries in Levels I, II, and III of development, the exceptions being Central African Republic with $+0.5$ in Level I, Greece, Yugoslavia, and Portugal with $+3.7$, $+2.0$, and $+1.3$, respectively, in Level III. Values of ASI or ASI' are positive in twelve of twenty countries in Level IV, and in all Level V countries except Venezuela, South Africa, and New Zealand, with -4.2, -1.6, and -0.2, respectively. The positive index for the Central African Republic is due to faulty enumeration of the population according to age groups. Venezuela and South Africa are countries where the economic indicators reflect an affluence not shared by large parts of the population.

The generally high proportions of children in the population of less-developed countries are reflected by values of AI_c which, like ASI, are negative for countries at the lower RDL levels and positive for almost all countries at higher levels of economic development. In RDL Level I, only Haiti has a positive AI_c ($+0.5$), due almost certainly to faulty enumeration of children in the census. In Level V, in contrast, all countries have positive AI_c except Venezuela (-3.8) and South Africa (-1.4). On the average, AI_c is strongly negative in Level I, II, and III countries, and strongly positive in Level V.

The values of AI_m and AI_f, either positive or negative, are usually much smaller than those of AI_c. In less developed countries, AI_m is predominantly negative, reenforcing the negative effects of AI_c on the crude activity rate levels, because of relatively large shares of the adult population consisting of teenage youths, whose activity rates are lower than those of men in middle adult ages. In more-developed countries, there are relatively fewer teenage youths, but on the other hand the proportions of elderly people, beyond retirement age, are relatively large. The result is mainly positive AI_f in the countries at Level I of development for which data were obtained, nearly neutral averages for Levels II, III, and IV, and a negative average for Level V. SI is quite small, on the average, in countries at all five levels of development, but it is important in a few countries where the sex ratio is unusually unbalanced as a result of migration, war losses, abnormal sex differences in mortality, or differential underenumeration of the sexes

87

in the census, and where the difference between levels of male and female activity rates is wide. Countries with the largest negative and positive values of SI are listed in Table 4B:

Table 4B

	SI		SI
Mozambique, 1950	−1.72	Pakistan, 1961	+1.67
Portugal, 1960	−1.49	Singapore, 1957	+1.29
East Germany, 1964	−1.21	Libya, 1964	+1.19
Spain, 1960	− .99	Ceylon, 1963	+ .96
West Germany, 1961	− .98		

To summarize, the outstanding feature of the cross-sectional picture of age structure effects is the contrast between the typically large negative values of AI_c in less-developed countries and large positive values of this index in highly developed countries. If, by lowering the birth rates of countries at Levels I and II of development, the proportions of children in their population were brought down to the levels that prevail in the most-developed countries, other factors remaining equal, the relative size of the labor force in Level I and II countries would be enlarged by more than seven workers per hundred of the total population, on the average. The result could be an appreciable help to efforts to raise income per head in the less developed countries, if the additional labor force could be employed at no less than the going average levels of earnings. This alone would obviously not go far, though, toward closing the economic gap between the "have" and "have-not" nations.

During the intervals between postwar censuses represented in the data compiled for the present study (mainly in the decade of the 1950s), there were few countries where the population structure changed in such a way as to lead to an increase in the crude activity rate. On the contrary, the predominant trend of age-sex indices was downward, both in less-developed and more-developed countries (see Table 4.4). In other words, where ASI was negative, it became more negative, and where it was positive, it became less positive in a majority of cases.

Negative changes of ASI or ASI' were recorded in all countries in Levels I, II, and III of development for which measures of intercensal changes were obtained. This trend was due mainly to in-

Development and size of labor force

Table 4.4. Intercensal changes of indices of population structure effects on levels of crude activity rates in countries at different levels of development

	Total	Level 1	Level II	Level III	Level IV	Level V
Age-sex index (ASI or ASI')						
Number of countries	58	3	10	11	17	17
With rising index	11	-	-	-	5	6
With falling index	47	3	10	11	12	11
Mean annual change	-.11	-.22	-.16	-.15	-.09	-.08
Effect of proportion of children under age 10 (AI$_c$)						
Number of countries	58	3	10	11	17	17
With rising index	20	-	1	1	9	9
With falling index	38	3	9	10	8	8
Mean annual change	-.05	-.28	-.11	-.09	+.02	.00
Effect of age structure of male population 10+ (AI$_m$)						
Number of countries	45	-	8	9	14	14
With rising index	3	-	-	1	1	1
With falling index	42	-	8	8	13	13
Mean annual change	-.07	-	-.03	-.04	-.07	-.08
Effect of age structure of female population 10+ (AI$_f$)						
Number of countries	45[a]	-	8	9	14[a]	14
With rising index	7	-	3	1	-	3
With falling index	37	-	5	8	13	11
Mean annual change	-.02	-	-.01	-.01	-.04	-.02
Effect of sex ratio in population 10+ (SI)						
Number of countries	58	3	10	11	17	17
With rising index	33	3	5	7	8	10
With falling index	25	-	5	4	9	7
Mean annual change	.00	+.01	-.01	+.01	-.01	+.01

[a] Including one country with no change in the index.

creasing proportions of child population, reflected by downward movements of AI$_c$, under the pressure of rising birth rates in some less-developed countries and a general trend of sharply decreasing infant and child mortality rates. Negative changes of AI$_m$ and AI$_f$ also contributed to the downward trend of the age-sex indices in a majority of less-developed countries.

Among the countries in Levels IV and V of development for which intercensal change measures were obtained, positive changes

89

of the age-sex indices were recorded in eleven cases and negative changes (mainly from larger to smaller positive values) in twenty-three cases. The countries where the largest positive changes of ASI or ASI' were recorded are listed in Table 4C. Annual increases in the range of $+.01$ to $+.04$ were recorded in Denmark, Sweden, United Kingdom, Italy, West Germany, Netherlands, and Hungary.

Table 4C

	Annual change of ASI or ASI'
Japan, 1950–60	$+.37$
Rumania, 1956–66	$+.12$
Hong Kong, 1961–66	$*+.11$
Austria, 1951–61	$*+.07$

*ASI' used as substitute for ASI.

The trends of AI_c in Level IV and Level V countries were divided almost equally between positive and negative directions, as the birth rates were rising during the 1950s in some more-developed countries and falling in others. Where falling birth rates pushed AI_c upward, however, the positive effect was overbalanced in a majority of cases by negative changes of AI_m and AI_f, due to shifts in the age structure of the adult population (related to earlier trends of birth rates). Slight positive changes of AI_m were recorded in only two cases, and positive AI_f changes in three cases among the twenty-eight countries in Levels IV and V for which data were obtained. These exceptional cases are listed in Table 4D.

It was an unusual and temporary constellation of demographic

Table 4D

	Annual change of AI_m	Annual change of AI_f
West Germany, 1950–61	$+.04$	$-.04$
Italy, 1951–61	$+.01$	$-.02$
Hungary, 1949–60	$-.02$	$.00$
United Kingdom, 1951–61	$-.06$	$+.02$
New Zealand, 1951–61	$-.09$	$+.01$
Australia, 1954–61	$-.13$	$+.01$

trends around the world during the 1950s that caused the age-sex indices to move downward almost everywhere at this time. In more developed countries before World War II, the secular trend of these indices was generally upward, reflecting the long-established general trend of decreasing birth rates in the economically more advanced regions of the world. This trend was reversed during the 1950s by the postwar "baby booms" in many of the more-developed countries, but the reversal was temporary, as the prevailing trend of birth rates in these countries turned downward again in the 1960s. In less-developed countries before World War II, the levels of birth rates and population structures were on the whole relatively constant. Here, too, the postwar trend of rising birth rates that contributed to negative changes of age-sex indices in some less-developed countries during the 1950s was a temporary phenomenon. A countertrend of falling birth rates started in several less-developed countries during the late years of the 1950s, and in a number of others during the 1960s. This trend seems likely to become more widespread in less-developed regions of the world in the future. So the generally negative trend of age-sex indices that appears in the data compiled for the present study, both in more-developed and less-developed countries, reflects a passing phase in the processes of demographic transition which is unlikely to be repeated in the decades ahead.[1]

Japan's experience in the 1950s was an outstanding exception. An extraordinarily rapid decline of the Japanese birth rate took place between 1947 and 1958, pushing the age-sex index sharply upward, with the result that the crude activity rate increased in spite of a decreasing trend of the male standardized activity rate. The trends in Japan between 1950 and 1965 are shown in Table 4E.

Although the decline of the birth rate was arrested about 1958, Japan's age-sex index continued to climb between 1960 and 1965. The full impact of the reduced birth rate upon the population structure would not be felt, in fact, before the early years of the 1970s,

---

[1] On prewar and early postwar demographic trends, see *Population Bulletin of the United Nations*, No. 6 (1962) for mortality and No. 7 (1963) for fertility. For trends in the late 1950s and in the 1960s, see the United Nations *Demographic Yearbooks*; and with reference to declining birth rates in less-developed countries, Dudley Kirk, "A New Demographic Transition?" in *Rapid Population Growth* (National Academy of Sciences Study Committee, 1970).

Development and size of labor force

Table 4E

	1950	1955	1960	1965
Crude birth rate[a]	30.2	23.7	18.2	17.2
Stand$_m$	74.7	73.2	72.7	71.3
Stand$_t$	43.4	43.8	44.1	43.1
Age-sex indices:				
ASI	+0.2	+1.6	+3.9	+6.6
AI$_c$	+0.4	+1.7	+4.3	+5.4
AI$_m$	−0.1	+0.1	−0.1	+0.9
AI$_t$	+0.2	+0.2	−0.1	+0.6
SI	−0.3	−0.3	−0.3	−0.3
Crude activity rate	44.0	45.1	47.2	49.1

[a]Averages for five-year periods preceding the given census years. Source: United Nations, *Demographic Yearbook* (1963, 1965).

when the birth cohorts of the late 1950s came of working age. These Japanese statistics afford a preview of the kinds of population structure changes exerting upward pressures upon crude activity rates that can be expected in the future in growing numbers of less-developed countries as a result of declining birth rates.

FIVE

The Decrease of Participation by Males in the Labor Force in the Process of Economic Development

5.1. *Causes of Decreasing Participation by Males*

A decrease of participation by males in income-producing work seems to take place almost universally in societies undergoing modern economic development. It was observed in the preceding chapter that in the cross section of census statistics, the mean level of male standardized activity rates declines progressively as the level of development of the countries rises. A similar pattern was observed in the United Nations study of a cross section of data of censuses taken around 1950.[1] The measures of labor force changes during postwar intercensal periods likewise indicate an almost universally decreasing trend accompanying the progress of economic development in countries around the world, with the possible exception of those at the lowest level of development, which are not adequately represented in the statistics (Table 5.1). This trend has been traced over many decades in historical series of census statistics of Western industrialized countries. It is apparent also in the historical statistics of some less-developed countries, although the statistical record is not adequate to verify the generality of the trend in less-developed regions of the world prior to World War II.[2]

The decreasing trend of male standardized activity rates does not imply that fewer men take part in the labor force during their lifetime, but that the extent of their participation is diminished by delayed entry into the labor force and by earlier retirement as

[1] United Nations, *Demographic Aspects of Manpower: Sex and Age Patterns of Participation in Economic Activities* (New York, 1958).

[2] For international compilation of such historical series, see *ibid.*, and Clarence Long, *The Labor Force under Changing Income and Employment* (Princeton, 1958), Appendix A. For secular trends in some less-developed countries, see: J. P. Ambannavar, "Changes in the Employment Patterns of the Indian Working Force, 1911–1961," *Developing Economies* (Tokyo, March 1970); Ghazi Farooq, "Labour Force Participation Rates in Pakistan, 1901–1961," *The Pakistan Development Review* 8, no. 1 (1968); Abdel-Fattah Nassef, *The Egyptian Labor Force: Its Dimensions and Changing Structure, 1907–1960* (Population Studies Center, University of Pennsylvania, Philadelphia, 1970).

Participation by males

Table 5.1. Levels and intercensal changes of male standardized activity rates in countries at different levels of development

	Total	Level I	Level II	Level III	Level IV	Level V
		Levels of $Stand_m$ or RAR_m, cross-sectional censuses				
Number of countries	100	20	20	20	20	20
Mean level of rates	76.8	81.0	80.1	76.0	73.7	73.1
Standard deviation	5.6	5.8	4.7	4.7	4.0	3.3
Frequency distribution:						
Under 70.0	10	-	1	2	2	5
70.0-74.9	28	3	1	5	10	9
75.0-79.9	35	5	6	10	8	6
80.0-84.9	20	8	9	3	-	-
85.0 and over	7	4	3	-	-	-
		Intercensal changes of $Stand_m$ or RAR_m				
Number of countries	58	3	10	11	17	17
Mean annual change	-.35	.00	-.29	-.43	-.46	-.26
Frequency distribution:						
+.10 or more	2	-	1	1	-	-
+.09 to -.09	9	2	2	-	1	4
-.10 to -.49	34	1	4	7	11	11
-.50 or more	13	-	3	3 .	5	2

economic development proceeds. In the cross-sectional view of age-specific activity rates of males (Table 5.2 and Figure 5.1), it can be seen that as the level of economic development rises, the mean levels of activity rates of males decrease in the age groups under 20, over 45, and especially over 65 years, while the mean rates for males in the central adult ages remain on a high plateau. In the tabulation of intercensal changes in the age-specific rates (Table 5.3), it likewise appears that among countries at each level of development from Level II to Level V, the prevailing trends were steeply downward in ages under 20 and over 65 years, while little change was recorded in the rates for the central age group of 30 to 44 years. Measures of intercensal changes in the age-specific rates are lacking for Level I countries.

The shortening at both ends of men's working life span is a result of several kinds of economic and social changes, typically entwined in the processes of economic development and modernization, which tend to diminish the opportunities and possibly also the willingness and capability of the young and the elderly to work for income. The freedom of the young to do so is also restricted, to an extent which is likely to increase as development progresses, by child-labor and compulsory school-attendance legislation. In the

Participation by males

Table 5.2. Levels of male age-specific activity rates in countries at different levels of development, cross-sectional censuses

Age groups	Total	Level I	Level II	Level III	Level IV	Level V
Number of countries	84	13	19	17	18	17

Mean levels of rates

15-19 years	65.6	75.5	69.6	62.8	60.5	61.6
20-29 years[a]	93.4	94.0	93.6	93.0	92.9	93.5
30-44 years[a]	97.3	97.5	97.6	96.8	97.1	97.5
45-64 years[a]	90.5	93.4	93.6	88.5	86.9	90.3
65 years and over[a]	50.3	63.4	67.7	52.3	40.3	29.5
20-24 years	90.5	91.5	90.8	90.0	89.7	90.5
25-29 years	96.3	96.5	96.4	96.0	96.1	96.5
30-34 years	97.4	97.3	97.5	97.0	97.3	97.9
35-39 years	97.5	97.7	97.7	97.0	97.3	97.8
40-44 years	97.0	97.5	97.5	96.5	96.8	96.9
45-49 years	96.4	97.3	97.2	95.5	95.7	96.7
50-54 years	94.4	96.0	95.8	92.6	92.9	95.0
55-59 years	90.4	93.8	93.6	87.7	86.8	91.0
60-64 years	80.5	86.7	88.0	78.4	72.3	78.3
65-69 years	65.0	78.6	80.0	66.4	56.1	45.8
70-74 years	50.7	64.2	69.9	53.4	40.3	27.4
75 years and over	35.2	47.5	53.2	37.1	24.5	15.2

Ranges of middle third

15-19 years	59.6-72.3	69.0-78.3	66.7-75.5	63.2-68.0	57.2-68.9	59.2-69.6
20-29 years	92.8-95.1	93.6-96.4	91.4-95.6	92.7-93.7	93.1-94.0	93.5-94.3
30-44 years	97.1-98.0	97.4-98.4	97.6-98.2	96.6-97.2	97.4-97.7	97.7-98.4
45-64 years	89.4-93.5	92.2-94.7	92.7-94.9	87.1-91.4	85.6-90.1	88.0-94.0
65 years and over	41.8-57.8	55.0-68.8	66.6-72.6	45.2-57.4	36.9-49.3	23.7-29.3

Standard deviations

15-19 years	13.1	15.6	11.5	12.8	13.8	12.3
20-29 years	3.6	4.2	3.9	2.2	4.1	2.7
30-44 years	1.5	1.4	1.1	1.1	2.1	1.4
45-64 years	4.4	2.7	3.1	5.6	5.2	4.5
65 years and over	13.8	15.5	12.2	15.5	11.7	14.0

[a] Unweighted average rates for 5-year age groups.

language of economic theory, the factors of employment opportunity are demand factors, while those of willingness, capability, and freedom to take advantage of employment opportunities are factors of supply.[3]

[3] Factors affecting the levels and trends of activity rates are discussed, with references to the findings of relevant studies, in: United Nations, *The Determinants and Consequences of Population Trends. New Summary of Findings on Interaction of Demographic, Economic and Social Factors* I (New York, 1973), 315–17.

95

Participation by males

Figure 5.1 Age-specific activity rates of males in countries at different
levels of development
(Mean values of rates according to cross-sectional censuses)

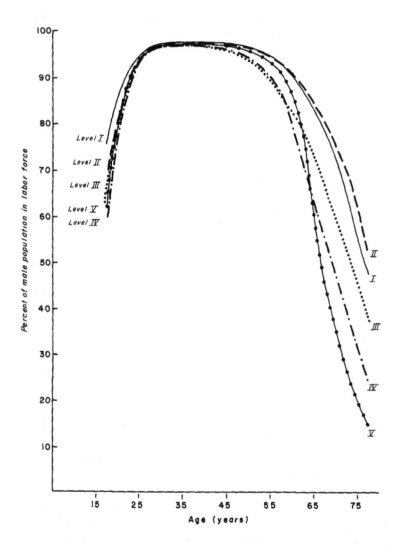

In many less-developed countries during recent times, the growth
of aggregate demand for labor seems to have been lagging behind
the increase in numbers of would-be workers, although the defects
of statistical measures of unemployment and underemployment for-
bid a definite generalization in this respect. (Demand for labor

96

Table 5.3. Intercensal changes of male age-specific activity rates in countries at different levels of development

Age groups	Total	Level II	Level III	Level IV	Level V
Number of countries	45	8	9	14	14
Mean annual changes:					
15-19 years	-1.05	-.71	-.98	-1.31	-1.10
20-29 years	-.06	-.05	-.08	-.08	-.06
30-44 years	+.01	+.04	-.02	+.01	-.00
45-64 years	-.16	-.10	-.27	-.33	+.04
65 years and over	-1.00	-.64	-.99	-1.55	-.67
20-24 years	-.16	-.12	-.16	-.22	-.14
25-29 years	+.03	+.02	-.01	+.06	+.03
30-34 years	+.04	+.05	-.00	+.06	+.04
35-39 years	+.01	+.04	-.02	+.00	+.02
40-44 years	-.03	+.03	-.04	-.03	-.06
45-49 years	-.03	-.00	-.07	-.04	+.03
50-54 years	-.06	-.03	-.16	-.12	+.04
55-59 years	-.13	-.10	-.27	-.27	+.09
60-64 years	-.44	-.26	-.57	-.90	-.02
65-69 years	-.98	-.44	-.92	-1.49	-.82
70-74 years	-1.08	-.68	-1.04	-1.68	-.73
75 years and over	-.95	-.82	-1.00	-1.48	-.47

should be understood in the present context to include opportunities for earning income by self-employment and for contributing to family income by work as an unpaid helper in a family enterprise, as well as demand in the wage-labor market.) Rapid growth of population due to improving conditions of health and mortality may be one factor tending to aggravate the shortage of employment opportunities. Unemployment and underemployment rates may be reduced as economic development advances and demand for labor expands with progress in capital formation, technology, rising incomes, and increasing effective demand for consumers' goods. Reduction of the birth rates, moderating the growth of population and labor supply, may also be helpful in this respect. Nevertheless, the increase in opportunities for employment of young and elderly workers may continue to lag behind the growth in these age groups of the population as a result of changes in the composition of labor demand.

The contraction in proportionate shares of agriculture, nonagricultural self-employment, and family enterprises in aggregate demand for labor, which goes almost universally with progress in modern economic development, is a major factor tending to restrict employment opportunities for the young and the elderly. For young people, family enterprise offers a relatively easy avenue of entry

97

into the labor force in the capacity of unpaid helpers. It is more difficult for them to establish themselves in the wage-labor market, where they face the competition of more experienced workers and their employment is often severely restricted by law. In many less-developed countries, in fact, a large majority of the labor force in ages under twenty years consists of unpaid family workers. Family enterprise, and especially self-employment, are havens also for the elderly, who may be handicapped in the competition for wage-earning jobs by physical disability, weakening health, outmoded skills, deficient education, and immobility. The competitive disadvantage of the elderly tends to increase with the progress of technology and shifts in the structure of labor demand, which put a growing premium on education and on occupational and residential mobility.

The shifting composition of demand for labor also plays an important role on the side of supply factors, tending to diminish the employment propensity of young people, that is, their willingness to join the labor force at an early age. The growing demand for educational qualifications in the better-paid jobs of the evolving modern economy furnishes a strong incentive for young people to continue longer in school before they go to work.

The effect of rising wages and levels of income upon the propensities of people to be employed is a question that has been debated in economic theory since the days of Adam Smith and earlier. It is postulated, on the one hand, that higher wages make employment more attractive but, on the other hand, that higher incomes make people less inclined to sacrifice leisure or alternative activities such as homemaking, school attendance, unpaid artistic or intellectual pursuits, etc., in order to earn still more income from employment. If both postulates are valid, the net effect on employment propensities of the linked trends of rising wages and incomes in the process of economic development is indeterminate in theory, and can only be discovered by empirical investigations.

There is, of course, little choice for those individuals who have no means of livelihood but the earnings of their jobs. Given higher wages, they may be inclined to work shorter hours and take more time for vacations, as workers in countries of increasing affluence have done during modern times, but these individuals do not have the alternative of remaining outside the labor force. The vast majority of men in middle adult ages are held in this position by the institutions and mores of most societies, and the position of spinsters and widows is often similar. The option of seeking an income-earning job or not is mainly for women with employed husbands, young people with parents able and willing to support them, and elderly people who can live on their savings or pensions, or who may be entitled by their seniority to look to relatives or the public for support.

As the level of wages rises, the need for young, elderly, and female members of families to be employed in order to achieve a desired level of family income may be diminished, and it may become easier for the primary breadwinners to save enough for early retirement. The growing income and wealth of the society also make it easier to provide, at social expense, education for the young and maintenance of the elderly in retirement. The question is whether such negative influences upon employment propensities outweigh the attraction of rising wages. The net effect may be different for males and females and for different age groups, it may not be the same in different cultural settings, and within a given setting it may change as economic development progresses.

So far as capability of income-producing work is concerned, a trend of improving health, education, and skills generally goes with modern economic development. But capability must be viewed in relation to the requirements of the job and the competitive position of the would-be worker in the labor market. From these angles, it is not clear whether today's workers in developed countries such as the United States are better qualified than those of a century ago. Although men of sixty-five or seventy years may generally be healthier now than they were formerly at the same age, it is not sure that as many are capable of continuing in employment, now that most of them have to meet the competition of younger workers in the wage-labor market instead of merely holding on as independent entrepreneurs or senior members of family enterprises. Seniority rights in the tenure of wage-earning jobs, fortified by trade-union organization, may not fully offset the competitive disadvantage of older workers.

It can be seen that the determinants of activity rates and their changes in the process of economic development are anything but simple. The factors of demand and supply are knottily entwined with one another, so that it is difficult to pick them apart cleanly. Propensity is related to the composition of employment opportunities as well as to the remunerations of the different types of jobs, capability varies with both opportunity and propensity, and

99

Participation by males

demand for labor is influenced both in its composition and its aggregate volume by the conditions of supply. The prices of labor, that is, wage rates, are both consequences and causal factors in the interaction of demand and supply.

Moreover, as noted in chapter 3, these factors of supply and demand are linked with cultural and institutional factors that are not the same in different societies, and which may be greatly altered in the process of economic development. The influence of cultural and institutional factors is especially important in the determinants of propensity to work for income. Fundamental here are the relative values attached, on the one hand, to employment, the income and other satisfactions that it provides, and, on the other hand, to leisure, education, and women's services as homemakers and mothers. Also fundamental are the norms for functional roles of individuals according to sex, age, and family relationships, and the forms of family structure.

Some econometric studies have been made in the United States and a few other countries with the aim of explaining differences in activity rates among areas within the country and changes of the rates during recent periods of time in terms of wage and income levels, unemployment rates, the composition of employment opportunities, and other factors.[4] In such studies the frame of cultural and institutional variables is taken as given, and assumed implicitly to be constant; thus the findings are culture-bound and time-bound. For example, when an estimate is obtained of the effect of a certain amount of increase in wages or incomes upon the activity rate of males over age sixty-five under the conditions existing in the United States around 1950 or 1960, it cannot be taken for granted that the effect would be similar in Italy or Japan, the Soviet Union or China, nor that it would have been similar in the United States of 1900. If econometric methods are to be used for analyzing factors of variations in broad international cross sections and long-range time series of labor-force participation measures, analytical models will be needed that take the principal cultural and institutional factors into account, along with the economic factors. The challenging problem of devising suitable models for this purpose and obtaining the relevant data is beyond the scope of the present study. The object of the following analysis is

[4] Results of a number of such studies in the United States are analyzed in William G. Bowen and T. Aldrich Finegan, *The Economics of Labor Force Participation* (Princeton, 1969).

less ambitious: to define the patterns of variations in male activity rates, related to economic development, which are apparent in our data on levels and recent changes of these rates in countries around the world, and see what hypotheses about causal factors they may suggest as orientation for future research.

5.2. Variations of Male Participation Among Countries in Early Stages of Development

The census statistics of the least-developed countries covered in this study imply that initially, in countries embarking upon modern economic development, there are wide variations in rates of participation in the production of income, especially by females, but also by males. In the cross section of male standardized activity rates (Table 5.1), while the countries at Levels I and II of development display distinctly higher rates, on the average, than those of more-developed countries, they are by no means uniformly high. Stand$_m$ as recorded in Level I and II countries ranges from *92.9 in Sudan (1956) down to 68.3 in Korea (1960), one of the lowest rates in the world-wide cross section. The same pattern of wide variations about a high average level appears in the cross section of age-specific male activity rates for the age groups of labor force entry and retirement. Degrees of disparity in the age-specific rates among countries at each development level are represented in Table 5.2 by the ranges of the middle third in rank-order arrays of the rates. Among Level I countries, for example, these ranges signify that the recorded activity rates of males in ages 15 to 19 are below 69.0 in one-third and above 78.3 in one-third of the cases. The range is even wider in the rates for ages 65 and over. The variations are seen from another angle in Table 5.4, where the countries are classified by types of age patterns of male activity rates, according to the method described in chapter 2. While patterns of early entry into the labor force and of late retirement predominate among Level I and II countries, six of the thirty-two countries at these low development levels exhibit late entry patterns, and ten exhibit medium or early retirement.

It has often been asserted as a general rule among preindustrial societies and those in early stages of modern economic development that nearly all able-bodied individuals of both sexes are required by economic necessity to take part in the work of producing subsistence from childhood to old age. The census statistics do not

101

Participation by males

Table 5.4. Types of age patterns of male activity rates in countries at different levels of development, cross-sectional censuses

	Total	Level I	Level II	Level III	Level IV	Level V
Total number of countries	84	13	19	17	18	17
HH: Early entry, late retirement	14	4	8	2	-	-
MH: Medium entry, late retirement	10	-	7	2	-	1
LH: Late entry, late retirement	4	2	1	1	-	-
HM: Early entry, medium retirement	8	4	-	1	3	-
MM: Medium entry, medium retirement	11	2	1	5	2	1
LM: Late entry, medium retirement	9	1	1	4	2	1
HL: Early entry, early retirement	6	-	-	1	1	4
ML: Medium entry, early retirement	7	-	-	-	3	4
LL: Late entry, early retirement	15	-	1	1	7	6
All early entry patterns	28	8	8	4	4	4
All medium entry patterns	28	2	8	7	5	6
All late entry patterns	28	3	3	6	9	7
All late retirement patterns	28	6	16	5	-	1
All medium retirement patterns	28	7	2	10	7	2
All early retirement patterns	28	-	1	2	11	14

bear out this idea, but it should be recalled that the statistics are distorted by errors and factors of noncomparability that almost certainly tend to exaggerate real differences in the patterns of activity rates, particularly among the least-developed countries. The truth is probably somewhere between the stereotype of nearly universal labor force participation and the picture of diversity that appears in these statistics. Ethnographic data and the results of detailed studies of agricultural labor in little-developed countries make it plain that customs governing the division of labor among sex and age groups in traditional agrarian societies are highly varied, and that the total input of labor per head of the population also differs widely from one society to another. At the same time, the ethnographic and agricultural labor survey data support the generalization that in such societies, as a rule, there are few individuals other than very young children and the disabled who do not share to some extent in income-producing activities. The roles of breadwinner and dependent are less distinct in such societies than they are in developed industrial societies; there is more community of participation in income production as well as in other activities.

It is hypothesized that if the labor force enumerations included all persons who take any part in work contributing to the production of income, the activity rates of both males and females from childhood to old age would be found to be generally very high in the traditional sectors of the least-developed economies; but measures taking into account the extent of each individual's involvement in such work would show wide differences from country to country in the rates for young and elderly males and for females. Comprehensive and reliable measures of the latter type, taking account of hours of work per day or week, and days or weeks per year, are not easy to obtain in a census, but only such measures can provide a satisfactory view of the dimensions and composition of the labor force in little-developed countries.

5.3. Economic Development and Changing Tempos of Labor Force Entry and Retirement

The trends toward later entry of males into the labor force and earlier retirement, associated with the progress of economic development, are marked with few exceptions both by differences between mean levels of age-specific male activity rates in less-developed and more-developed countries, and by intercensal changes of the rates in countries at each level of development. (See Tables 5.2 and 5.3 and Figure 5.1.) Influences of extraneous factors or faulty and incomparable measures could account for the exceptions that appear in these data (higher average levels of activity rates of men over 60 years of age in Level II countries than in Level I, higher in Level V than in Level IV for age groups below 65, and some instances of small positive average intercensal changes in age groups between 25 and 60).

However, as noted above, the averages for Level I and II countries conceal a great deal of diversity in levels of the rates among individual countries within these groups, and the same is true to a lesser extent of countries at the higher levels of development. The ranges of middle thirds of the distributions and the standard deviations of the rates for major age groups, shown at the foot of Table 5.2, make it appear that in the rates for the labor-force entry ages, there is more difference, on the whole, among countries within the same group of relative development level than there is between groups. It is only in the ages of sixty-five years and over that the differences between groups are marked distinctly in the sense that, in most instances, there is little or no overlap between ranges of the middle thirds of the rates for countries in the different quintile groups of relative development level.

103

Participation by males

What takes place during the course of economic development and modernization is not merely a decrease in the extent of labor-force participation by males in the youngest and eldest age groups, but also, at the same time, an increasing polarization of economically active and inactive phases in the life cycle. In the traditional sectors of little-developed economies, the entry of young males into income-producing activities and the withdrawal of elderly men are commonly gradual processes. The boy takes a gradually increasing part in production as he matures and gains knowledge and skill through experience, while the old man's activity diminishes gradually as his powers decline. In more-developed countries, labor-force entry and retirement are more abrupt. The young and the elderly take little or no part in production during phases of the life cycle that lengthen as development progresses.

Economic development seems typically to entail a greater change in the conditions of retirement than in the conditions of entry of males into the labor force. The classification of countries by types of age patterns of male activity rates, in Table 5.4, confirms that, with few exceptions, late-retirement patterns go with a relatively low level of economic development, and early retirement with a high level. Of the thirty-five countries in Levels IV and V, twenty-five display early-retirement and nine medium retirement-patterns, and the only one with late retirement is Venezuela (a country which, as mentioned previously, is less developed so far as the conditions of a majority of the people are concerned than the economic indicators make it appear to be). Among less-developed countries, early-retirement patterns appear only in South Korea (Level II), Taiwan, and Mauritius (Level III). The correspondence between tempo of entry into the labor force and level of economic development is not so close. Although early-entry patterns occur most frequently in countries at the lowest development levels, and late-entry most frequently in those at the highest development levels, numerous exceptions appear in the statistics. The most remarkable exceptions are the early-entry patterns in four countries at Level V, namely, the United Kingdom, Denmark, West Germany, and Austria (HL), and late-entry patterns in three countries at Level I, namely, Liberia and Nigeria (LH) and Khmer Republic (LM). With reference to the latter three cases, it should be noted that the census figures may not reflect the actual conditions very accurately; but one should not be too ready to discredit

104

measures merely because they deviate from the norms of countries at given levels of development.[5]

The association with the level of development is marked not only more consistently but also more strongly in male activity rates for ages 65 and over than for 15 to 19. In ages 65 and over, the average level of male activity rates for Level v countries is less than half the average for Level ı or ıı, while the corresponding difference in ages 15 to 19 is less than one-fifth. The implication is that economic development and related social changes may have had a greater impact on the tempo of retirement than on the tempo of entry of males into the labor force. The variations in frequency of very early entry into the labor force, before the age of 15, are not, however, represented in this comparison because of the low reliability of the measures. If accurate measures were available, they would undoubtedly show wide differences in activity rates of the age group 10 to 14 between the least-developed and most-developed countries. Very few boys and girls under age 15 are employed in highly developed countries, while in little-developed countries, children of this age very commonly take some part, and often a significant part, in income-producing activities, especially in agriculture.

The measures of intercensal changes (Table 5.3) show male activity rates decreasing about as steeply during the postwar years in ages 15 to 19 as in 65 and over, and considerably more steeply in 15 to 19 in Level v countries. The apparent contradiction here between the cross-sectional differences and the intercensal changes is probably explained by a difference between the trends in the period since World War II and earlier trends, which presumably brought about the present differences between male activity rate patterns in more-developed and less-developed countries. There is reason to think that the pace of decline in activity rates of males under age 20 may have quickened since the war, particularly in less-developed countries, with increased emphasis in governmental policy upon the

[5] In the case of Liberia, the anomaly may be due partly to the fact that unemployed persons were not included in the census tabulations of the labor force, according to information given in the report of the International Labour Office, *Labour Force Projections, 1965–1985. Part VI. Methodological Supplement, First Edition, 1971* (Geneva, 1973). However, the observation that the activity rates recorded for Liberian males in ages 15 to 19 were relatively low in the rural as well as the urban sector (see Appendix Table A.9) makes it seem doubtful that omission of the unemployed would fully account for the anomaly.

Participation by males

promotion of education and growing popular belief in the value of education.

To see whether the association between economic development and levels of male activity rates appears to be similar in varied cultural and institutional settings, Tables 5.5 and 5.6 have been drawn

Table 5.5. Mean levels of male standardized activity rates in countries at different levels of developm in each region, cross-sectional censuses

Levels of development	All regions[a]	Region 1	Region 2	Region 3	Region 4	Region 5	Region 6	Region 7	Reg 8
Total									
Number of countries	100	15	9	7	16	22	9	7	11
Mean level of rates	76.8	79.3	76.5	81.2	77.0	79.0	73.8	74.2	72.5
Level I									
Number of countries	20	12	1	2	5	1	-	-	-
Mean level of rates	81.0	79.0	92.9	82.6	81.5	85.0	-	-	-
Level II									
Number of countries	20	3	2	3	7	7	-	-	-
Mean level of rates	80.1	80.5	78.5	82.0	76.3	83.4	-	-	-
Level III									
Number of countries	20	-	6	2	3	7	2	1	-
Mean level of rates	76.0	-	73.1	78.5	72.7	79.0	77.2	76.2	-
Level IV									
Number of countries	20	-	-	-	1	6	4	2	1
Mean level of rates	73.7	-	-	-	72.7	73.2	73.0	72.5	75.8
Level V									
Number of countries	20	-	-	-	-	1	3	4	10
Mean level of rates	73.1	-	-	-	-	78.3	72.5	74.5	72.6
Differences between mean levels of rates[b]									
Level I-II	-0.9	+1.5	(-14.4)	-0.6	-5.2	(-1.6)	-	-	-
Level II-III	-4.1	-	-5.4	-3.5	-3.6	-4.4	-	-	-
Level III-IV	-2.3	-	-	-	(0.0)	-5.8	-4.2	(-3.7)	-
Level IV-V	-0.6	-	-	-	-	(+5.1)	-0.5	+2.0	(-3.2)

[a]Including 9 countries in regional group 9 (Miscellaneous).
[b]Mean rate for each level of development subtracted from mean rate for next higher level of development. Parentheses signify that only a single country is represented at one of the two levels.

up, showing mean levels of the standardized and age-specific rates in countries at different levels of development within each region. On the whole, the regional patterns are similar to the pattern of the pooled data for all regions: with few exceptions, the mean levels of the standardized rates and of the specific rates for both labor-force entry and retirement ages decline as the level of development rises, and in most cases the decline is greater in ages over 65 than in 15 to 19. The most remarkable exception is Japan, the single country in Level IV in South and East Asia (region 4), where the rate for males over 65 is above the average of the least developed countries in the region. Venezuela, the sole country in Level V in Latin America (region 5), is another exception, but this is indeed

106

Participation by males

Table 5.6. Mean levels of male age-specific activity rates in countries at different levels of development in each region, cross-sectional censuses

Age groups	Total	Level I	Level II	Level III	Level IV	Level V	Levels I-II	Levels II-III	Levels III-IV	Levels IV-V
1. Tropical Africa										
Number of countries	8	6	2	-	-	-				
15-19 years	73.6	74.6	70.5	-	-	-	-4.1	-	-	-
20-29 years	93.8	93.2	95.6	-	-	-	+2.4	-	-	-
30-44 years	97.4	97.1	98.4	-	-	-	+1.3	-	-	-
45-64 years	94.0	93.3	95.9	-	-	-	+2.6	-	-	-
65 years and over	66.6	63.1	76.9	-	-	-	+13.8	-	-	-
2. Arab countries										
Number of countries	7	-	2	5	-	-				
15-19 years	58.5	-	64.7	56.1	-	-	-	-8.6	-	-
20-29 years	91.4	-	91.0	91.5	-	-	-	+0.5	-	-
30-44 years	96.2	-	96.8	96.0	-	-	-	-0.8	-	-
45-64 years	89.0	-	93.0	87.5	-	-	-	-5.5	-	-
65 years and over	55.3	-	61.2	42.1	-	-	-	-19.1	-	-
3. Other Moslem countries										
Number of countries	5	2	2	1	-	-				
15-19 years	74.7	80.1	72.7	68.0	-	-	-7.4	(-4.7)	-	-
20-29 years	93.7	94.4	93.0	93.7	-	-	-1.4	(+0.7)	-	-
30-44 years	97.1	96.5	97.3	97.7	-	-	+0.8	(+0.4)	-	-
45-64 years	92.2	92.4	94.7	86.9	-	-	+2.3	(-7.8)	-	-
65 years and over	65.9	63.3	78.7	45.4	-	-	+15.4	(-33.3)	-	-
4. South and East Asia										
Number of countries	16	5	7	3	1	-				
15-19 years	63.2	74.4	60.0	55.7	51.6	-	-14.4	-4.3	(-4.1)	-
20-29 years	92.1	92.6	90.7	91.8	92.4	-	-1.9	+0.9	(+0.6)	-
30-44 years	97.1	97.9	96.8	96.3	97.7	-	-1.1	-0.5	(+1.4)	-
45-64 years	89.5	92.4	90.5	81.9	91.5	-	-1.9	-8.6	(+9.6)	-
65 years and over	41.6	46.3	47.2	17.5	50.8	-	+0.9	-29.7	(+33.3)	-
5. Latin America, Spain, and Portugal										
Number of countries	22	1	7	7	6	1				
15-19 years	71.1	78.3	79.1	69.8	63.6	62.1	(+0.8)	-9.3	-6.2	(-1.5)
20-29 years	94.3	94.8	96.3	94.5	91.6	94.8	(+1.5)	-1.8	-2.9	(+3.2)
30-44 years	97.2	97.1	98.3	97.5	95.6	98.0	(+1.2)	-0.8	-1.9	(+2.4)
45-64 years	91.4	94.7	95.9	92.6	83.9	94.0	(+1.2)	-3.3	-8.7	(+10.1)
65 years and over	61.3	78.9	73.7	63.2	40.2	69.0	(-5.2)	-10.5	-23.0	(+28.8)
6. Eastern Europe										
Number of countries	4	-	-	-	3	1				
15-19 years	52.4	-	-	-	54.3	46.8	-	-	-	(-7.5)
20-29 years	93.4	-	-	-	92.7	90.8	-	-	-	(-1.9)
30-44 years	98.2	-	-	-	98.2	97.9	-	-	-	(-0.3)
45-64 years	84.9	-	-	-	86.1	81.2	-	-	-	(-4.9)
65 years and over	34.4	-	-	-	38.1	23.0	-	-	-	(-15.1)
7. Middle Europe										
Number of countries	7	-	-	1	2	4				
15-19 years	63.4	-	-	66.5	63.6	73.0	-	-	(-2.9)	+9.4
20-29 years	92.9	-	-	93.1	96.4	93.7	-	-	(+3.3)	-2.7
30-44 years	97.0	-	-	96.6	96.8	97.3	-	-	(+0.2)	+0.5
45-64 years	87.3	-	-	87.0	85.3	88.4	-	-	(-1.7)	+3.1
65 years and over	29.6	-	-	43.8	30.1	25.8	-	-	(-13.7)	-4.3
8. Northwestern Europe, Northern America, and Oceania										
Number of countries	11	-	-	-	1	10				
15-19 years	59.8	-	-	-	62.8	59.6	-	-	-	(-3.2)
20-29 years	92.7	-	-	-	93.1	92.6	-	-	-	(-0.5)
30-44 years	97.4	-	-	-	97.4	97.4	-	-	-	(0.0)
45-64 years	91.0	-	-	-	92.6	90.9	-	-	-	(-1.7)
65 years and over	27.7	-	-	-	51.8	25.3	-	-	-	(-26.5)

The "Differences[a]" span covers the Levels I-II, Levels II-III, Levels III-IV, and Levels IV-V columns.

[a]
Mean rate for each level of development subtracted from mean rate for next higher level of development.
Parentheses signify that only a single country is represented at one of the two levels.

an example of the proverbial "exception that proves the rule." On the whole, the data show little cause for doubting the generality, in varied settings, of the decrease in activity rates of males in entry and retirement ages associated with progress in economic development. The present compilation of data is not well suited to this kind of analysis, however, because only narrow ranges of development levels are represented in most of the regions and numbers are small in many cells of the table, often only one or two countries. It would be better to use data for provinces or economic regions within countries as the units of analysis. In that way, it might be possible to do a better job of disentangling the variations associated with economic development from the influences of culture, social institutions, and other factors. It was not feasible in this study to compile data for subnational areas.

5.4. Convergence in Trends of Male Participation

A conspicuous feature of the cross-sectional frequency distribution of levels of male standardized activity rates (Table 5.1) is that the differences among countries diminish progressively as the level of economic development rises. Thus the standard deviations of the rates diminish from 5.8 among countries in Level I to 3.3 in Level v. It is mainly the elimination of very high rates that causes the standard deviations as well as the mean levels of the rates to decrease with rising level of development. Rates above 85 are eliminated in the progression from Levels I and II to III, and rates above 80 are eliminated in Levels IV and V. This pattern suggests that during the course of economic development, participation by males in the labor force may tend to decrease more in countries where it is relatively high than in those where it is relatively low, so that the trends converge toward a relatively uniform, low level at an advanced stage of development. This hypothesis finds some support also in the data on intercensal changes, which show greater decreases of male standardized activity rates, on the whole, in countries where the rates were relatively high at the beginning of the intercensal periods than where they were relatively low (Table 5.7), although the pattern does not hold very consistently when the figures for countries at different levels of development are considered separately. One factor that would tend to produce such a pattern of convergence is the increase of urbanization associated with economic development, since the levels of male standardized

Table 5.7. Intercensal changes of male standardized and age-specific activity rates in countries classified by levels of the rates at the beginning of the intercensal period and by level of development

(N = number of countries; Mean = mean annual intercensal change in activity rates)

Initial levels of rates	Total		Levels I-II		Level III		Level IV		Level V	
	N	Mean	N	Mean	N	Mean	N	Mean	N	Mean
Standardized rates										
Total	58	-.35	13	-.22	11	-.43	17	-.46	17	-.26
Under 75.0	11	-.27	1	-.08	1	-.36	4	-.40	5	-.18
75.0-79.9	22	-.30	2	-.10	2	-.34	8	-.36	10	-.27
80.0-84.9	16	-.33	4	+.03	7	-.47	4	-.48	1	-.20
85.0 and over	9	-.57	6	-.46	1	-.37	1	-1.38	1	-.62
Specific rates, ages 15-19										
Total	45	-1.06	8	-.71	9	-.98	14	-1.31	14	-1.10
Under 65.0	8	-1.17	1	-.02	1	-1.59	4	-1.48	2	-.93
65.0-79.9	21	-1.00	-	-	4	-.66	8	-.87	9	-1.27
80.0 and over	16	-1.10	7	-.81	4	-1.14	2	-2.69	3	-.70
Specific rates, ages 65 and over										
Total	45	-1.00	8	-.64	9	-.99	14	-1.55	14	-.67
Under 40.0	12	-.66	-	-	1	-.38	1	-.65	10	-.69
40.0-59.9	12	-1.17	-	-	1	+.14	9	-1.44	2	-.59
60.0-74.9	15	-1.20	3	-.49	6	-1.19	4	-2.02	2	-.66
75.0 and over	6	-.86	5	-.74	1	-1.51	-	-	-	-

activity rates are less disparate in urban than in rural populations, as shown in chapter 2. The validity of the apparent pattern of convergence in the cross-sectional data may be questioned, however, on the ground that the disparity of the rates is exaggerated, to a greater extent in less-developed than in more-developed countries, as a result of error and noncomparability in the census measures. Moreover, the pattern of convergence is not marked so clearly in the cross-sectional distributions of age-specific activity rates for males in ages of labor-force entry and retirement (see the standard deviations of the age-specific rates at the foot of Table 5.2), nor in the intercensal changes of the age-specific rates, particularly for ages 15 to 19 (see Table 5.7).[6] On the whole, the data compiled for this study do not give unequivocal support to the hypothesis that the trends in participation by males in the labor force tend to draw together toward relatively uniform levels as economic develop-

[6] The defects of the indicators of level of development are partly responsible for the failure of a clear pattern of convergence to show up in the cross-sectional distributions. In Level v, for example, if the anomalous cases of Venezuela and South Africa are left out, the mean level of activity rates for males sixty-five years of age and over is reduced from 29.5 to 25.3, and the standard deviation from 14.0 to 8.0.

ment progresses. It is beyond the scope of this study to test the validity of this hypothesis by reviewing the patterns of long-range past trends in countries now at high levels of development.[7]

5.5. Logistic Trends of Decreasing Male Participation

As noted in the preceding chapter, both the cross-sectional pattern of mean levels of male standardized activity rates and their mean intercensal changes among countries at different levels of development suggest that the decreasing trend of participation by males in the labor force during the course of economic development may typically follow a curve of logistic form: falling slowly if at all during early stages of development, more rapidly during middle stages, and more slowly again during advanced stages. Let us call this the logistic hypothesis. Such logistic trends appear in long-range time series of many economic and demographic variables. They imply a transition from one relatively stable state of affairs to another, such as the transitions from high to low levels of mortality and fertility that have taken place during modern times in countries leading the march of economic development.

The mean intercensal changes of male activity rates according to age groups in countries at different levels of development (Table 5.3) display a generally logistic pattern of decrease of the rates for both ages of entry and ages of retirement from the labor force. The pattern of cross-sectional levels of these rates (Table 5.2) is also consistent with the logistic hypothesis on the whole, but it suggests that the timetable of changes in the activity rates in relation to stages of economic development might commonly be different for labor-force entry ages and retirement ages. Between Level I and Level II, the average level of the rates already drops sharply in ages 15 to 19 and slightly in 20 to 29 while it remains constant in 45 to 64 and rises in 65 and over. Between Levels II and IV, the average rates decrease both in entry and retirement ages, but more steeply in the latter. From Level IV to V, the curves

---

[7] A pattern of convergence was observed in an historical study of trends in activity rates of males in the states of the United States between 1870 and 1950. See S. Kuznets, A. R. Miller, and R. A. Easterlin, *Population Redistribution and Economic Growth, United States, 1870–1950* II (Philadelphia, 1960), 16–23. Convergence was pronounced in the trends of refined activity rates in the total male population 10 years of age and over and specific rates of ages 10 to 15 and 65 and over, but not so clearly marked in the ages of 16 to 24.

of average levels of the rates turn upward in ages 15 to 19, 20 to 29, and especially 45 to 64, while continuing downward with unabated speed in 65 and over.

The implication of this cross-sectional picture is that economic development and related processes of modernization may commonly begin at a relatively early stage to take a strong effect on the tempo of entry of young males into the labor force, while a strong impact on the tempo of retirement is delayed. Conversely, in countries in more advanced stages of development, the trend of activity rates would seem to have levelled off in the ages of entry and ages of early retirement, while it continued steeply downward in the primary ages of retirement.

This interpretation of the cross-sectional differences is predicated on the supposition that present levels of male activity rates in less-developed countries are representative of their former levels in countries that are now more developed. Such a supposition is, of course, uncertain, if only because today's more-developed and less-developed countries are to a large extent segregated in different regions of the world, with different cultural heritages and social institutions. It is important as a test of validity of the interpretation to examine patterns of variations of the activity rates in relation to economic development in varied cultural settings, and it is regrettable that our data for regional groups of countries afford such limited scope for this analysis.

As far as they go, however, the regional data are generally consistent with the logistic hypothesis. In the regional tabulation of mean intercensal changes of male standardized activity rates (Table 5.8) there is no exception to the logistic pattern in any region. There are more irregularities in the patterns of intercensal changes in age-specific rates (Table 5.9) and cross-sectional mean levels of the standardized rates (Table 5.5) but if figures that refer to only a single country are disregarded, only one deviation from the logistic pattern remains in Table 5.5: the precocious decrease from Level I to Level II in South and East Asia (region 4). This is not really out of line with the trends indicated by the pooled data for all regions, because it results mainly from a sharp decrease, from Level I to Level II in South and East Asia, in mean level of the activity rates for ages 15 to 19, in accord with the hypothesis of relatively early impact of economic development upon the tempo of entry into the labor force. In other cases, cross-sectional mean levels of the standardized rates either decrease by relatively small

111

Participation by males

Table 5.8. Intercensal changes of male standardized activity rates in countries at different levels c
development in each region

(N = number of countries; C = mean annual change)

Regional groups	Total N	C	Level I N	C	Level II N	C	Level III N	C	Level IV N	C	Level N
All regions[a]	58	-.35	3	.00	10	-.29	11	-.43	17	-.46	17 -
1. Tropical Africa	-	-	-	-	-	-	-	-	-	-	-
2. Arab countries	1	-.66	-	-	1	-.66	-	-	-	-	-
3. Other Moslem countries	3	-.75	-	-	1	-.44	2	-.91	-	-	-
4. South and East Asia	9	-.26	3	.00	3	-.34	2	-.38	1	-.20	-
5. Latin America, Spain & Portugal	16	-.24	-	-	5	-.10	6	-.27	4	-.31	1 -
6. Eastern Europe	7	-.72	-	-	-	-	2	-.95	4	-.64	1 -
7. Middle Europe	6	-.29	-	-	-	-	-	-	2	-.58	4 -
8. Northwestern Europe, Northern America, and Oceania	11	-.26	-	-	-	-	-	-	1	-.36	10 -

a
Including 6 countries in regional group 9 (Miscellaneous).

amounts or increase in the progression from Level I to II and from
IV to V, with larger decreases from II to III and from III to IV. To be
sure, increases are not prescribed by the logistic hypothesis at any
stage of development, but as noted in the preceding section, oc-
casional instances of higher rates for more-developed than for less-
developed countries could easily be due to extraneous factors.

Our data and the above analysis, so far as they go, bear out
the logistic hypothesis of declining male activity rates, and suggest
that the timing of decline of the rates in relation to stages of the
development process may be different for males in the labor-force
entry and retirement ages. These findings are tentative, however;
the hypotheses need testing with cross-sectional data for component areas of various countries, long-range historical time series
of activity rates, and more detailed analytical models. In any event,
it would be rash to put much trust in the results of this kind of
analysis for inferences about future trends in little developed African, Asian, and Latin American countries when and if they reach
the levels of development now prevailing in Europe, northern
America, and Oceania. It is also worth noting that, if the logistic
trends are to lead eventually to stable levels of male activity rates,
few of the most economically advanced countries seem yet to be
drawing near that state. Substantial decreases continued during
postwar intercensal periods in a majority of Level V countries,
although the pace of the trend was noticeably slower than that of
the decreases recorded in Levels III and IV.

112

Table 5.9. Intercensal changes of male age-specific activity rates in regional
groups of countries by levels of development

Age groups	Total	Level I	Level II	Level III	Level IV	Level V
3. Other Moslem countries						
Number of countries	2	-	1	1	-	-
Mean annual change:						
15-19 years	-1.33	-	-1.40	-1.27	-	-
20-29 years	-.22	-	-.21	-.23	-	-
30-44 years	-.05	-	+.01	-.12	-	-
45-64 years	-.48	-	-.08	-.87	-	-
65 years and over	-1.72	-	-.66	-2.79	-	-
4. South and East Asia						
Number of countries	4	-	1	2	1	-
Mean annual change:						
15-19 years	-1.18	-	-.02	-1.86	-1.01	-
20-29 years	-.02	-	+.17	-.13	-.06	-
30-44 years	+.07	-	+.10	+.07	+.04	-
45-64 years	-.15	-	-.30	-.22	+.13	-
65 years and over	-.49	-	-1.63	-.12	-.08	-
5. Latin America, Spain, and Portugal						
Number of countries	15	-	5	6	3	1
Mean annual change:						
15-19 years	-.71	-	-.59	-.63	-.77	-1.56
20-29 years	-.02	-	-.04	+.04	+.03	+.05
30-44 years	+.01	-	+.03	-.04	+.03	+.19
45-64 years	-.14	-	-.06	-.18	-.29	+.13
65 years and over	-1.02	-	-.26	-.98	-1.22	-.19
6. Eastern Europe						
Number of countries	3	-	-	-	3	-
Mean annual change:						
15-19 years	-1.96	-	-	-	-1.96	-
20-29 years	-.09	-	-	-	-.09	-
30-44 years	+.02	-	-	-	+.02	-
45-64 years	-.65	-	-	-	-.65	-
65 years and over	-2.56	-	-	-	-2.56	-
7. Middle Europe						
Number of countries	5	-	-	-	2	3
Mean annual change:						
15-19 years	-.89	-	-	-	-1.50	-.48
20-29 years	-.05	-	-	-	-.15	+.01
30-44 years	-.06	-	-	-	-.08	-.06
45-64 years	-.23	-	-	-	-.51	-.05
65 years and over	-1.17	-	-	-	-1.79	-.76
8. Northwestern Europe, Northern America, and Oceania						
Number of countries	10	-	-	-	1	9
Mean annual change:						
15-19 years	-1.23	-	-	-	-1.62	-1.18
20-29 years	-.12	-	-	-	-.37	-.10
30-44 years	-.00	-	-	-	-.00	-.00
45-64 years	+.04	-	-	-	-.00	+.05
65 years and over	-.65	-	-	-	-.64	-.65

5.6. Effects of the Speed of Economic Development

It has been shown that the speed of decline in male activity rates varies with the level of the rates and the level of economic development. Another factor is the speed of development. To see how the trends of the rates during intercensal periods varied in this respect, countries are classified by two indicators of the speed of development: annual rate of increase in real gross domestic product per head, and annual increment in the percent share of nonagricultural industries in total employment or labor force. For brevity, these are labelled "GDP growth rate" and "increase of nonagricultural share," respectively. Mean intercensal changes of male standardized activity rates and of specific rates for ages 15 to 19 and 65 and over are shown in Table 5.10 for countries classified by these two indicators (see the technical notes on the indicators, Appendix H).

Among the countries that were developing most rapidly according to either indicator, the male activity rates decreased appreciably more, on the average, than they did among countries that were making slower progress in economic development. This pattern is marked in the mean intercensal changes of activity rates in both age groups 15 to 19 and 65 and over, as well as in the changes of the standardized rates. It may be due partly to the influence of the level of development as well as the speed of development, since the speed of development and the decrease of male activity rates were both relatively fast, on the average, among countries at Levels III and IV of development. When the figures for countries at different levels of development are considered separately, however, the association between speed of development and decrease of male activity rates seems to hold fairly well up to Level IV (although there are irregularities, which could easily be due to random variations in the means for small numbers of countries). The association seems to disappear among the countries in Level V, suggesting that at this level of development, variations of speed of development may no longer have much effect on the trends of male activity rates.

Conversely, reading Table 5.10 horizontally instead of vertically so as to compare mean intercensal changes of activity rates among countries at different levels of development within each category of GDP growth rate and increases of nonagricultural share in employment, one sees the logistic curve repeated with

114

Table 5.10. Intercensal changes of male standardized and age-specific activity
rates in countries cross-classified by levels of development and
indicators of the speed of development

(N = number of countries; Mean = mean annual intercensal change
in activity rates)

Indicators of speed	Total		Levels I-II		Level III		Level IV		Level V	
of development	N	Mean	N	Mean	N	Mean	N	Mean	N	Mean

Changes of male standardized activity rates

Total, all countries	58	-.35	13	-.22	11	-.43	15	-.44	17	-.26
GDP growth rate:										
Under 2.0 percent	16	-.25	6	-.17	2	-.32	3	-.33	5	-.27
2.0-3.9 percent	20	-.39	4	-.30	6	-.46	2	-.38	8	-.25
4.0 percent & over	15	-.43	-	-	1	-.53	10	-.48	4	-.27
Not available	7	-.39	3	-.24	2	-.38	2	-.62	-	-
Increase of nonagricul-tural share:[a]										
Under .40 percent	13	-.17	7	-.06	2	-.44	1	-.32	3	-.22
.40-.79 percent	24	-.31	5	-.37	4	-.19	7	-.41	8	-.23
.80 percent & over	18	-.43	-	-	4	-.43	8	-.52	6	-.32
Not available	3	-.82	1	-.66	1	-1.37	1	-.44	-	-

Changes of male activity rates in ages 15-19

Total, all countries	45	-1.06	8	-.71	9	-.98	14	-1.31	14	-1.10
GDP growth rate:										
Under 2.0 percent	14	-.74	5	-.44	2	-.96	2	-.28	5	-1.14
2.0-3.9 percent	17	-1.04	3	-1.16	5	-.63	2	-1.60	7	-1.13
4.0 percent & over	11	-1.33	-	-	-	-	9	-1.42	2	-.92
Not available	3	-1.80	-	-	2	-1.86	1	-1.70	-	-
Increase of nonagricul-tural share:[a]										
Under .40 percent	10	-.64	5	-.37	2	-.80	1	-.55	2	-1.17
.40-.79 percent	19	-1.04	2	-1.24	4	-.74	5	-1.10	8	-1.10
.80 percent & over	15	-1.38	-	-	3	-1.41	8	-1.53	4	-1.08
Not available	1	-1.32	1	-1.32	-	-	-	-	-	-

Changes of male activity rates in ages 65 and over

Total, all countries	45	-1.00	8	-.64	9	-.99	14	-1.55	14	-.67
GDP growth rate:										
Under 2.0 percent	14	-.93	5	-.63	2	-1.10	2	-1.88	5	-.78
2.0-3.9 percent	17	-.93	3	-.67	5	-1.30	2	-1.36	7	-.73
4.0 percent & over	11	-1.41	-	-	-	-	9	-1.67	2	-.23
Not available	3	-.30	-	-	2	-.12	1	-.65	-	-
Increase of nonagricul-tural share:[a]										
Under .40 percent	10	-.83	5	-.37	2	-1.36	1	-2.38	2	-.69
.40-.79 percent	19	-.76	2	-.87	4	-.72	5	-.96	8	-.64
.80 percent & over	15	-1.39	-	-	3	-1.10	8	-1.82	4	-.74
Not available	1	-1.58	1	-1.58	-	-	-	-	-	-

[a]
Annual increase in percent share of nonagricultural industries in total
employment.

few irregularities on each line of the table. So the logistic pattern
of decreasing male activity rates does not seem to be explained
merely by the fact that countries at the middle level of development were developing more rapidly, on the average, than those
at the lowest and highest levels.

Participation by males

The two indicators of speed of development considered here are not independent of each other. Kuznets observes[8] that both the GDP growth rate and the rate of shifts in industrial structure are linked positively with the rate of technological change, as the latter affects both productivity and the relative demand for labor in different industry sectors. Moreover, the relative shares of different industries in the total demand for final products shift as the level of real income per head rises. But the correlation between GDP growth rates and increase in the nonagricultural share in employment is not perfect (see Appendix H, Table H.3). It is interesting to ask which of the two indicators of speed of development appears to be more closely associated with changes in male activity rates. Some indications on this score are given by Table 5.11, where mean intercensal changes of standardized and age-specific male activity rates are shown in a cross classification of countries

Table 5.11. Intercensal changes of male standardized and age-specific activity rates in countries cross-classified by growth rate of gross domestic product per head and rate of increase in nonagricultural share in employment

(N = number of countries; Mean = mean annual change of activity rate)

Increase of nonagricultural share in employment[a]	Total[b]		GDP growth rate under 2.0%		GDP growth rate 2.0-3.9%		GDP growth rate 4.0% and over	
	N	Mean	N	Mean	N	Mean	N	Mean
Changes of male standardized activity rates								
Total	58	-.35	16	-.25	20	-.39	15	-.43
Under .40 percent	13	-.17	7	-.15	5	-.24	-	-
.40-.79 percent	24	-.31	7	-.24	10	-.28	2	-.30
.80 percent & over	18	-.43	1	-.62	4	-.35	12	-.45
Changes of male activity rates in ages 15-19								
Total	45	-1.06	14	-.74	17	-1.04	11	-1.33
Under .40 percent	10	-.64	7	-.48	3	-1.00	-	-
.40-.79 percent	19	-1.04	5	-.79	10	-1.03	2	-1.09
.80 percent & over	15	-1.38	1	-1.73	4	-1.11	9	-1.38
Changes of male activity rates in ages 65+								
Total	45	-1.00	14	-.93	17	-.93	11	-1.41
Under .40 percent	10	-.83	7	-.85	3	-.80	-	-
.40-.79 percent	19	-.76	5	-.87	10	-.70	2	-1.06
.80 percent & over	15	-1.39	1	-1.13	4	-1.61	9	-1.49

a
Annual increase in percent share of nonagricultural industries in total employment.
b
Totals include countries for which GDP growth rate and increase in nonagricultural share were not available.

[8] Simon Kuznets, *Modern Economic Growth; Rate, Structure, and Spread* (New Haven and London, 1966), p. 156.

by the two indicators of speed of development. When the rate of increase in nonagricultural share in employment is held constant, the association between the GDP growth rate and intercensal changes of the activity rates to a large extent fades out. On the other hand, the association between the rate of increase in non-agricultural share and changes in the activity rates seems to be largely independent of the GDP growth rate. These observations suggest tentatively that the trends of participation by males in the labor force may be influenced more directly by changes in the structure of employment as they affect conditions of employment opportunity than by the trends of earnings and income as they affect the propensity to be employed. This tentative inference calls for testing by further analysis, including consideration of other aspects of the changes in employment structure (industrial and occupational composition of the nonagricultural sector, and shares of employees, self-employed, and family workers in employment), which are outside the scope of the present study.

5.7. Effects of Urbanization and Changing Male Participation Rates in Rural and Urban Sectors

The changes in national activity rates which take place during the course of economic development can be considered as results of increasing urbanization, together with changes of the rates within the rural and urban population sectors. The effect of increasing urbanization on national activity rates of males is almost always negative, since the urban rates are almost universally lower than the rural rates, as shown in chapter 2. Changes of male activity rates within both rural and urban sectors during the course of development are also likely to be negative, but the rural and urban trends may not be parallel, because the changes in employment opportunities, earnings and income levels, and other factors in the development process are likely to be different in rural and urban sectors.

Levels and intercensal changes of rural and urban male activity rates in countries at different levels of development are portrayed in Tables 5.12 and 5.13. The cautions in chapter 2 with regard to weaknesses of the rural and urban data should be recalled, and caution should be doubled now that the data are spread thinner with the classification by levels of development of countries. These data will not, in fact, support definite conclusions. They can only

117

Participation by males

Table 5.12. Levels and intercensal changes of rural and urban male standardized activity rates in countries at different levels of development

	Total	Level I	Level II	Level III	Level IV	Level V
Levels of $Stand_m$ or RAR_m, cross-sectional censuses						
Number of countries	41	4	12	10	9	6
Mean levels of rates:						
National totals	75.6	78.0	79.4	76.7	72.5	69.9
Rural	78.5	79.2	82.6	80.4	76.4	69.9
Urban	71.0	71.0	72.0	71.6	70.7	69.3
Urban-rural difference[a]	-7.5	-8.2	-10.6	-8.8	-5.7	-0.6
Frequency distribution of rural rates:						
Under 70.0	5	-	-	1	1	3
70.0-74.9	8	1	2	-	2	3
75.0-79.9	9	1	2	3	3	-
80.0-84.9	12	1	3	5	3	-
85.0 and over	7	1	5	1	-	-
Frequency distribution of urban rates:						
Under 70.0	15	1	4	3	3	4
70.0-74.9	18	2	4	5	5	2
75.0-79.9	8	1	4	2	1	-
80.0-84.9	-	-	-	-	-	-
85.0 and over	-	-	-	-	-	-
Intercensal changes of $Stand_m$ or RAR_m						
Number of countries	16	-	5	4	5	2
Mean annual changes:						
National totals	-.31	-	-.41	-.37	-.30	-.02
Rural	-.20	-	-.23	-.17	-.19	-.23
Urban	-.32	-	-.43	-.48	-.20	-.02

[a]
Urban minus rural rate.

furnish some tentative indications of patterns of changes in rural and urban activity rates accompanying economic development, and of the effects of increasing urbanization.

The data on intercensal changes are especially weak as they refer to only sixteen countries, nine of which belong to region 5 (Latin America, Spain, and Portugal). They suggest tentatively that during the postwar years, standardized activity rates of males in countries at all levels of development were generally decreasing in both rural and urban sectors. The only exceptions among the sixteen countries are small increases of urban rates recorded in Japan, Puerto Rico, and the United States.

The cross-sectional sample of levels of rural and urban activity rates is more ample, but still badly unbalanced in regional distribution, with fourteen of the forty-one countries belonging to region

118

Table 5.13. Levels of rural and urban male age-specific activity rates in
countries at different levels of development, cross-sectional
censuses

Age groups	Total	Level I	Level II	Level III	Level IV	Level V
Number of countries	36	4	11	9	8	4
			Mean rural rates			
15-19 years	71.8	70.8	75.8	79.2	68.6	52.0
20-29 years	94.2	91.9	94.9	96.6	94.1	89.6
30-44 years	97.1	96.4	97.8	97.9	96.7	95.2
45-64 years	92.8	91.6	95.0	93.6	91.2	89.2
65 years and over	60.9	61.5	73.5	64.9	52.8	32.4
			Mean urban rates			
15-19 years	50.2	53.5	49.9	50.4	51.1	45.7
20-29 years	88.8	86.2	88.5	90.9	88.4	88.4
30-44 years	95.8	92.6	96.3	96.7	95.6	96.4
45-64 years	87.3	86.3	88.5	87.7	84.1	90.3
65 years and over	45.7	51.9	55.5	46.8	37.0	27.4
			Urban-rural differences[a]			
15-19 years	-21.6	-17.3	-25.9	-28.8	-17.5	-6.3
20-29 years	-5.4	-5.7	-6.4	-5.7	-5.7	-1.2
30-44 years	-1.3	-3.8	-1.5	-1.2	-1.1	+1.2
45-64 years	-5.5	-5.3	-6.5	-5.9	-7.1	+1.1
65 years and over	-15.2	-9.6	-18.0	-18.1	-15.8	-5.0

[a]
Urban minus rural rates.

5 (Latin America, Spain, and Portugal). The pattern of cross-sectional differences according to levels of development of countries, in the rural and urban male standardized rates, does not agree very well with the trends indicated by the smattering of data on intercensal changes. While the average levels of the standardized rates for males in the rural sector decline as the level of development rises, it is not so with the urban rates. The average of the urban rates is already low in the four Level I countries represented in the cross section, and it does not decline substantially or consistently as the level of development rises. Only in Level V does the average of the urban rates fall appreciably below that of Level I, and even here the difference is not impressive. So it seems that the decrease in average cross-sectional level of national total standardized activity rates of males, moving up the scale of relative development levels, is brought about almost entirely by decreasing rates in the rural sector and by the decrease in the proportionate share of rural population in the total, without any substantial change in average level of the urban rates. Studying the averages of age-

119

specific rates (Table 5.13), one sees, however, a well-defined pattern of diminishing activity of men over age sixty-five in the urban as well as the rural sector, with rising level of development. It is the failure of a corresponding trend to appear in the rates for males under age twenty in the urban sector that accounts for the small differences, according to levels of development, in the cross-sectional average levels of urban male standardized rates. In other words, while the generality of the trend toward earlier retirement of males from the labor force with progress in economic development is confirmed both for urban and rural sectors, our cross-sectional data do not bear out the generality in the urban sector of the trend toward later entry into the labor force.

As the cross-sectional average level of male standardized activity rates in the rural sector declines with rising level of development, while the average of the urban rates remains relatively constant, the urban-rural difference diminishes. The difference almost disappears when Level v of development is reached; rural and urban male standardized activity rates in these highly developed countries are nearly equal on the average, both on a low plane. This narrowing of the urban-rural difference is apparent both in the average rates for males in the ages of retirement and for those in the ages of entry into the labor force. However, average levels of the specific rates for males in ages 15 to 19 and 65 and over among Level v countries are still appreciably lower in the urban than in the rural population.

A point worth noting in Table 5.13 is that the average levels of the rural male activity rates exceed the urban averages by a wider margin in ages 15 to 19 than in ages over 65, without exception among countries at each level of development. In this respect, the urban-rural differences are unlike the differences between more-developed and less-developed countries. As noted above, the latter differences are wider and more consistent in the ages over 65 than in 15 to 19.

In little-developed countries, changes of activity rates in the urban population will not ordinarily have a great effect on the trends of national total rates, because the share of urban population in the total is ordinarily small. As economic development and urbanization advance, changes within the urban sector become more influential, while the influence of changes within the rural sector diminishes. The increase of urbanization is an important factor making for decreasing trends of national total male activity rates in countries in early stages of development, but its effect tends to diminish in later stages because of narrowing of the difference between rural and urban rates. The diminishing effect of increasing urbanization is one of the causes of the logistic trend of decreasing national male activity rates in the course of economic development.

The rural and urban data also reveal an important aspect of the convergence in trends of national male activity rates that may go with progress in economic development. Consider the distributions of levels of rural and urban male standardized activity rates among countries at different development levels (Table 5.12). The pattern of wide variations among less-developed countries and increasing concentration of rates at low levels as development progresses is marked most strongly in the rural rates, while the urban rates are confined within a narrower range from the start. It can be seen that the movement of national total rates toward equality on a low plane comes about mainly by elimination of high rates in the rural sector, together with the decreasing weight of the rural sector in the total.

The rural-urban convergence—that is, closing the gap between levels of male activity rates in rural and urban sectors within countries—can be viewed as an aspect of diffusion of modernization in economic organization and styles of life from cities to rural communities, with a lag that diminishes as economic development progresses. The lag diminishes partly as a result of the increase of urbanization, as the influence of the cities upon the rural communities intensifies with the growing preponderance of the former in the population and economy of the nation. In addition, economic development involves growing integration of rural communities with the cities in a common market for labor as well as for products; there is increasing movement between rural and urban areas of migrants, commuters, shoppers, and visitors; the rural-urban dichotomy of the social as well as the economic organization tends to break down. The progressive urbanization of the rural population is especially visible in the United States, where a growing share of the dwindling minority of rural residents consists of commuters to the cities, while even the farmers and others who work in rural communities become more and more citified in their life style.

Participation by males

Before summing up the principal results of the analysis in this chapter, let us take up the question of how the patterns of women's participation in the labor force evolve in the process of modern economic development. An overview of salient findings with reference to both sexes will be found in the concluding chapter.

SIX

Changes in Women's Participation in the Labor Force in the Process of Economic Development

6.1. Factors of Increasing or Decreasing Participation by Females

Economic development in some countries has brought an increase in participation by women in the labor force, partly or wholly compensating for the decrease in men's participation, while in other countries, women's participation also has decreased.[1] In the United States, for example, females in the labor force increased from 16.6 percent of the female population ten years of age and over in 1890 to 31.3 percent in 1960, while in Belgium, the rate dropped from 32.6 in 1890 to 23.5 in 1961. The trend since the beginning of the census record has been predominantly upward in Sweden; downward in Switzerland; upward in Japan; downward in Egypt, India, and Pakistan. In Great Britain, the 1961 census showed almost the same rate as was recorded in 1851, although there were some ups and downs in the meantime. In France and the Netherlands, the recorded trends have been unsteady: upward during some periods of their modern economic development, downward during other periods. The changes of female standardized activity rates during postwar intercensal periods present a similar mixture of rising, falling, and level trends among countries at each level of economic development (Table 6.1).

The trends of women's activity rates in countries undergoing economic development are influenced by the same kinds of factors of changing opportunity, propensity, and capability of employment discussed in the preceding chapter with reference to males. But while the net effect is generally negative in the case of males in labor-force entry and retirement ages, it may be either negative

[1] In addition to the compilations of historical data in United Nations, *Demographic Aspects of Manpower* (New York, 1958) and Clarence Long, *The Labor Force under Changing Income and Employment* (Princeton, 1958), Appendix A, historical series of measures of female participation rates in a number of countries are analyzed in C. E. V. Leser, "Trends in Women's Work Participation," *Population Studies* 12 (1958), 100–10. Series for India, Pakistan, and Egypt are assembled in the works of Ambannavar, Farooq, and Nassef cited in chapter 5, note 2.

Women's participation

Table 6.1. Levels and intercensal changes of female standardized activity rates in countries at different levels of development

	Total	Level I	Level II	Level III	Level IV	Level V
Levels of Stand$_f$ or RAR$_f$, cross-sectional censuses						
Number of countries	100	20	20	20	20	20
Mean level of rates	32.0	47.8	26.3	19.5	32.0	34.2
Standard deviation	19.0	25.1	16.0	14.1	12.5	10.8
Frequency distribution:						
Under 10.0	11	3	3	5	-	-
10.0-19.9	21	1	5	9	5	1
20.0-29.9	23	1	7	2	5	8
30.0-39.9	14	2	1	2	4	5
40.0-49.9	12	2	2	-	3	5
50.0-59.9	9	3	1	2	3	-
60.0-69.9	4	2	1	-	-	1
70.0 and over	6	6	-	-	-	-
Intercensal changes of Stand$_f$ or RAR$_f$						
Number of countries	58	3	10	11	17	17
Mean annual change	-.10	+.06	-.44	-.14	-.05	+.04
Frequency distribution:						
+.50 or more	3	-	1	-	2	-
+.10 to +.49	17	-	-	5	2	10
-.09 to +.09	16	1	4	3	5	3
-.10 to -.49	13	2	2	2	5	3
-.50 or more	9	-	3	1	3	2
Relative volatility [a]	1.1	0.2	2.1	1.5	0.9	0.9

[a] Mean annual change irrespective of sign, as percentage of mean level of rates.

or positive for females, according to the circumstances of each country at each stage of its development.

Whether economic development brings an increase or a decrease of opportunities for women to be employed depends to a great extent on the relative proportions of female workers employed in the fields that expand and in those that contract in the process of development. The expansion of the nonagricultural share in labor demand at the expense of agriculture makes for increasing opportunity for women in countries where the female share in nonagricultural employment is larger than in agriculture, as in Latin American countries, and for decreasing opportunity in the opposite case, as in the majority of South and East Asian countries. Also important in this respect is the distribution of female workers among fields of employment within the nonagricultural sector. Domestic service, for example, is one of the fields in which employment tends to contract as economic development goes forward, and the effect of this contraction varies with the relative importance of domestic

124

Table 6.2. Levels and intercensal changes of rural and urban female standardized activity rates in countries at different levels of development

	Total	Level I	Level II	Level III	Level IV	Level V
Cross-sectional levels of Stand$_f$ or RAR$_f$						
Number of countries	41	4	12	10	9	6
Mean levels of rates:						
National total	27.4	49.2	25.4	17.9	30.7	27.7
Rural	26.2	51.2	25.4	15.7	30.0	22.6
Urban	25.0	31.3	20.9	20.4	29.0	30.7
Urban-rural difference[a]	-1.2	-19.9	-4.5	+4.7	-1.0	+8.1
Frequency distribution of rural rates:						
Under 10.0	8	-	4	3	1	-
10.0-19.9	14	1	2	5	4	2
20.0-29.9	7	-	2	1	-	4
30.0-39.9	1	-	1	-	-	-
40.0-49.9	6	1	2	1	2	-
50.0-59.9	1	-	-	-	1	-
60.0-69.9	1	-	-	-	1	-
70.0 and over	3	2	1	-	-	-
Frequency distribution of urban rates:						
Under 10.0	5	1	2	2	-	-
10.0-19.9	8	1	4	1	2	-
20.0-29.9	16	-	5	6	3	2
30.0-39.9	9	1	-	1	3	4
40.0-49.9	1	-	-	-	1	-
50.0-59.9	1	-	1	-	-	-
60.0-69.9	1	1	-	-	-	-
70.0 and over	-	-	-	-	-	-
Intercensal changes of Stand$_f$ or RAR$_f$						
Number of countries	16	-	5	4	5	2
Mean annual changes:						
National totals	-.06	-	-.24	+.11	-.18	+.32
Rural	-.07	-	-.25	+.25	-.12	+.34
Urban	+.05	-	-.04	+.07	+.02	+.27
Urban-rural difference	+.12	-	+.21	-.18	+.14	-.07

a
Urban minus rural rate.

service as a field of employment for women in different countries. Collver and Langlois emphasized this point in their study of the economic activities of women in the metropolitan populations of countries at different levels of development. Table 6A shows their findings of the mean rates of participation by females in all industries, domestic service, and other industries in a cross section of census statistics for the metropolitan areas of twenty-five countries.[2]

[2] Andrew Collver and Eleanor Langlois, "The Female Labor Force in Metropolitan Areas: An International Comparison," *Economic Develop-*

Women's participation

Table 6A

	Least developed countries	Medium-level countries	Most developed countries
Number of countries	8	10	7
Mean levels of female participation rates in metropolitan areas:[a]			
All industries	28	34	39
Private domestic service	11	9	3
Other industries	17	25	36

[a] Females in the labor force per hundred female population fifteen to sixty-four years of age.

Likewise, the contraction of family enterprise in the process of economic development has a negative effect on women's employment opportunities, which may be overbalanced or not by expansion in other fields. In the cross section of census data compiled for the present study, mean levels of female standardized activity rates, including and excluding unpaid family workers (in national total populations), vary in relation to the levels of economic development, as shown in Table 6B.

Table 6B

	No. of countries	All status categories[a]	Unpaid family workers	Others
Level I	10	49.4	31.7	17.7
Level II	17	24.6	9.4	15.2
Level III	17	19.6	6.0	13.6
Level IV	17	31.9	8.0	23.9
Level V	17	34.2	2.9	31.3

[a] Mean rates differ from those shown in Table 6.1 because they refer only to countries for which the numbers of female unpaid family workers were obtained.

ment and Cultural Change 10 (1962), Table 2, p. 373. Material used by permission of the University of Chicago Press.

Of course, the effect of decreasing participation in unpaid family work, agriculture, domestic service, or any other contracting field upon the trend of overall activity rates is not measured simply by the amount of decrease in the participation rate in the contracting field, since the levels and trends of participation in different kinds of employment are not independent of one another. But the shrinkage of opportunities in such fields during the course of economic development has a depressing effect on the trend of total participation by females in the labor force, and this may be greater or less than the positive effect of growing opportunities in other fields.

In addition to the changes in structure of labor demand according to occupation, industry, and status, the trends of employment opportunity for women may be modified by changes in the shares of the sexes in employment within various fields. In the United States and other countries in recent times, women have come to be regarded as fit for many jobs formerly reserved for men. Women may also take over occupations by default of male workers, or they may be forced out by male competition, as seems to have happened in some occupations in India, for example, since the early years of the present century.

In the factors of changing propensity to take advantage of available opportunities for employment, there are important differences between females and males, due to the fact that females generally have greater domestic responsibilities that compete with income-producing jobs for their time and energies. This competition tends to be abated as economic development progresses, by increasing mechanization and other technological advances in domestic work, and by the shift out of the domestic sphere of a host of activities such as food preparation, laundry, etc. If other factors were neutral, a generally increasing trend of participation by women in the labor force might be expected on this account. If fertility decreases, as it has done in all countries that have reached high levels of development, this, too, may have a positive effect on the trend of female activity rates. This is, in fact, one of the arguments commonly used to support claims of important economic advantages from the promotion of family planning and other antinatalist policies. Decreasing infant and child mortality rates, by the same reasoning, should produce an opposite effect. But the importance of effects of decreasing fertility and mortality upon activity rates of females is uncertain. While it is true, as data from many countries

127

have confirmed, that women who have young children in their care are less likely to be employed outside the home than those who do not, it does not necessarily follow that, given more freedom from maternal responsibilities, many more women would choose to be employed. Moreover, changes in fertility and child mortality rates do not have proportionate effects on women's maternal responsibilities. Whether or not a woman feels free to leave home for work is likely to depend more on whether she has any young children or not than on the number of children.[3] Fertility and child mortality rates may change considerably without much effect on the number of women who have at least one young child. Some negative correlation has nevertheless been observed between female activity rates and ratios of children to women of childbearing ages in the population of different countries.[4]

Women's appetite for income-earning jobs, like that of males in the ages of labor-force entry and retirement, may be whetted by rising wages and at the same time dulled by rising family incomes. In recent studies in the United States and a few other countries, attempts have been made to estimate these opposing influences on women's activity rates by regression analyses with women's earnings and the earnings of husbands or levels of family income as independent variables.[5] It would be rash, though, to suppose that the results of such analyses referring to the conditions of a given country in a given stage of its development would hold true in the varied cultural and institutional settings of other countries or other times in the same country. Especially for married women, the choice between domestic activities or leisure and work for income is influenced, more than it is for men, by the system of relative values that prevails in the particular society at the particular time. It is possible that the changes in these relative values which take place during the course of economic development might be a primary factor shaping the secular trends of female activity rates.

[3] For example, see Elizabeth Waldman and Anne M. Young, "Marital and Family Characteristics of Workers, March 1970," *Special Labor Force Report No. 130* (U.S. Department of Labor, Bureau of Labor Statistics, 1971).

[4] Collver and Langlois, "The Female Labor Force in Metropolitan Areas."

[5] Among others, see William G. Bowen and T. Aldrich Finegan, *The Economics of Labor Force Participation* (Princeton, 1969); Glen Cain, *Married Women in the Labor Force* (Chicago, 1966); and Robert Leroy, *Essai sur la population active* (Louvain, 1968).

128

6.2. Effects of Expansion of the Nonagricultural Share in Employment and Changing Female Shares in Agricultural and Nonagricultural Employment

The decreasing trend of male activity rates accompanying economic development was considered in chapter 5 as a composite of effects of changing rates in the rural and the urban population, together with the increasing share of urban population in the total. The trends of female activity rates can likewise be considered as made up mainly of three components: changes of female shares in agricultural and in nonagricultural employment, and the effect of the increasing relative share of nonagricultural employment in the total. Each of these three components may be either positive or negative.

It was observed in chapter 2 that during postwar intercensal periods, female shares in both agricultural and nonagricultural employment increased in some countries and decreased in others, with a slight negative balance of changes on the average in the agricultural sector and a slight positive balance in the nonagricultural sector among the countries for which data were obtained. The picture is similar with respect to the trends in countries at each level of economic development (Table 6.4), except that the positive average change of FS_{nonag} does not appear among countries in Levels I and II.

The effect of the relative expansion of the nonagricultural sector upon the trend of female activity rates is positive in countries where the female share is larger in nonagricultural than in agricultural employment, and negative in the opposite circumstances. The differences among countries in this respect follow distinct regional patterns, as shown in chapter 3. If other factors were constant, the expansion of the nonagricultural sector that goes with economic development would bring increasing female activity rates in almost all Arab and Latin American countries and all those of northwestern Europe, northern America, and Oceania while the effects would be opposite in South and East Asia and Eastern Europe, and mixed in other regions. The strength of the positive or negative effect in each country depends, of course, on the width of the difference between the female shares in the two sectors of employment, as well as on the speed of increase of the nonagricultural share in total employment.

It was observed in the preceding chapter that in the case of males, the effect of increasing urbanization upon the trend of their

129

Women's participation

Table 6.3. Levels of female shares in agricultural and nonagricultural employment in countries at different levels of development, cross-sectional censuses

	Total	Level I	Level II	Level III	Level IV	Level V
Number of countries	91	16	19	18	19	19

Female shares in agricultural employment (FS_{ag})

	Total	Level I	Level II	Level III	Level IV	Level V
Mean level	22.4	33.0	18.7	14.4	27.5	21.0
Standard deviation	18.6	18.3	15.6	14.8	19.8	17.9
Frequency distribution:						
Under 10.0	36	3	9	10	5	9
10.0-19.9	15	2	2	4	3	4
20.0-29.9	7	1	2	1	2	1
30.0-39.9	11	1	4	1	4	1
40.0-49.9	9	6	1	1	-	1
50.0 and over	13	3	1	1	5	3

Female shares in nonagricultural employment (FS_{nonag})

	Total	Level I	Level II	Level III	Level IV	Level V
Mean level	26.8	23.4	27.0	21.6	30.1	31.6
Standard deviation	11.5	15.7	11.7	11.0	7.4	6.0
Frequency distribution:						
Under 10.0	10	3	2	5	-	-
10.0-19.9	13	5	4	3	1	-
20.0-29.9	31	3	4	5	10	9
30.0-39.9	27	3	5	4	6	9
40.0-49.9	9	1	4	1	2	1
50.0 and over	1	1	-	-	-	-

Table 6.4. Intercensal changes of female shares in agricultural and nonagricultural employment in countries at different levels of development

	Total	Level I	Level II	Level III	Level IV	Level V
Number of countries	54	3	10	9	15	17

Female shares in agricultural employment (FS_{ag})

	Total	Level I	Level II	Level III	Level IV	Level V
Mean annual change	-.13	-.04	-.14	-.09	-.07	-.22
Frequency distribution:						
+.50 or more	3	-	-	-	2	1
+.10 to +.49	14	-	2	4	5	3
+.09 to -.09	14	2	4	1	2	5
-.10 to -.49	13	1	3	3	2	4
-.50 or more	10	-	1	1	4	4
Relative volatility[a]	1.5	0.2	1.4	1.5	1.7	1.9

Female shares in nonagricultural employment (FS_{nonag})

	Total	Level I	Level II	Level III	Level IV	Level V
Mean annual change	+.10	-.01	-.04	+.17	+.13	+.14
Frequency distribution:						
+.50 or more	5	-	-	1	3	1
+.10 to +.49	21	1	4	4	3	9
+.09 to -.09	14	1	3	3	4	3
-.10 to -.49	11	-	2	1	4	4
-.50 or more	3	1	1	-	1	-
Relative volatility[a]	1.0	1.4	1.1	0.9	1.1	0.8

a
Mean annual change irrespective of sign, as percentage of mean level of rates.

activity rates tended to diminish as the level of economic development rose, because of narrowing differences between male activity rates in rural and urban populations. No corresponding tendency of narrowing differences between female shares in agricultural and nonagricultural employment with rising level of economic development is apparent in our data (Table 6.3). The data suggest that positive or negative FS_{ag} — FS_{nonag} differences tend to persist as economic development goes forward, and although the trends in the two sectors may not be parallel within countries, there is little evidence of either convergent or divergent trends predominating.

6.3. The U–Curve Hypothesis

It was observed in chapter 4 that the cross-sectional mean levels of female activity rates form a U-shaped pattern in relation to levels of economic development, suggesting that a typical trend in countries in process of economic development might be one of decreasing participation by women in the labor force during early stages and increasing again during later stages of development. Let us call this the U-curve hypothesis.

Sinha noted such a U-shaped pattern in the cross section of female standardized activity rates from censuses taken around 1950, compiled by the United Nations.[6] He proposed an explanation for it along the following lines. In early stages of economic development, opportunities for employment of women diminish as a result of the contraction in agriculture and in traditional occupations and industries within the nonagricultural sector. Although demand for labor is growing in other occupations and industries, women are at a disadvantage in competition with men for these jobs under the conditions of unemployment and underemployment that commonly plague countries in early stages of development. At the same time, the rising level of family incomes relaxes pressure upon women to be employed as supplementary earners. The trend of diminishing opportunity is reversed in later stages, when

[6] J. N. Sinha, "Dynamics of Female Participation in Economic Activity in a Developing Economy," United Nations World Population Conference, 1965, document WPC/285, Session A.5 (mimeographed); referring to the data compiled in United Nations, *Demographic Aspects of Manpower*. The U-shaped pattern was found also in the I.L.O. study of the cross-section of female activity rates recorded in various countries as of 1960, and was taken as a basis for I.L.O. labor force projections for the period 1965–1985. International Labour Office, *Labour Force Projections 1965–1985, Part VI, Methodological Supplement, First Edition, 1971* (Geneva, 1973).

larger growth of labor demand in the modern industries and occupations overbalances the contraction in traditional fields of employment; and women's propensity to take advantage of these opportunities is enhanced by rising wages, now overbalancing the
disincentive due to higher family incomes. Sinha found empirical
support for this hypothesis in Indian data, comparing levels and
trends of female activity rates in different parts of the country
and among different socio-economic groups of the population, as
well as in the international cross section of labor force measures.

The U-shaped pattern of cross-sectional mean levels of female
standardized activity rates in relation to levels of economic development can be seen in Table 6.1. Similar patterns appear in the
mean levels of rural and urban standardized rates (Table 6.2)
and female shares in agricultural and nonagricultural employment
(Table 6.3), although the mean of FS_{nonag} is higher in Level II
than in Level I, and the means of both FS_{ag} and rural $Stand_f$ are
lower in Level v than in Level IV. The data make it appear that the
downslope of the mean $Stand_f$ on the left arm of the U, from Level
I to III, is due mainly to diminishing participation by females in the
rural and agricultural sectors, while the upslope on the right arm,
from Level III to V, is due mainly to increasing participation in the
urban and nonagricultural sectors. These observations are in general agreement with Sinha's interpretation.

In the mean levels of female activity rates by age groups (Table
6.5), the U-curve is quite regular in ages 15 to 19, 20 to 24, and
55 to 59. Between ages 25 and 54 and between 60 and 69, the pattern is modified to the extent that the mean rates in Level v are
lower than in Level IV. In ages 70 to 74 and 75 and over, the
Level v means fall below both Level IV and Level III, giving the
curve a downward trend throughout except that the average is
higher in Level IV than in Level III. Subject to this reservation as
regards Level IV countries, the cross-sectional data suggest that
economic development typically brings a continuously decreasing
trend in the tenacity of females, as well as males, in the labor force
at advanced ages. Unlike the trend for males, the frequency of early
entry of females into the labor force seems to increase with economic development above a medium level. Less consistently, the
data indicate an upturn in average height of female activity rates
in the central adult ages at higher levels of economic development.

These observations suggest an addendum to Sinha's interpretation of factors that make for the U-shaped trend. For young males,

Women's participation

Table 6.5. Levels of female age-specific activity rates in countries at different levels of development, cross-sectional censuses

	Total	Level I	Level II	Level III	Level IV	Level V
Number of countries	84	13	19	17	18	17
Mean levels of rates:						
15-19 years	36.4	50.6	28.1	22.1	34.0	51.5
20-29 years[a]	37.6	52.6	28.2	22.2	42.8	46.4
30-44 years[a]	34.0	54.1	28.2	19.6	38.3	34.8
45-64 years[a]	29.3	45.3	26.9	16.7	31.0	30.4
65 years and over[a]	11.8	19.5	15.8	7.7	10.3	7.0
20-24 years	40.8	52.6	29.4	24.4	45.6	55.6
25-29 years	34.4	52.6	27.2	20.1	39.9	37.2
30-34 years	33.2	53.5	27.3	19.1	37.9	33.5
35-39 years	33.9	54.1	28.1	19.6	38.1	34.8
40-44 years	34.8	54.6	29.4	20.0	39.0	36.1
45-49 years	34.5	53.5	29.5	19.6	38.3	36.3
50-54 years	32.5	50.5	28.6	18.0	35.2	34.6
55-59 years	28.2	43.6	26.6	15.9	28.6	30.1
60-64 years	21.8	33.4	22.8	13.2	21.6	20.6
65-69 years	16.4	26.6	19.5	10.7	15.3	11.9
70-74 years	11.7	19.5	16.2	7.8	10.4	6.2
75 years and over	7.2	12.4	11.6	4.8	5.2	2.9
Standard deviations of rates:						
15-19 years	18.4	30.6	16.0	13.1	12.9	18.0
20-29 years	18.7	31.0	15.8	14.9	17.8	12.3
30-44 years	19.4	30.9	17.6	14.1	20.1	12.4
45-64 years	16.4	25.4	17.4	13.5	14.4	9.7
65 years and over	9.8	14.3	14.3	6.7	5.6	2.8

[a]
Unweighted average rates for 5-year age groups.

the decrease of activity rates in the process of development is the obverse of lengthening years in school; but for females, the relationship between trends in school attendance and labor force participation is more elastic. In the process of development, the activity rates of young females may rise concurrently with lengthening education. For married women in more developed countries, the smaller size of families and concentration of child-bearing in the early years of marriage are favorable to increased activity rates in middle age.

So the age patterns as well as the overall levels of female activity rates may change in the process of economic development, with the changing life cycle of marriage and the family and changing conditions of employment opportunity for women according to age, marital status, and family composition. The distributions of types of age curves of female activity rates among countries at different levels of development (Table 6.6) are interesting in this connection. The central peak or plateau and late peak patterns (Types A

133

Women's participation

Table 6.6. Types of age patterns of female activity rates in total, rural, and urban sectors of countries at different levels of development, cross-sectional censuses

	Total	Level I	Level II	Level III	Level IV	Level V
National totals						
Total number of countries	84	13	19	17	18	17
A. Central peak or plateau	14	7	5	-	2	-
B. Late peak	8	3	2	1	2	-
C. Early peak						
C-1. Without shoulder	21	1	1	8	7	4
C-2. Peak and shoulder	14	1	4	4	1	4
D. Double peak						
D-1. Early peak higher	19	-	4	3	4	8
D-2. Late peak higher	8	1	3	1	2	1
Rural						
Total number of countries	36	4	11	9	8	4
A. Central peak or plateau	10	3	3	-	4	-
B. Late peak	4	1	2	1	-	-
C. Early peak						
C-1. Without shoulder	5	-	-	2	2	1
C-2. Peak and shoulder	5	-	2	3	-	-
D. Double peak						
D-1. Early peak higher	6	-	2	1	1	2
D-2. Late peak higher	6	-	2	2	1	1
Urban						
Total number of countries	36	4	11	9	8	4
A. Central peak or plateau	4	1	2	-	1	-
B. Late peak	4	3	1	-	-	-
C. Early peak						
C-1. Without shoulder	15	-	5	6	5	1
C-2. Peak and shoulder	2	-	-	-	1	1
D. Double peak						
D-1. Early peak higher	8	-	1	3	2	2
D-2. Late peak higher	3	-	2	-	-	1

and B) are found mainly in little-developed countries, where most of the women in the labor force are unpaid family workers or employed at home in handicraft industries, retail trade "in the front room," and other such activities that combine easily with the role of the housewife and mother. The double-peaked pattern that has evolved recently in the United States and some other highly developed countries seems especially fitting to the small size of families, the early termination of child-bearing, and the predominance of wage labor in the modern urban-industrial society. In fact, nine of seventeen Level v countries in the cross section have Type D patterns, but such patterns are found also in a number of less-developed countries, including seven of the nineteen in Level II.

134

The distribution of types of age patterns of female activity rates is apparently not so closely tied to economic development and demographic modernization as one might think. Regional influences are important. For example, the fact that early-peaked patterns (Type C) predominate among the Spanish and Portuguese-language countries is mainly responsible for a high concentration of such patterns in Level III.

To resume the discussion of the U-curve hypothesis: if it is true, as the pattern of cross-sectional differences suggests, that the trend of overall female activity rates sometimes follows a U-shaped curve in countries in process of economic development, it is certainly not a universal rule. The historical statistics of Western industrialized countries make it plain that women's participation in the labor force does not invariably increase in advanced stages of economic development, although there do seem to be more instances of increasing than of decreasing trends in the recorded recent experiences of today's most developed countries. Whether decreases or increases predominated among these countries during earlier stages of their development is an open question. The data on changes during the postwar intercensal periods also deny the U-curve hypothesis as a generalization, particularly with regard to the trends in more developed countries.

Intercensal increases and decreases of female standardized activity rates were almost balanced among Level IV countries (Table 6.1), and while increases were recorded in a majority of those at Level V, the average annual change in this group was only slightly positive. The data give stronger support to the hypothesis as regards decreasing activity rates of females in less-developed countries. Negative intercensal changes were indeed predominant among Level II countries; a large increase was recorded in only one of these (Nicaragua) and small increases, less than .10 per annum, in two others (El Salvador and Paraguay). For Level I, the measures of intercensal changes in three countries are not an adequate sample, but it is noteworthy that little change in either female or male activity rates was recorded in two of these three (Nepal and Sabah). At least in Nepal, there was not much economic development going on during the intercensal period.

The intercensal changes of female shares in agricultural and non-agricultural employment (Table 6.4) present a less definitely patterned picture, with a mixture of increasing and decreasing trends in both sectors among countries at each level of development. The

135

average changes in FS_{ag} are negative both in less-developed and more-developed countries. Average FS_{nonag} changes are positive in Levels IV and V, in accord with the U-curve hypothesis, but they are neutral in Level II. The pattern of changes in rural and urban female standardized activity rates (Table 6.2) would probably be similar if these data had the same coverage of countries.

One reason why the intercensal changes in measures of female participation in the labor force do not conform better with the patterns of cross-sectional differences is that the latter are affected to an important extent by extraneous factors associated fortuitously with the levels of economic development. The different regional distributions of countries at different levels of development have a good deal to do with shaping the U-curves of the cross-sectional means. Especially important in this connection is the fact that thirteen of the twenty countries in Level III belong to regions 2 and 5 (Arab and Latin American countries), where female activity rates and female shares in agricultural employment are generally very low.

The corresponding figures are tabulated for each region in Table 6.7. It is especially interesting to compare the patterns of regions 4 and 5, which cover the widest ranges of development levels with considerable numbers of countries. In region 4 (South and East Asia), the mean levels of female standardized activity rates decrease from Level I to III as a result of decreasing relative participation by females in agriculture together with negative effects of the shift in the agricultural-nonagricultural structure of employment, while female shares in nonagricultural employment remain on an almost constant mean level. In Japan, alone in Level IV, the high levels of all three female labor force participation measures cause the regional curves of all three to turn upward from Level III according to the U-curve pattern, but the upturn here has little significance, since it depends on the statistics of only one country. In region 5 (Latin America, Spain, and Portugal), if the single figures for Bolivia in Level I and Venezuela in Level V are left out of account, there is no U-curve. The mean female standardized activity rate rises from Level II to IV, chiefly as a result of positive effects of the expanding share of the nonagricultural sector, and in spite of decreasing average female shares in nonagricultural employment.

The figures for region 6 (Eastern Europe) are also interesting, although the numbers of countries are rather small. Here the mean

136

le 6.7. Levels of female standardized activity rates and female shares in agricultural and nonagricultural employment in countries at different levels of development within each region, cross-sectional censuses (N = number of countries)

	Total N	Total Mean	Level I N	Level I Mean	Level II N	Level II Mean	Level III N	Level III Mean	Level IV N	Level IV Mean	Level V N	Level V Mean
Female standardized activity rates (Stand$_f$ or RAR$_f$)												
All regions	100	32.0	20	47.8	20	26.3	20	19.5	20	32.0	20	34.2
Tropical Africa	15	45.1	12	45.8	3	42.7	-	-	-	-	-	-
Arab countries	9	11.1	1	39.7	2	7.7	6	7.4	-	-	-	-
Other Moslem countries	7	42.3	2	42.2	3	48.7	2	32.7	-	-	-	-
South and East Asia	16	36.0	5	46.8	7	30.6	3	28.1	1	44.1	-	-
Latin America, etc.	22	19.2	1	58.4	7	15.2	7	17.6	6	19.7	1	17.3
Eastern Europe	9	50.0	-	-	-	-	2	46.0	4	50.5	3	51.9
Middle Europe	7	38.6	-	-	-	-	1	34.7	2	34.1	4	41.8
Northwestern Europe, etc.	11	29.6	-	-	-	-	-	-	1	30.5	10	29.6
Miscellaneous	9	33.2	1	75.2	-	-	-	-	6	29.3	2	23.7
Female shares in agricultural employment (FS$_{ag}$)												
All regions	91	22.4	16	33.0	19	18.7	18	14.4	19	27.5	19	20.9
Tropical Africa	10	27.9	8	27.7	2	28.2	-	-	-	-	-	-
Arab countries	8	7.6	1	28.5	2	6.4	5	4.0	-	-	-	-
Other Moslem countries	4	24.6	1	14.2	2	38.9	1	6.4	-	-	-	-
South and East Asia	16	33.5	5	37.2	7	29.6	3	30.7	1	51.8	-	-
Latin America, etc.	21	6.9	1	45.2	7	3.9	7	7.4	5	3.4	1	3.6
Eastern Europe	7	50.0	-	-	-	-	1	42.5	4	51.0	2	51.8
Middle Europe	7	38.3	-	-	-	-	1	39.6	2	30.8	4	41.7
Northwestern Europe, etc.	11	9.5	-	-	-	-	-	-	1	11.1	10	9.3
Miscellaneous	9	28.2	1	46.9	-	-	-	-	6	29.4	2	15.5
Female shares in nonagricultural employment (FS$_{nonag}$)												
All regions	91	26.8	16	23.4	19	27.0	18	21.6	19	30.1	19	31.6
Tropical Africa	10	19.7	8	16.2	2	33.6	-	-	-	-	-	-
Arab countries	8	12.5	1	37.4	2	13.4	5	7.2	-	-	-	-
Other Moslem countries	4	16.1	1	7.3	2	19.0	1	19.1	-	-	-	-
South and East Asia	16	23.5	5	21.9	7	23.0	3	24.2	1	33.0	-	-
Latin America, etc.	21	31.6	1	37.0	7	35.7	7	30.4	5	27.4	1	27.3
Eastern Europe	7	35.4	-	-	-	-	2	26.0	4	33.3	2	41.2
Middle Europe	7	32.3	-	-	-	-	1	20.6	2	32.9	4	34.9
Northwestern Europe, etc.	11	30.4	-	-	-	-	-	-	1	35.0	10	29.9
Miscellaneous	9	31.3	1	59.6	-	-	-	-	6	28.0	2	26.8
Difference between female shares in agricultural and nonagricultural employment[a]												
All regions	91	+4.4	16	-9.6	19	+8.3	18	+7.2	19	+2.6	19	+10.7
Tropical Africa	10	-8.2	8	-11.5	2	+5.4	-	-	-	-	-	-
Arab countries	8	+4.9	1	+8.9	2	+7.0	5	+3.2	-	-	-	-
Other Moslem countries	4	-8.5	1	-6.9	2	-19.9	1	+12.7	-	-	-	-
South and East Asia	16	-10.0	5	-15.3	7	-6.6	3	-6.5	1	-18.8	-	-
Latin America, etc.	21	+24.7	1	-8.2	7	+31.8	7	+23.0	5	+24.0	1	+23.7
Eastern Europe	7	-14.6	-	-	-	-	1	-16.5	4	-17.7	2	-10.6
Middle Europe	7	-6.0	-	-	-	-	1	-19.0	2	+2.1	4	-6.8
Northwestern Europe, etc.	11	+20.9	-	-	-	-	-	-	1	+23.9	10	+20.6
Miscellaneous	9	+3.1	1	+12.7	-	-	-	-	6	-1.4	2	+11.3

[a] S$_{nonag}$ minus FS$_{ag}$.

Stand$_f$ rises gradually from Level III to Level V, conforming with the U-curve hypothesis. The increase is marked more definitely in the female shares in both agricultural and nonagricultural employment; counteracting effects of the shift in employment structure cushion the impact on female standardized activity rates. For the rest of the regions, narrow ranges of development levels and small numbers of countries deprive the figures of much meaning. So far as they go, they indicate varied and irregular patterns.

To summarize, the hypothesis of predominantly decreasing trends of female activity rates during early stages of economic development is supported fairly well, on the whole, both by the cross-sectional differences between mean levels of the rates for countries at Levels I, II, and III of development and by the measures of changes between postwar censuses. It is particularly in the agricultural sector that women's share in the labor force seems frequently to diminish as economic development progresses from a low to a medium level. The data give no clear indication of a parallel trend predominating in the nonagricultural sector. Unlike the decrease of male activity rates, the shrinking relative size of the female labor force during early stages of development does not appear to be broadly representative of experiences in individual countries, but only the average result of decreasing trends in some countries and increasing trends in others. The different effect of the expansion in relative share of nonagricultural employment is one of the factors that make for such diversity of experiences.

The increase of women's participation in the labor force in later stages of development, postulated by the U-curve hypothesis, appears in the statistics of some of the more developed countries but not in others. It is not clear whether this can be expected to take place in a majority of countries as they progress from medium to high development levels. The increase or decrease of female shares in the nonagricultural labor force becomes the crucial factor in the trend in advanced stages. Increases predominated during postwar years among the countries in Level v, but the fact that nearly all these countries belong to the European cultural family makes uncertainty about the trend in varied cultural settings. Where an increasing trend has been recorded, it has been confined in most cases to women in the ages between twenty and sixty-five years.

6.4. Convergence in Trends of Participation by Females

The tendency toward equality in levels of male activity rates among countries in process of economic development, indicated somewhat equivocally by the analysis in the preceding chapter, is marked more conspicuously in the statistics for females, with the difference that the trends of the female rates converge toward the middle instead of the lower end of the range.

In the cross section of female standardized activity rates (Table 6.1), there is great disparity in levels of the rates among less-developed countries. Both the highest and the lowest rates in the cross section are found in countries at Levels I–III. Moving up the scale of development levels, the distributions of the rates converge into a medium range. The frequency of rates between 20 and 50 increases from five out of twenty countries in Level I to eighteen out of twenty in Level V, where only the Soviet Union remains with Stand$_f$ above 50 and only Venezuela below 20. The convergence has a downward bias in the progression from Level I to III, where very high rates are eliminated, while some very low rates persist, and an upward bias from Level III to V, where the very low rates are eliminated, and thus the U-curve of mean levels is formed. The degree of convergence, as measured by the difference in standard deviations of the rates between Level I and Level V, is much greater in the female than it is in the male standardized activity rates (compare Tables 5.1 and 6.1). Yet the levels of female activity rates remain much more disparate than those of males among the most-developed countries.

The pattern of convergence appears in the cross-sectional distributions of both rural and urban female standardized activity rates (Table 6.2) but it is more pronounced in the urban. It is marked strongly also in the distributions of female shares in non-agricultural employment (Table 6.3) but not consistently in the agricultural sector. Among age groups, convergence is most pronounced in the activity rates of women over age 65, as indicated by the pattern of standard deviations of the age-specific rates in Table 6.5. There is less convergence in the rates for age groups between 20 and 65 and still less in ages below 20, although even in the activity rates of females in ages 15 to 19 the standard deviation is much smaller in Level V than in Level I.

The convergence in the cross-sectional distributions is probably in part an artifact of faulty statistics, as noncomparability and error exaggerate the disparity of the rates to a greater extent among less-developed than among more-developed countries. But the tabulations of intercensal changes (Tables 6.8 and 6.9) also display some tendency of convergence. On the whole, although the patterns are not marked strongly, the higher the levels of female standardized

Women's participation

Table 6.8. Intercensal changes of female standardized activity rates in countries classified by level of the rate at the beginning of the intercensal period and by level of development

Initial levels of rates	Number of countries			Mean annual change of rates
	Total	+	-	
Total, all levels of development				
Total	58	28	30	-.10
Under 20.0	14	9	5	+.10
20.0-29.9	17	7	10	-.08
30.0-39.9	11	6	5	+.03
40.0-49.9	8	3	5	-.14
50.0 and over	8	3	5	-.66
Levels I-II				
Total	13	5	8	-.32
Under 20.0	4	2	2	+.06
20.0-39.9	4	1	3	-.52
40.0 and over	5	2	3	-.47
Level III				
Total	11	6	5	-.15
Under 20.0	6	4	2	+.12
20.0-39.9	3	1	2	-.14
40.0 and over	2	1	1	-.96
Level IV				
Total	17	6	11	-.05
Under 20.0	3	2	1	+.17
20.0-39.9	8	2	6	+.04
40.0 and over	6	2	4	-.26
Level V				
Total	17	11	6	+.04
Under 20.0	1	1	-	+.00
20.0-39.9	13	9	4	+.09
40.0 and over	3	1	2	-.20

+ = number of countries with increasing rates.
- = number with decreasing rates.

activity rates and female shares in nonagricultural employment, the more likely they were to decrease, and the lower the levels, the more likely to increase. The data on intercensal changes agree with the pattern of cross-sectional differences also in showing little tendency of convergence in female shares in the agricultural labor force. Convergence has also been observed in long-range past trends of female activity rates among Western countries, and among the states in the United States.[7]

[7] C. E. V. Leser, "Trends in Women's Work Participation"; S. Kuznets, A. R. Miller, and R. A. Easterlin, *Population Redistribution and Economic Growth, United States, 1870–1950* II (Philadelphia, 1960), 23–29.

Table 6.9. Intercensal changes of female shares in agricultural and nonagricultural employment in countries classified by levels of female shares at the beginning of the intercensal period and by level of development

Agricultural sector				Nonagricultural sector			
Initial levels of FS$_{ag}$	No. of countries Total	+	-	Mean change	Initial levels of FS$_{nonag}$	No. of countries Total	+	-	Mean change

Initial levels of FS$_{ag}$	Total	+	-	change	Initial levels of FS$_{nonag}$	Total	+	-	change
Total, all levels of development									
Total	54	25	29	-.13	Total	54	34	20	+.10
Under 10.0	19	10	9	+.03	Under 20.0	8	6	2	+.23
10.0-19.9	7	2	5	-.30	20.0-29.9	22	14	8	+.12
20.0-39.9	15	4	1	-.31	30.0-39.9	21	13	8	+.08
40.0 and over	13	9	4	+.05	40.0 and over	3	1	2	-.33
Levels I-II									
Total	13	3	10	-.12	Total	13	6	7	-.04
Under 20.0	6	1	5	-.16	Under 20.0	5	3	2	+.79
20.0-39.9	3	1	2	-.02	20.0-29.9	3	1	2	-.31
40.0 and over	4	1	3	-.09	30.0 and over	5	2	3	-.11
Level III									
Total	9	5	4	-.09	Total	9	7	2	+.16
Under 20.0	6	3	3	-.11	Under 20.0	2	2	-	+.15
20.0-39.9	1	-	1	-.42	20.0-29.9	3	2	1	+.14
40.0 and over	2	2	-	+.15	30.0 and over	4	3	1	+.19
Level IV									
Total	15	8	7	-.07	Total	15	10	5	+.12
Under 20.0	5	2	3	-.09	Under 20.0	1	1	-	+.58
20.0-39.9	6	3	3	-.20	20.0-29.9	7	6	1	+.29
40.0 and over	4	3	1	+.15	30.0 and over	7	3	4	-.12
Level V									
Total	17	9	8	-.22	Total	17	11	6	+.14
Under 20.0	9	6	3	+.08	Under 20.0	-	-	-	-
20.0-39.9	5	-	5	-.91	20.0-29.9	9	5	4	+.13
40.0 and over	3	3	-	+.02	30.0 and over	8	6	2	+.16

+ = number of countries with increasing female share.
- = number with decreasing female share
Mean change = mean annual change of female shares.

Increasing urbanization and the shift from agriculture to non-agricultural industries make for such convergence because participation by females differs less from country to country in the urban and nonagricultural sectors of the labor force than it does in the rural and agricultural sectors. Within the nonagricultural sector, if female shares in employment are high in little-developed countries, it means almost certainly that there are many women employed in family enterprises, traditional handicraft manufactures, domestic service, and other fields that are bound to contract as

141

economic development goes forward. Where the FS_{nonag} is lower at the start, there is less scope for negative effects of contraction in such fields, and positive effects of expanding employment opportunities in other fields can more easily predominate. Finally, economic development and associated social changes may loosen the grip of traditions that have dictated large or small shares for women in various fields of economic activity in preindustrial societies.

6.5. Logistic Trends of Participation by Females

In the transition from low or high to medium levels of female activity rates, do the trends commonly take a logistic form, so that the female rates, like those of males, tend to become stabilized as well as equalized among countries at high levels of development? Such a tendency is suggested by the measures of relative volatility of female standardized activity rates during intercensal periods in countries at different levels of development (Table 6.1). The rates were most volatile, that is, moving most rapidly upward or downward, on the average, among Level II and III countries, and considerably more stable in Levels IV and V. But this logistic pattern does not appear in the relative volatility of female shares within either the agricultural or the nonagricultural sector (Table 6.4). FS_{ag}, on the contrary, seems to become more and more volatile as the level of development rises, while the relative volatility of FS_{nonag} displays no consistent pattern related to the level of economic development. So the greater stability of $Stand_f$ in more-developed countries appears to be due mainly to the diminished weight of the agricultural sector rather than to abated speed of changes in female participation within either agricultural or nonagricultural employment. The highly volatile FS_{ag} has diminishing influence on the movements of female activity rates as the agricultural share in total employment dwindles. Since the high volatility of FS_{ag} is probably due in large part to varying definitions, enumeration procedures, and quality of reporting from one census to the next, it follows that the appearance of logistic trends in female standardized activity rates may be largely an illusion, due to faults in the measures of intercensal changes, diminishing as the level of development rises.

6.6. Speed of Economic Development and Volatility of Participation by Females

If it is true that women's participation in the labor force is affected to an important extent by the changing structure of employment and the rising levels of income and wages in the course of economic development, it is reasonable to suppose that the volatility of female activity rates should be associated positively with the indicators of speed of economic development, as the changes in male activity rates appear to be. But the expected associations do not show up in the tabulation of relative volatility of female standardized activity rates and female shares in employment sectors for countries classified by GDP growth rate per head and annual increase in percent share of the nonagricultural sector in total employment (Table 6.10). On the contrary, there seems to be a negative association instead of the expected positive one between the GDP growth rate and relative volatility of $Stand_f$ and FS_{ag}, while no consistent patterns of association appear either between GDP growth rate and the relative volatility of FS_{nonag}, or between the increase in nonagricultural share in total employment and relative volatility of any of the three measures of female participation. That the hypothesized patterns do not show up in the data does not necessarily mean that they do not exist in reality; they may be hidden by faults in the statistics or by influences of extraneous factors. Indeed, it must be so at least so far as the effect of expansion of the nonagricultural sector upon the changes of female activity rates is concerned.

6.7. Substitution of Sexes in the Labor Force

According to another hypothesis, decreasing participation by males in the labor force might have a positive influence on the trend of participation by females or, conversely, the decrease of male participation might be hastened by increasing female participation. Long found indications of such mutually compensating trends of participation by the two sexes in his study of the historical statistics of the United States and a number of European countries.[8] To test the hypothesis of male-female substitution, the intercensal changes of female standardized activity rates and female shares in agricultural and nonagricultural employment are tabulated in relation to

[8] Long, *The Labor Force under Changing Income and Employment.*

143

Women's participation

Table 6.10. Relative volatility of female standardized activity rates and female shares in agricultural and nonagricultural employment in countries classified by level of development and indicators of speed of development

Indicators of speed of development	Total N	Total R.V.	Levels I-II N	Levels I-II R.V.	Level III N	Level III R.V.	Level IV N	Level IV R.V.	Level V N	Level V R.V.
Female standardized activity rates (Stand$_f$)										
Total, all countries	58	1.1	13	1.4	11	1.5	17	0.9	17	0.9
GDP growth rate:										
Under 2.0 percent	16	1.6	6	2.2	2	0.3	3	1.4	5	1.5
2.0-3.9 percent	20	1.3	4	1.3	6	2.7	2	0.6	8	0.8
4.0 percent and over	15	0.7	-	-	1	0.2	10	0.8	4	0.6
Not available	7	1.0	3	0.8	2	0.7	2	1.9	-	-
Increase of nonagricultural share:[a]										
Under .40 percent	13	1.1	7	1.1	2	1.4	1	2.2	3	0.7
.40-.79 percent	24	1.2	5	1.5	4	1.2	7	1.1	8	1.1
.80 percent and over	18	0.8	-	-	4	0.7	8	0.8	6	0.9
Not available	3	2.1	1	3.7	1	3.5	1	0.2	-	-
Female shares in agricultural employment (FS$_{ag}$)										
Total, all countries	54	1.5	13	0.9	9	1.5	15	1.7	17	1.9
GDP growth rate:										
Under 2.0 percent	16	3.4	6	2.3	2	2.8	3	3.2	5	4.4
2.0-3.9 percent	18	2.1	4	0.6	4	4.9	2	1.5	8	2.9
4.0 percent and over	13	0.8	-	-	1	0.4	8	1.3	4	0.1
Not available	7	1.1	3	0.2	2	0.8	2	2.9	-	-
Increase of nonagricultural share:[a]										
Under .40 percent	12	1.3	7	0.8	1	0.7	1	7.2	3	1.8
.40-.79 percent	23	2.3	5	0.7	4	3.3	6	2.4	8	4.2
.80 percent and over	18	1.0	-	-	4	0.7	8	1.3	6	0.8
Not available	1	5.6	1	5.6	-	-	-	-	-	-
Female shares in nonagricultural employment (FS$_{nonag}$)										
Total, all countries	54	1.0	13	1.2	9	0.9	15	1.1	17	0.8
GDP growth rate:										
Under 2.0 percent	16	0.9	6	1.3	2	0.5	3	0.9	5	0.8
2.0-3.9 percent	18	0.5	4	0.4	4	0.8	2	0.7	8	0.5
4.0 percent and over	13	1.2	-	-	1	2.9	8	1.0	4	1.3
Not available	7	2.1	3	2.8	2	0.8	2	3.1	-	-
Increase of nonagricultural share:[a]										
Under .40 percent	12	0.9	7	1.0	1	0.8	1	1.2	3	0.7
.40-.79 percent	23	0.9	5	1.3	4	0.6	6	1.2	8	0.7
.80 percent and over	18	1.0	-	-	4	1.3	8	1.0	6	1.0
Not available	1	3.4	1	3.4	-	-	-	-	-	-

N = number of countries; R.V. = relative volatility, i.e. mean annual intercensal change irrespective of sign, in percentage of mean level of rates or female shares.

[a]Annual increase in percent share of nonagricultural industries in total employment.

the intercensal changes of male standardized rates (Tables 6.11 and 6.12). The hypothesized negative association with the changes of male standardized rates does not show up in the changes of female standardized rates or female shares in agricultural employment, but a somewhat irregular pattern of such association does

144

Table 6.11. Intercensal changes of female standardized activity rates in countries classified by intercensal change of male standardized activity rate and by level of development

Intercensal change of Stand$_m$	Number of countries			Mean annual change of Stand$_f$
	Total	+	-	
Total, all levels of development				
Total	58	28	30	-.10
+.33 to -.19	15	8	7	-.06
-.20 to -.49	21	11	10	-.01
-.50 or more	22	9	13	-.22
Levels I-II				
Total	13	5	8	-.32
+.33 to -.19	7	3	4	-.27
-.20 to -.49	2	1	1	-.00
-.50 or more	4	1	3	-.57
Level III				
Total	11	6	5	-.15
+.33 to -.19	1	-	1	-.46
-.20 to -.49	5	3	2	-.03
-.50 or more	5	3	2	-.26
Level IV				
Total	17	6	11	-.05
+.33 to -.19	1	1	-	+.88
-.20 to -.49	7	2	5	-.11
-.50 or more	9	3	6	-.10
Level V				
Total	17	11	6	+.04
+.33 to -.19	6	4	2	+.07
-.20 to -.49	7	5	2	+.07
-.50 or more	4	2	2	-.07

+ = number of countries with increasing or constant Stand$_f$.
- = number of countries with decreasing Stand$_f$.

appear in the changes of female shares in nonagricultural employment. On the whole, the more the male standardized activity rate decreased, the greater was the likelihood of an increase in FS$_{nonag}$ and the more positive was the net balance of increases and decreases of female shares in the nonagricultural employment sector.[9]

The data in Table 6.12 are not adequate to demonstrate the existence of a significant correlation between the intercensal changes of Stand$_m$ and FS$_{nonag}$. The numbers of observations are small and the pattern of differences is not very regular. It does not require

[9] With constant participation by females, of course, decreasing participation by males in nonagricultural employment would push the female share up, but this is not a sufficient explanation of the apparent association.

145

Women's participation

Table 6.12. Intercensal changes of female shares in agricultural and nonagricultural employment in countries classified by intercensal change of male standardized activity rate and by level of development

Intercensal change of Stand$_m$	Total number of countries	Changes of FS$_{ag}$			Changes of FS$_{nonag}$		
		+	-	Mean	+	-	Mean
Total, all levels of development							
Total	54	25	29	-.13	34	20	+.10
+.33 to -.19	15	5	10	-.22	7	8	-.04
-.20 to -.49	20	9	11	-.06	13	7	+.05
-.50 or more	19	11	8	-.44	14	5	+.26
Levels I-II							
Total	13	3	10	-.13	6	7	-.03
+.33 to -.19	7	1	6	-.18	2	5	-.21
-.20 to -.49	2	1	1	-.20	1	1	+.19
-.50 or more	4	1	3	-.17	3	1	+.20
Level III							
Total	9	5	4	-.09	7	2	+.17
+.33 to -.19	1	-	1	-.79	-	1	-.36
-.20 to -.49	5	2	3	-.10	4	1	+.10
-.50 or more	3	3	-	+.17	3	-	+.44
Level IV							
Total	15	8	7	-.07	10	5	+.13
+.33 to -.19	1	1	-	+.71	1	-	+.49
-.20 to -.49	6	2	4	-.11	3	3	-.12
-.50 or more	8	5	3	-.12	6	2	+.25
Level V							
Total	17	9	8	-.22	11	6	+.14
+.33 to -.19	6	3	3	-.33	4	2	+.11
-.20 to -.49	7	4	3	-.03	5	2	+.12
-.50 or more	4	2	2	-.38	2	2	+.21

+ = number of countries with increasing or constant female share.
- = number of countries with decreasing female share.
Mean = mean annual change of female shares.

any tests of statistical significance to see that random variations might easily account for much of the apparent association, and it does not take great imagination to envisage the possibility of extraneous factors shaping the pattern. The hypothesis of male-female substitution in the nonagricultural labor force is therefore not confirmed, but neither is it denied by these observations.

SEVEN

Review of Principal Findings

The data compiled for this study afford two views of variations in labor-force participation rates and other aspects of labor-force dimensions in relation to economic development: the cross-sectional view of the status quo at recent census dates in a hundred countries at different levels of development, and the dynamic view of changes accompanying the progress of economic development in fifty-eight countries during intervals between recent censuses. Both views are seriously distorted by flaws in the statistics, and the relationships in question are distorted, in addition, by influences of factors that have little or nothing to do with economic development. Inferences from these data about changes in labor force dimensions that go with economic development are therefore uncertain at many points. The inferences that merit most confidence are those which are supported by well-defined, consistent patterns of variations both in the cross section and in the intercensal changes, and are also in accord with long-range trends observed in historical studies of various countries. Other less firmly supported inferences may be considered as hypotheses to be tested by further research.

7.1. Conditions at the Start of Economic Development

The census statistics of the least-developed countries included in the cross section show great diversity of labor-force participation rates ("activity rates" in the simplified terminology of this study) of women and of young and elderly males. Although the diversity is almost certainly exaggerated by errors and noncomparability in the measures, other evidence confirms that traditional customs with regard to the division of labor according to sex and age in preindustrial and little-industrialized societies are varied. While certain sex-age groups may contribute relatively little to production, however, it appears to be the general rule in the traditional sectors of such societies that nearly all able-bodied persons except young children take some part in the production of income at least in seasons of peak labor requirements. The diverse patterns of activity rates recorded in the censuses of the least developed countries reflect differences in the reporting of individuals who take part in

147

income-producing activities only to a relatively minor extent or seasonally, as well as differences in the extent of participation by the various sex-age groups. In the process of development, as productive functions formerly performed by household or community groups are taken over by specialized units, the roles of income producers and dependents become more distinct. The picture of changes in labor force dimensions associated with economic development that appears in the statistics must be viewed in the context of this change in the organization of production.

7.2. Changes in Activity Rates of Males in the Process of Development

In all societies, production of income[1] is a primary function of men in the central adult ages, and there is no evidence of economic development having brought an important change in this respect in any society. Activity rates above 95 percent in the male population of ages 30 to 44 years have been recorded almost universally in censuses of different countries and different times, and no general pattern of variations in relation to economic development is apparent. But the rates in younger and older age groups of males display a tendency to decrease as economic development goes forward, a tendency that is most pronounced and most consistently marked in the statistics for ages under 20 and over 65. This signifies a trend of rising average age of entry of males into the labor force and falling average age of retirement—that is, curtailment of men's working lives at both ends, which causes the overall level of male participation in the labor force to decline.

The trend toward earlier retirement that goes with economic development and the associated processes of modernization is reflected in the cross section of census statistics by a wide difference between more-developed and less-developed countries in mean levels of male activity rates in the ages of 65 and over: a mean of 63.4 percent among the least-developed quintile of countries (Level I) and 29.5 percent among the most-developed quintile (Level V). Some increase in the frequency of earlier retirement, before age 65, is indicated by a smaller difference in mean levels of activity rates of males in the ages of 45 to 64: 93.4 percent for Level I

[1] It should be recalled that "income," in the context of this study, does not necessarily refer to money earnings; see the discussion of the concept of the labor force in chapter 1.

and 90.3 percent for Level V. The delayed entry of young males into the labor force, with prolonged education, in more-developed countries is represented by activity rates in ages 15 to 19 averaging 61.6 percent in Level V, as compared with 75.5 percent in Level I countries. It is noteworthy that the difference here is much smaller than in the ages of 65 and over, and the pattern is also less consistent. The censuses of several little-developed African and Asian countries show activity rates of males in ages 15 to 19 below those recorded in some of the most-developed countries in Western and central Europe. Census data on children under age 15 in the labor force are fragmentary and relatively unreliable, but certainly very few children of this age are employed in highly developed countries, while their participation in the labor force is considerable in many less-developed countries.

Long-range historical series of census statistics for Western industrialized countries confirm what the cross-sectional pattern of differences between more-developed and less-developed countries suggests, that the age at which males enter the labor force has tended generally to rise and the age of retirement to fall as economic development progressed. Among countries outside the Western industrialized group, the record of historical statistics is not adequate to show how general these trends were before World War II. During the postwar intercensal periods considered in this study, however, decreasing activity rates of males 15 to 19 and 65 years of age and over were recorded, with few exceptions, among countries in all parts of the world, at all levels of economic development, and in varied cultural settings. Reservations as regards the generality of these trends since World War II refer only to countries in the lowest quintile of economic development levels, where intercensal change measures were too few for an adequate sample, and particularly to the tropical African region, where such measures were entirely lacking.

7.3. Changes in Activity Rates of Females in the Process of Development

Activity rates of females in the youngest and oldest age groups, like those of males, tend generally to decrease in the process of economic development, although this trend is marked less distinctly and less consistently in the statistics for females. In the adult female population between the ages of the late teens and the sixties,

149

economic development and modernization may bring either an increasing or a decreasing trend of participation in the labor force, depending on the cultural setting and other circumstances in each country. As the circumstances change during the course of a country's development, the direction of this trend may be reversed. Thus as economic development progresses, the overall level of participation by females in the labor force rises in some countries, falls in others, and oscillates in still others. During the intercensal periods considered in this study, increases of female standardized activity rates were recorded in twenty-eight countries and decreases in thirty-one, with little change in the average level. A similar, mixed picture of rising and falling trends appears in long-range historical series of census measures of female activity rates in countries where such series are available.

A U-shaped pattern of cross-sectional differences in average levels of female activity rates among countries at successively higher levels of development suggests that these rates might ordinarily tend to decrease during early stages of economic development *and to increase again during later stages;* but this suggestion is not borne out either by long-range historical statistics or by the data on changes in female activity rates during recent intercensal periods. On the contrary, a mixture of rising trends in some countries and falling trends in others appears both in long-range series and in the recent intercensal change data for countries at all development levels. The U-shaped pattern of cross-sectional average levels of these rates reflects, at least in part, influences of extraneous factors unrelated to economic development, as well as errors and biases in the measures. There is some reason for expecting, however, that in the future, as traditions about female and male social roles are modified, women may generally take an increasing part in the labor force in countries at the higher levels of economic development.

7.4. *Trends in Rural and Urban, Agricultural and Nonagricultural Sectors*

The changes in structure of the society and economy and accompanying changes in life styles, which take place in the process of economic development, play important parts in bringing about changes in labor-force dimensions. The organization of production in specialized, market-oriented units, taking over former produc-

150

tive functions of household and community groups, has already been mentioned. Other important structural changes include increasing urbanization, contraction of the relative share of agriculture in employment, decline of self-employment, and growing dominance of the employee class. These structural changes affect opportunities for women, the young, and the elderly to be employed, while also influencing their propensities to take advantage of employment opportunities. The results of this study provide some indications of the effects of urbanization and the agriculture-nonagriculture shift upon activity rates, although the view of these questions is limited by shortcomings of the data.

Although data on the labor force in rural and urban sectors were obtained for only forty-one countries (with data by age groups in thirty-six of these), and although this sample is badly unbalanced in regional distribution, these data as well as the results of earlier research make it clear that activity rates of males are almost universally lower in urban than in rural populations, particularly in the youngest and oldest age groups. The cross-sectional mean levels of male activity rates in ages 15 to 19 were 71.8 percent in the rural and 50.2 percent in the urban sectors, and the corresponding figures for ages 65 and over were 60.9 and 45.7 percent, respectively. By inference, the rates are generally lower also among males in nonagricultural than in agricultural households.

For women, in addition to the rural and urban data, measures of their participation in agriculture and in nonagricultural industries were obtained in the form of percent shares of females in total employment within each sector. These could be derived from the statistics of ninety-one countries. Greater participation by women in urban and nonagricultural sectors than in rural and agricultural sectors is indicated by the statistics of some countries, while the opposite difference appears in other countries. The variations in this respect exhibit distinct regional patterns. For example, women's participation appears to be relatively greater in the agricultural than in the nonagricultural sector in most countries of South and East Asia and Eastern Europe, while the opposite pattern prevails in Latin America, Spain, and Portugal, northwestern Europe, northern America, Australia, and New Zealand. Although there is evidence of women's share in the agricultural labor force being understated in the census statistics of countries in the latter regions, the pattern of female migration from rural to urban areas suggests that opportunities for women's employment in the rural

151

and agricultural sectors are indeed relatively restricted in those regions.

The implication of these data is that certainly in the case of males, and probably in the case of females, the increase of urbanization and expansion of the nonagricultural share in total employment are important factors in the trends of activity rates that accompany economic development. But the activity rate trends can by no means be explained in terms of these structural changes alone. In the cross section of rural and urban male activity rates, the mean levels of the rates for younger and older age groups decrease progressively within both sectors as the level of development rises. Measures of intercensal changes in rural and urban rates were found only for a grossly inadequate sample of sixteen countries, of which data by age were given for twelve. So far as they go, these data also indicate generally decreasing activity rates of young and elderly males in both rural and urban sectors. For females as well, the mixed pattern of increases in some countries and decreases in others appears in the intercensal changes of female standardized activity rates within both rural and urban population sectors, and of female shares within both agricultural and nonagricultural sectors of employment. It was beyond the scope of this study to attempt to compare these changes during postwar intercensal periods with the records of long-range past trends in rural and urban or agricultural and nonagricultural sectors in various countries.

7.5. Hypotheses of Convergence in Trends of Activity Rates

The results of the analysis suggest some hypotheses with regard to typical patterns in the trends of participation by males and females in the labor force related to the levels of the participation rates, levels of development of the countries, and the speed of their progress in economic development. If these hypotheses are validated by further research, they may be helpful in efforts to predict future changes in labor-force dimensions in individual countries for purposes of policy-making and planning, although the findings of the present analysis make it plain that predictions taking only these factors into account would often go wide of the mark.

In the case of females, the data suggest that the higher the rate of their participation in the labor force at a given stage in a country's development, the greater is the likelihood of their participation diminishing as economic development progresses; and conversely, the lower the level of their participation, the more likely it is to increase. This hypothesis is supported, first, by the pattern in the cross-sectional distribution of levels of female standardized activity rates. These rates vary over an extremely wide range among the least-developed countries, and as the level of development rises the frequencies of both low and high rates diminish, so that the distributions converge into a medium range of rates among the most-developed countries. Female standardized rates between 20 and 50 percent are recorded in only five of the twenty countries in Level I of development, while eighteen of the twenty countries in Level V have rates within this medium range. A similar pattern of convergence toward the middle of the range appears in the cross section of female shares in employment in the nonagricultural sector, but not in agriculture. Second, the data on intercensal changes agree in showing that within the nonagricultural sector, the higher the female share at the beginning of the intercensal period, the more likely it was to decrease, and the lower the initial level, the more likely to increase. Third, further support for the hypothesis of convergence is found in the results of historical studies of long-range trends of female activity rates in Western industrialized countries and in the states of the United States.

A suggested interpretation of these observations is that in the process of economic development, the overall rates of participation by females in the labor force tend to move from high or low toward medium levels as a result of converging trends in female participation in nonagricultural employment, together with the growing proportionate share of the nonagricultural sector in total employment. (Female shares in employment as reported in the censuses do not vary so widely among countries within the nonagricultural sector as they do in agriculture.) A high female share in nonagricultural employment in a little-developed country implies almost certainly that many women are employed in family enterprises, domestic service, and/or other fields that contract as economic development progresses; thus the stage is set for a relatively large contraction of opportunities for women's employment in nonagricultural industries. Where the initial level of women's employment in the nonagricultural sector is lower, increasing opportunities in expanding fields of employment are more likely to overbalance the contraction in family enterprise, domestic service, etc.

153

Although the empirical support for this hypothesis seems to be fairly substantial, two reservations should be noted. First, the differences in levels of female activity rates among the less-developed countries, as recorded in the censuses, are almost certainly exaggerated as a result of factors of noncomparability and error, which have less influence on the data for more-developed countries. Thus the degree of convergence in the cross-sectional distributions of female standardized activity rates with rising level of development is exaggerated. The same reservation applies with less force to the data on women's participation in the nonagricultural sector. Second, most of the countries at the highest levels of development have a European cultural heritage, and this fact may be a part of the explanation of their clustering in the medium range of female shares in nonagricultural employment. Further study of variations of these measures among regions within countries, where the influences of cultural factors as well as error and noncomparability would be minimized, would be helpful in clarifying these questions.

A corresponding hypothesis of convergence in the case of males is that their activity rates in labor-force entry and retirement ages tend to decrease in the process of development, more rapidly where they are relatively high than where they are relatively low, thus drawing together toward a relatively uniform, low level at an advanced stage of development. Some historical evidence of this was found in an earlier study of long-range trends in the states of the United States. The data analyzed in the present study support this hypothesis at some points, but not consistently throughout. There is more definite evidence of convergence in the trends of activity rates of males over age 65 than in the ages of 15 to 19.

7.6. Hypotheses of Logistic Trends of Activity Rates

The results of the analysis suggest that the trends of participation in the labor force by males in the ages of labor-force entry and retirement may commonly follow curves of logistic form, decreasing slowly during early stages of economic development, more rapidly during middle stages, and more slowly again during later stages, and that they may eventually be stabilized at low levels in countries at advanced stages of development. This hypothesis is in accord with the patterns of both cross-sectional differences and recent intercensal changes of male standardized activity rates and specific rates for ages 15 to 19 and 65 and over,

154

although there are some differences between the patterns of the rates for the two age groups, and the intercensal change data are inadequate for a reliable indication of the trends in the least-developed countries. For females, the patterns of intercensal changes in their standardized activity rates also suggest logistic forms of the trends of increase in some countries and decrease in others, but this pattern is not apparent in the intercensal changes of female shares in either agricultural or nonagricultural employment.

A tendency to produce trends of logistic form is inherent in the influences of structural changes such as urbanization, the expansion of the nonagricultural share in employment, and the decline of family enterprise and self-employment. The influence of these changes upon male and female activity rates weakens in the advanced stage of the development process, if only because the share of the rural sector in the population and the shares of agriculture, self-employment, and family enterprise in the labor force are reduced to small minorities, in which further decreases can no longer have a great impact upon overall trends. With regard to urbanization, the data analyzed in this study suggest that its influence is weakened further in countries at the higher levels of development by a tendency of the differences between rural and urban activity rates to narrow as development progresses. In some of the most highly developed countries, little difference in this respect now remains between rural and urban sectors.

Both the patterns of differences in a cross-section and those of changes in various countries during a relatively brief period of time are, however, unreliable bases for inferences about the forms of long-term trends in labor-force dimensions in countries undergoing economic development. Although the stated hypotheses with regard to logistic forms of the long-term trends are strengthened by the observation that the indications from the cross section and the intercensal change measures are in general agreement, this is not enough to warrant definite conclusions.

7.7. Associations between Indicators of the Speed of Economic Development and Changes in Activity Rates

The intercensal changes in measures of participation by males and females in the labor force were examined in relation to two indicators of the speed of economic development of countries during the intercensal periods: the growth rate of gross domestic product

155

per head and the rate of expansion in the proportionate share of the nonagricultural sector in employment. Although no very strong, consistent patterns of association were found, it appeared on the whole that the faster the pace of development, the greater was the average annual decline in male standardized activity rates and in specific rates for males in ages 15 to 19 and 65 and over. The trends of male participation in the labor force seem to have been influenced more by the shift in the agricultural-nonagricultural balance of employment than by the growth of gross domestic product per head. When the former indicator was held constant, the association between the latter indicator and the changes in male activity rates tended to fade out. These findings suggest the hypothesis that the shifts in employment structure and related changes in life styles that go with economic development have generally negative net effects on opportunities and propensities of young and elderly males to work for income, while the increases of wages and incomes related directly to the growth of gross domestic product per head may have mixed positive and negative effects. The rather weak and irregular patterns of association found in this analysis of changes in various countries during relatively short recent periods of time do not, however, furnish a basis for definite conclusions.

In the case of females, the speed of increases or decreases in their standardized activity rates and their shares in agricultural and nonagricultural employment were not found to vary in a consistent relationship with either of the two indicators of speed of economic development. Although it is possible that influences of the shifts in employment structure and the growth of gross domestic product per head upon women's participation in the labor force were obscured by faults in the statistics or by the influence of extraneous factors, the failure of consistent relationships to show up implies that the trends of women's participation are governed to a large extent by factors not closely linked with these aspects of economic development. With less emphasis, the same inference with regard to males can be drawn from the results of the analysis. The importance of the roles of noneconomic factors is even more clearly apparent in the varied levels of the labor-force participation measures, especially for females, among countries in similar economic circumstances. The differences among regional groups of countries indicate that cultural, institutional, and other factors related to the regional grouping play a more important part than do factors related to the level of economic development in determining the patterns of women's participation in income-producing employment.

7.8. Effects of Age Structure of the Population

In addition to the changing rates of participation by males and females, the trends in relative size of the labor force in proportion to total population are influenced by changes in population structure associated with economic development. All countries that have achieved high levels of development have experienced a considerable decrease of fertility, lowering the proportion of child to adult population, and thus tending to raise the crude activity rate. This positive effect of decreased fertility has been only partly offset by the negative effect of decreased infant and child mortality, which moderates the shrinkage in the proportion of child population. The consequent advantage of more-developed over less-developed countries in population structure is more than enough, on the average, to compensate for the lower level of male activity rates in the more-developed countries. In the cross section of recent census statistics, if the population structure in the least-developed countries (Level I) had been the same as in the most-developed countries (Level v), with the levels of male and female age-specific activity rates as recorded in the censuses, the average crude activity rate of the Level I countries would have been about 50 percent instead of 44.2 percent, as recorded. This would have made possible an appreciably higher level of income per head, provided that the additional workers could have been employed at the going level of productivity.

While positive effects of population structure changes in countries moving from low to high levels of development may be expected in the long run, provided that a considerable decrease of fertility materializes, short-term effects of this factor upon the ratio of income producers to consumers may sometimes be negative. In fact, they were preponderantly negative in countries around the world during the decade of the 1950s, to which the intercensal change measures considered in this study mostly refer. This was a period of temporarily rising fertility in many of the more-developed countries and some less-developed countries, and of rapidly

157

falling mortality rates in less-developed countries generally. Negative effects of population structure changes were recorded during the intercensal periods in all less-developed countries (Levels I–III) and a majority of more-developed countries. With participation by males in the labor force generally decreasing and mixed trends in female participation, the net result was a downward trend of crude activity rates, that is growth of the labor force did not keep pace with the growth of population, in all but five of the fifty-eight countries for which measures were obtained. These conditions were unusual and transitory; on the whole, more favorable trends of population structure may be expected in the future, especially if the decrease of fertility observed in a number of less-developed countries during the 1960s and early 1970s becomes general in less-developed regions of the world.

7.9. Indications for Further Research

Several avenues of further research are suggested for testing and elaborating the findings and hypotheses presented here. First, the data of more recent censuses furnish material for updating the statistical picture, and especially for extending and clarifying the view of trends in labor force dimensions among countries at relatively low levels of development. In many of these countries, data of only one census in the period of 1946–1966 could be found, and in many others, there were only two census benchmarks, giving uncertain indications of changes because of uncertainty about the effects of changed definitions, procedures, and reporting errors. When three or more benchmarks are given, the trends can be assessed with more confidence.

Second, a comprehensive review of available historical series of census data on the labor force of various countries would be valuable for testing consistency between the patterns of long-range past trends and those of the recent intercensal changes and cross-sectional differences analyzed in the present study, as well as for examining other patterns and relationships with aspects of economic development. In spite of the limitations of long-range historical statistics, which are confined for the most part to Western industrialized countries, and which do not reach back to the earliest stages of their modern economic development, it is important to make the fullest possible use of this source of information about relationships between economic development and changing labor-force dimensions.

The third avenue suggested is study, at the subnational level, of cross-sectional differences and intercensal changes of labor-force dimensions in different regions within countries that exhibit significant variations in economic development and other relevant conditions. Whole countries are not ideal units for the kinds of analysis attempted in this study; they are too heterogeneous in dimensions of the labor force and conditions of economy as well as in culture and social institutions. Moreover, the patterns of variations within countries are much less affected than those between countries by errors and biases in the census measures and by the differences in definitions. Coordinated studies of regional variations within a number of countries at different levels of economic development in different regions of the world could do much to improve knowledge of the kinds of patterns and relationships considered in the present study.

Fourth, as the view of variations of labor-force participation measures in space and time is extended in the ways suggested above, these data may be subjected to more intensive and rigorous statistical analyses than could be undertaken in the present study, including the construction and empirical testing of appropriate multivariate models to estimate the influences of economic and other factors. It will be important in such analyses to take into account the nonlinearity of relationships which is apparent in the findings of the present study. Above all, it will be important to incorporate, as well as possible in such models, the principal cultural and institutional variables that influence international differences in labor-force participation patterns and their changes within countries in the process of development.

Finally, the most important need is to improve the measures of the labor force, especially in less-developed countries. A satisfactory view of the variations of labor-force dimensions within and between such countries and their changes in the process of development will never be achieved until measures are provided that take into account the varying degrees of involvement of individuals in activities that contribute to the production of income. Although the censuses of many countries provide some information on this score, in the form of classifications of individuals by hours of work per week, weeks of employment per year, etc., there is too little standardization of such classifications to make broad international comparisons feasible, and the statistics of scarcely any country provide a full view of the different aspects of degree of participation in the labor force. Without this, a satisfactory measure of employment, which is one of the most important economic variables, cannot be obtained.

Country Tables

Table A.1. Principal measures of participation in the labor force for countries, censuses of 1946-1966

Country	Census years	Crude activity rate	Standardized activity rates, ages 10 and over — Males	Females	Females ex.UPFW[a]	Refined activity rates, ages 10 and over — Males	Females	Females ex.UPFW[a]	Female shares in employment FS_ag	FS_nonag	Relat level devel ment
1. Tropical Africa[c]											
Botswana	1964	47.4	-	-	-	71.6	66.7	65.3	52.3	27.1	I
Central African Rep.	1960	55.7	75.0	73.5	7.5	79.8	84.6	6.4	-	-	I
Dahomey	1961	53.3	-	-	-	87.3	81.0	-	-	-	I
Ghana	1960	41.0	76.8	49.8	41.5	76.1	48.4	39.6	36.6	42.2	II
Guinea	1954/55	51.7	80.7	70.8	3.6	80.7	76.5	3.4	-	-	I
Liberia	1962	40.5	71.9	38.9	-	74.6	40.7	10.2	41.6	12.3	I
Namibia	1960	38.6	84.0	24.4	-	84.0	24.2	-	19.7	25.1	II
Nigeria	1963	34.1	78.1	25.8	-	75.7	24.6	-	9.6	43.4	I
Senegal	1960/61	44.0	-	-	-	80.7	53.9	-	-	-	II
Sierra Leone	1963	41.6	-	-	-	77.1	42.8	7.3	42.3	16.5	I
Togo	1958/60	45.0	-	-	-	89.5	61.7	-	-	-	I
Zaire	1955/57	51.4	-	-	-	73.1	73.3	-	59.4	0.9	I
1a. Portuguese Africa											
Angola	1960	29.4	-	-	-	77.9	6.9	6.8	5.3	13.4	I
Mozambique	1950	29.1	83.2	6.5	-	80.5	7.1	-	11.5	2.1	I
Portuguese Guinea	1950	29.7	83.1	1.0	-	82.8	.9	-	0.0	14.6	I
2. Arab countries											
Algeria	1966	21.6	-	-	-	65.7	2.6	-	1.8	7.7	III
Iraq	1957	28.2	84.8	3.1	-	83.8	3.1	-	1.8	6.0	III
Jordan	1961	22.8	70.4	3.8	3.1	63.2	3.8	3.1	5.2	6.3	III
Libya	1964	25.8	70.7	4.5	2.8	69.6	4.4	2.7	2.1	7.8	III
Morocco	1960	28.0	77.4	9.5	6.6	76.9	9.2	6.5	7.8	17.5	II
Sudan	1956	44.8	-	-	-	92.9	39.7	-	28.5	37.4	I
Syria	1960	25.9	74.8	7.8	5.5	71.2	7.8	5.5	9.2	8.3	III
Tunisia	1966	30.2	72.2	22.8	-	68.1	22.1	4.8	-	-.	III
United Arab Rep.	1947	35.6	88.3	9.7	6.5	87.8	9.8	6.5	10.9	6.0	
	1960	29.0	79.7	5.9	4.6	77.9	6.0	4.6	5.1	9.3	II
3. Other Moslem countries[d]											
Iran	1956	32.0	83.8	9.2	-	83.9	9.2	7.6	4.3	16.6	
	1966	30.2	79.2	12.3	9.9	77.0	12.5	10.0	6.4	19.1	III
Turkey	1955	56.1	89.6	68.9	5.8	89.5	69.4	5.8	53.3	8.3	
	1960	52.5	87.0	62.8	-	86.2	62.7	8.0	51.7	8.1	II
	1965	48.8	85.2	54.8	4.6	83.4	54.6	4.4	49.6	7.9	
4. South and East Asia											
Ceylon	1946	39.2	76.6	25.3	-	76.1	24.8	-	25.3	18.0	
	1953	36.8	72.4	27.2	-	72.8	26.6	23.4	27.6	20.4	
	1963	32.6	71.5	20.3	-	69.3	20.1	19.0	24.8	15.7	II
India	1961	43.0	81.4	39.4	23.4	81.1	39.9	23.5	35.6	20.6	II
	NSS[e]	40.0	79.4	32.1	-	79.4	32.7	-	-	-	
Indonesia	1961	35.9	78.3	29.5	-	79.8	29.4	-	26.1	30.0	II
Japan	1950	44.0	74.7	43.4	17.2	74.4	43.9	17.5	48.9	29.0	
	1955	45.1	73.2	43.8	20.0	73.4	44.1	20.1	50.1	31.5	
	1960	47.2	72.7	44.1	24.8	72.4	44.0	24.4	51.8	33.0	IV
	1965	49.1	71.3	43.1	-	73.6	44.6	-	51.5	34.9	
Khmer Republic	1962	43.6	76.0	52.3	-	73.1	52.6	-	45.5	28.0	I
Korea, South	1960	31.0	68.3	24.4	-	65.6	24.4	10.5	30.4	25.6	II
Malaysia:											
West Malaysia	1947	38.9	-	-	-	77.0	26.9	20.6	28.0	14.3	
	1957	34.5	75.7	26.1	-	74.8	26.2	21.3	32.2	13.8	II
Sabah	1951	46.3	-	-	-	83.7	42.7	-	35.2	12.0	
	1960	42.3	82.3	40.4	10.6	83.8	41.8	10.5	33.5	16.4	I
Sarawak	1947	56.2	-	-	-	92.2	65.0	-	44.0	8.4	
	1960	44.2	83.2	49.5	8.2	82.8	50.8	8.2	43.1	12.4	II
Mauritius	1952	32.6	72.4	18.9	18.7	74.4	18.8	18.6	23.4	17.2	
	1962	27.4	68.8	15.3	15.1	65.8	14.3	14.2	19.2	17.7	III

Table A.1. (continued)

Country	Census years	Crude activity rate	Standardized activity rates, ages 10 and over — Males	Females	Females ex.UPFW[a]	Refined activity rates, ages 10 and over — Males	Females	Females ex.UPFW[a]	Female shares in employment FS$_{ag}$	FS$_{nonag}$	Relative level of development[b]
4. South and East Asia (continued)										
pal	1952/54	50.0	-	-	-	83.7	54.1	-	41.9	24.8	
	1961	49.1	84.2	53.1	-	83.6	54.4	-	41.8	20.5	I
kistan	1961	33.5	84.5	13.7	-	84.4	13.8	4.4	14.2	7.3	I
lippines	1960	32.0	75.2	24.9	-	71.1	24.4	16.5	14.8	42.7	II
ukyu Islands	1950	42.6	75.9	49.3	-	71.4	48.5	25.3	50.6	36.2	
	1955	42.1	73.9	51.5	-	71.7	51.7	28.8	51.7	38.6	
	1960	40.9	71.8	50.4	31.1	67.7	48.7	29.8	51.9	40.2	III
iwan	1956	33.2	77.3	18.6	-	79.8	20.2	10.9	20.9	14.8	III
ailand	1947	53.6	-	-	-	79.6	72.0	19.8	49.8	37.3	
	1954	57.0	82.4	77.3	-	81.6	79.4	11.0	51.2	31.9	
	1960	53.2	80.6	74.7	-	79.6	75.3	13.8	50.8	37.2	I
5. Latin America, Spain, and Portugal										
gentina	1947	40.8	-	-	-	80.6	21.2	21.2	5.4	24.7	
	1960	37.9	73.8	21.5	-	75.0	21.0	-	5.9	25.4	IV
livia	1950	50.0	85.0	58.4	-	84.1	59.0	19.0	45.2	37.0	I
azil	1950	33.0	82.0	12.8	10.4	80.8	13.6	10.8	7.4	25.4	
	1960	32.3	78.6	16.2	-	77.0	16.5	13.2	10.0	26.3	III
ile	1952	36.4	76.6	23.7	-	76.2	24.0	23.1	6.5	33.0	
	1960	32.5	74.0	19.7	-	72.4	19.7	19.5	3.6	29.8	IV
lombia	1951	33.7	82.5	17.6	16.8	80.3	17.8	16.9	4.6	35.1	
	1964	29.6	77.8	17.6	16.7	73.5	17.4	16.5	4.8	34.1	III
sta Rica	1950	34.1	85.9	14.5	-	83.8	15.0	14.5	3.2	30.1	
	1963	29.7	81.0	14.9	14.5	77.0	14.8	14.3	1.7	32.4	III
ba	1953	36.7	79.0	17.0	-	78.8	17.2	-	1.8	21.0	IV
minican Republic	1960	28.1	80.3	9.7	9.1	75.9	9.3	8.7	1.8	25.2	II
uador	1950	39.0	83.7	32.3	-	81.5	32.1	30.3	13.8	40.7	
	1962	32.8	85.2	15.9	14.8	82.3	15.8	14.7	5.0	30.5	II
. Salvador	1950	35.2	86.4	15.9	-	84.4	16.2	15.4	3.2	39.8	
	1961	32.1	83.5	16.5	16.2	80.3	16.5	16.1	2.9	41.3	II
atemala	1950	34.2	86.6	12.5	11.3	85.2	12.6	11.3	2.5	34.4	
	1964	30.7	84.1	11.6	10.4	81.0	11.5	10.2	2.4	32.1	II
nduras	1961	30.1	85.1	11.7	11.3	82.2	11.9	11.4	1.0	39.2	II
xico	1950	32.4	84.4	12.4	-	81.7	12.2	-	NA	NA	
	1960	30.6	78.4	16.3	-	74.5	16.0	15.9	10.8	26.4	III
icaragua	1950	33.7	89.3	12.7	-	86.9	12.6	12.3	2.3	38.5	
	1963	30.9	82.8	19.4	18.5	78.8	18.7	17.7	5.1	42.4	II
anama	1950	35.0	79.5	20.0	-	78.7	20.3	18.0	5.6	34.5	
	1960	33.2	76.8	21.2	20.3	74.3	21.0	20.0	3.1	37.3	III
araguay	1950	33.4	82.5	21.3	-	78.5	21.0	-	9.9	38.0	
	1962	32.2	82.3	21.7	-	77.3	21.1	18.7	9.2	38.9	II
ru	1961	31.5	76.4	19.8	-	73.0	19.7	17.2	13.8	30.0	III
rtugal	1950	39.6	80.3	21.4	20.5	81.1	21.0	20.1	15.3	29.8	
	1960	38.5	83.6	16.8	16.4	83.9	16.0	15.6	7.4	26.2	III
uerto Rico	1950	27.3	63.6	18.5	-	60.4	18.5	18.0	1.8	36.5	
	1960	25.4	61.5	18.4	-	55.0	17.1	16.8	1.7	31.3	IV
pain	1950	38.6	80.7	13.9	-	83.3	14.2	12.5	7.9	23.4	
	1960	38.1	77.9	16.9	13.6	80.2	16.4	13.2	NA	NA	IV
ruguay	1963	39.2	72.9	24.9	-	73.4	24.1	23.9	4.0	29.6	IV
enezuela	1950	33.9	80.5	17.3	16.0	79.4	17.5	16.2	5.1	27.9	
	1961	31.2	78.3	17.3	17.1	76.2	17.2	17.0	3.6	27.3	V
6. Eastern Europe										
lbania	1955	53.4	-	-	-	84.7	63.2	-	-	-	
	1960	44.9	-	-	-	77.8	53.1	-	-	-	III
ulgaria	1956	54.5	72.9	53.5	-	77.9	55.7	39.2	50.5	31.0	
	1965	51.9	66.0	53.7	-	69.2	53.9	-	54.7	35.5	IV
zechoslovakia	1947	48.1	-	-	-	78.1	39.3	22.0	49.1	26.7	
	1961	47.2	69.7	47.6	-	70.1	45.5	45.0	49.5	38.2	V

163

Table A.1. (continued)

Country	Census years	Crude activity rate	Standardized activity rates, ages 10 and over Males	Females	Females ex.UPFW[a]	Refined activity rates, ages 10 and over Males	Females	Females ex.UPFW[a]	Female shares in employment FS_ag	FS_nonag	Rel lev dev me
				6.	Eastern Europe (continued)						
Germany, East	1964	49.1	-	-	-	73.4	46.6	-	-	-	
Hungary	1949	45.2	78.1	30.5	-	81.3	30.0	-	29.7	28.2	
	1960	49.0	78.4	40.2	-	80.9	39.8	31.2	37.5	33.6	
Poland	1950	52.1	-	-	-	80.7	52.5	-	-	-	
	1960	48.3	-	-	-	76.3	51.4	30.7	54.7	34.8	
Rumania	1956	61.7	85.0	65.8	-	87.7	67.1	-	53.6	26.4	
	1966	54.2	71.2	56.5	-	73.5	57.2	21.4	57.3	29.2	
U.S.S.R.	1959	52.2	-	-	-	74.4	61.5	51.7	54.0	44.2	
Yugoslavia	1953	46.3	80.0	38.4	-	80.9	38.3	15.9	41.2	20.6	
	1961	45.0	-	-	-	76.6	39.0	18.6	42.5	26.0	II
				7.	Middle Europe						
Austria	1951	48.5	-	-	-	76.6	40.7	27.4	52.6	32.0	
	1961	47.7	74.7	47.3	36.0	73.1	41.8	31.3	53.0	36.6	
Finland	1950	49.2	76.3	46.8	-	79.6	48.3	30.2	40.5	40.9	
	1960	45.8	72.2	43.4	-	72.1	42.4	31.3	35.3	41.6	I
France	1954	45.4	73.0	35.9	26.7	76.1	35.5	26.3	35.0	33.4	
	1962	42.8	71.4	35.2	29.2	70.6	32.5	26.4	32.3	33.4	
Germany, West	1950	46.3	75.7	39.9	29.1	75.0	36.3	25.2	54.7	30.4	
	1961	47.9	76.1	43.5	35.3	76.6	38.9	30.2	54.7	34.3	
Greece	1961	44.9	76.2	34.7	15.0	77.6	33.5	14.5	39.6	20.6	II
Italy	1951	43.5	80.4	27.4	20.5	80.8	26.0	19.7	24.6	25.5	
	1961	39.9	72.9	24.8	20.7	73.5	23.0	19.0	26.3	24.2	I
Switzerland	1950	49.8	76.5	41.7	-	81.5	40.5	38.4	32.9	36.1	
	1960	49.3	76.0	41.0	-	79.2	38.8	37.0	26.6	35.2	
			8.	Northwestern Europe, Northern America, and Oceania							
Australia	1947	42.2	76.4	25.0	24.9	79.9	23.0	22.9	4.9	25.8	
	1954	41.2	76.8	27.1	-	79.6	24.0	23.7	6.6	25.3	
	1961	40.2	74.8	28.5	28.3	75.2	25.6	25.4	8.7	27.1	
Belgium	1947	41.2	72.2	23.7	21.1	74.5	22.0	19.6	14.5	24.8	
	1961	38.2	69.1	27.4	25.1	69.1	23.5	21.3	16.3	27.5	*
Canada	1951	38.1	73.4	22.4	21.7	75.8	21.8	21.1	3.8	26.3	
	1961	36.0	68.6	27.1	25.9	68.3	26.0	24.7	10.4	29.6	*
Denmark	1950	48.2	78.1	42.2	-	80.2	39.4	-	23.4	37.1	
	1960	45.7	76.6	35.9	-	76.4	33.1	30.8	9.4	35.4	*
Ireland	1951	43.8	79.5	31.7	28.0	79.9	28.9	25.7	13.6	34.3	
	1961	39.9	75.8	30.5	28.6	74.2	26.6	25.0	11.1	35.0	I*
Netherlands	1947	40.2	-	-	-	77.7	24.5	18.3	22.6	26.4	
	1960	36.4	73.4	23.3	21.1	72.0	20.1	18.1	9.1	23.9	*
New Zealand	1951	38.2	73.8	25.6	25.4	74.7	22.5	22.4	7.1	26.9	
	1956	37.6	74.0	26.2	26.0	74.2	23.2	23.0	6.9	26.9	
	1961	37.1	73.5	27.0	26.8	72.1	24.2	24.0	7.8	28.0	*
Norway	1950	42.9	76.6	26.8	-	80.8	24.6	23.6	7.5	29.3	
	1960	39.8	72.8	24.5	-	74.3	22.0	-	4.6	27.3	*
Sweden	1950	44.1	75.1	30.1	29.2	79.0	27.8	27.0	8.5	31.0	
	1960	43.9	71.3	32.4	31.4	72.5	29.7	28.6	8.7	33.1	*
	1965	45.2	68.6	35.9	33.5	70.6	34.5	31.7	22.7	35.1	
United Kingdom	1951	46.4	77.7	36.8	36.6	80.5	32.4	32.2	10.1	31.9	
	1961	46.7	76.3	38.3	37.8	77.7	34.3	33.8	8.8	33.6	*
United States	1950	39.8	68.7	26.3	25.5	73.1	27.0	26.1	8.3	30.3	
	1960	39.1	69.2	31.3	30.7	69.7	31.3	30.6	9.3	33.6	*
				9.	Miscellaneous						
Cyprus	1960	42.0	-	-	-	77.1	36.0	18.2	53.5	20.0	IV
Guyana	1946	39.9	79.9	29.8	-	79.9	29.7	27.9	23.8	31.3	
	1960	31.2	76.2	22.8	-	73.1'	21.8	19.7	15.5	26.8	IV
Haiti	1950	59.4	86.6	75.2	-	84.4	74.4	31.9	46.9	59.6	I
Hong Kong	1961	38.7	73.4	33.2	-	76.5	32.3	29.2	35.8	28.1	IV
	1966	39.2	-	-	-	72.5	36.2	32.8	40.1	32.5	

Table A.1. (continued)

Country	Census years	Crude activity rate	Standardized activity rates, ages 10 and over			Refined activity rates, ages 10 and over			Female shares in employment		Relative level of development[b]
			Males	Females	Females ex.UPFW[a]	Males	Females	Females ex.UPFW[a]	FS_ag	FS_nonag	

9. Miscellaneous (continued)

Country	Census years	Crude activity rate	Males	Females	Females ex.UPFW[a]	Males	Females	Females ex.UPFW[a]	FS_ag	FS_nonag	Relative level of development[b]
␣el	1961	33.9	-	-	-	65.6	23.9	22.1	18.9	26.5	V
␣ica	1953	42.8	79.0	40.4	36.1	77.8	41.6	37.2	24.8	50.8	
	1960	38.4	75.5	38.5	-	74.0	38.3	35.7	16.4	49.3	IV
␣gapore	1947	39.0	-	-	-	79.6	16.4	15.9	11.8	13.3	
	1957	33.2	73.5	18.8	16.6	76.6	19.2	17.0	34.5	16.3	IV
	1966	29.9	69.6	20.8	19.2	64.4	19.8	18.3	24.1	21.5	
␣h Africa	1946	45.4	85.7	35.3	-	85.4	36.1	-	28.4	28.8	
	1960	35.7	77.0	23.5	-	76.1	23.3	-	12.0	27.2	V
␣idad & Tobago	1946	39.2	78.4	26.8	26.3	80.2	27.2	26.6	18.6	27.4	
	1960	33.6	74.0	26.5	25.0	71.2	25.4	24.0	20.5	27.6	IV

cluding unpaid family workers.

lues of the component indices from which the index of relative level of development for each country was de-
ved are given in Appendix H, Table H.1.

rtuguese Africa is also included in Tropical Africa.

e also Guinea and Senegal (Tropical Africa), Indonesia and Pakistan (South and East Asia), Albania (Eastern
rope).

erages of rates derived from results of National Sample Survey rounds 14 (1958-59) and 15 (1959-60).

Table A.2. Principal measures of participation in the labor force for rural and urban parts of countries, censuses of 1946-1966

Country	Census years	Rural					Urban				
		Crude activity rate	Standardized activity rates, 10+		Refined activity rates, 10+		Crude activity rate	Standardized activity rates, 10+		Refined activity rates, 10+	
			Males	Females	Males	Females		Males	Females	Males	Females
1. Tropical Africa											
Central African Rep.	1960	56.0	76.0	74.9	80.4	86.0	54.8	72.1	69.1	77.7	79.8
Guinea	1954/55	52.8	81.1	73.7	81.0	79.7	40.3	77.4	38.4	78.6	39.4
Ghana	1960	40.4	77.5	49.7	76.0	48.6	43.6	73.8	50.5	76.4	47.4
Liberia	1962	41.3	73.3	41.1	76.4	43.1	32.7	61.2	12.6	62.2	12.1
2. Arab countries											
Algeria	1966	21.3	-	-	66.3	1.5	22.0	-	-	64.7	4.4
Morocco	1960	27.7	80.6	7.9	79.6	7.4	27.8	69.7	11.3	71.5	11.3
Tunisia	1966	32.0	75.2	28.8	70.5	27.8	27.5	68.5	14.2	64.9	13.8
U.A.R.	1947	34.6	-	-	85.1	10.5	32.2	-	-	76.2	8.4
	1960	29.3	-	-	79.9	5.3	27.7	-	-	70.1	8.7
3. Other Moslem countries[a]											
Iran	1956	32.1	86.7	9.2	86.6	9.2	31.8	78.5	9.4	78.5	9.3
	1966	31.5	84.8	14.0	82.6	14.3	28.3	72.2	9.9	69.2	9.9
Turkey	1955	60.5	93.0	84.2	92.3	84.5	41.2	78.7	16.3	82.0	16.6
	1960	58.5	91.8	82.2	90.4	81.9	35.6	75.2	8.3	77.1	8.3
	1965	55.3	90.8	74.6	88.6	74.2	33.5	73.7	8.2	73.8	8.1
4. South and East Asia											
Ceylon	1963	32.6	72.3	21.8	69.4	21.6	33.0	68.8	13.8	68.7	13.7
India	1961	44.9	83.7	44.2	83.0	44.8	34.4	71.7	16.0	73.1	15.9
Indonesia	1961	36.5	80.1	30.6	81.5	30.4	32.7	69.6	23.7	70.6	23.8
Japan	1950	47.0	76.9	52.1	75.3	51.6	39.1	70.6	29.6	73.1	31.2
	1955	47.7	75.3	53.3	74.2	52.7	43.0	71.6	36.7	72.8	37.7
	1960	49.2	74.1	54.0	71.9	52.6	46.1	71.9	38.6	72.6	39.2
	1965	49.8	72.0	50.4	71.0	49.9	48.9	71.1	39.8	74.7	42.0
Korea, South	1960	32.5	71.5	27.3	68.1	27.1	27.0	60.4	17.0	59.4	17.8
Pakistan	1961	33.8	86.6	15.0	86.5	15.2	31.1	73.2	5.0	73.6	4.7
Thailand	1954	59.0	84.1	81.3	83.3	83.6	36.0	65.2	33.1	65.4	33.7
5. Latin America, Spain, and Portugal											
Argentina	1947	37.7	-	-	81.2	14.0	42.7	-	-	80.3	24.6
	1960	38.4	81.0	23.7	73.2	23.1	36.4	71.0	13.9	80.1	13.8
Chile	1952	34.5	81.8	14.0	79.6	13.6	37.6	72.5	28.4	73.7	29.5
	1960	31.8	81.0	8.7	78.2	8.4	32.8	70.2	23.6	69.4	23.8
Colombia	1951	33.1	85.0	12.6	82.4	12.2	34.6	78.2	23.7	76.7	24.7
	1964	30.2	84.4	10.8	80.4	10.2	29.1	71.3	22.6	66.4	22.9
Costa Rica	1950	32.7	88.7	7.5	86.3	7.8	36.8	79.8	25.0	65.4	26.4
	1963	28.6	84.7	7.4	80.6	7.5	31.9	73.8	25.6	69.8	25.6
Cuba	1953	35.3	84.0	11.5	82.2	11.4	37.7	74.4	19.8	76.2	20.5
Ecuador	1962	33.4	89.7	11.2	87.2	11.0	32.0	77.0	23.2	72.9	23.2
El Salvador	1950	34.0	89.3	9.0	87.2	9.2	37.2	80.5	25.5	79.0	26.3
	1961	31.2	87.8	8.2	84.8	8.3	33.6	76.3	27.4	72.7	27.6
Guatemala	1950	33.0	88.8	7.3	87.1	7.4	37.7	79.8	25.4	79.3	26.3
	1964	30.0	87.2	5.2	84.3	5.2	32.1	77.6	22.0	74.3	22.0
Mexico	1960	29.7	79.8	11.6	75.6	11.0	31.6	76.9	20.5	73.4	20.4
Nicaragua	1950	34.5	92.6	7.5	90.6	7.3	32.3	81.8	20.0	78.8	20.4
	1963	31.4	88.7	11.7	85.8	11.0	30.2	73.3	28.5	69.4	27.8
Panama	1950	32.6	83.9	11.4	81.4	11.5	38.7	71.3	30.1	74.2	31.7
	1960	31.1	82.8	9.1	79.6	9.1	36.0	68.6	32.6	67.5	32.8
Peru	1961	30.1	79.4	16.4	75.4	16.1	33.0	73.4	23.3	70.5	23.6
Portugal	1960	37.3	85.5	12.9	85.2	12.4	42.8	76.1	28.7	79.5	27.0
Puerto Rico	1950	25.9	67.1	14.2	61.9	14.0	29.2	58.7	23.3	58.3	23.8
	1960	22.4	62.8	12.3	53.6	11.0	29.2	59.8	24.4	56.8	23.6
Spain	1950	38.3	83.2	10.6	85.3	10.9	39.1	76.0	18.9	79.9	19.2

166

Table A.2. (continued)

Country	Census years	Rural Crude activity rate	Rural Standardized activity rates, 10+ Males	Rural Standardized activity rates, 10+ Females	Rural Refined activity rates, 10+ Males	Rural Refined activity rates, 10+ Females	Urban Crude activity rate	Urban Standardized activity rates, 10+ Males	Urban Standardized activity rates, 10+ Females	Urban Refined activity rates, 10+ Males	Urban Refined activity rates, 10+ Females
				6. Eastern Europe							
Bulgaria	1956	59.6	76.6	64.3	80.8	65.9	44.4	66.2	33.7	72.2	35.9
				7. Middle Europe							
Finland	1960	44.6	73.9	41.6	72.4	39.9	47.6	68.9	45.6	71.8	46.0
Greece	1961	49.0	81.1	45.0	81.1	43.3	39.6	70.1	22.4	73.4	21.4
			8. Northwestern Europe, Northern America, and Oceania								
Canada	1961	31.5	68.0	18.7	64.7	17.2	38.0	68.6	30.2	69.9	29.3
New Zealand	1951	36.2	-	-	75.4	17.4	39.8	-	-	74.0	26.0
	1956	35.1	-	-	75.0	17.5	39.6	-	-	73.5	27.0
	1961	34.1	-	-	72.5	17.7	39.1	-	-	71.8	27.9
Norway	1960	38.1	74.1	20.0	74.6	17.4	43.3	69.7	32.2	73.6	30.3
Sweden	1960	41.1	72.6	25.9	72.0	22.3	46.4	70.0	37.6	73.0	36.1
	1965	43.0	69.9	30.2	68.2	26.6	45.8	68.1	37.2	71.4	36.6
United States	1950	35.0	70.2	18.4	70.6	18.2	42.6	67.7	30.1	74.4	31.4
	1960	35.3	68.6	25.0	66.3	24.3	40.8	69.5	33.7	71.2	34.0
				9. Miscellaneous							
Cyprus	1960	45.2	-	-	78.2	45.2	36.1	-	-	75.2	19.7
Guyana	1946	38.5	-	-	80.8	27.3	41.1	-	-	77.3	34.7
	1960	29.8	77.7	18.4	73.9	17.1	34.8	73.7	31.8	71.0	31.2
Israel	1961	31.9	-	-	63.7	28.4	34.5	-	-	66.1	22.8

a
See also Guinea (Tropical Africa), Indonesia and Pakistan (South and East Asia).

Table A.3. Annual changes in principal measures of participation in the labor force for countries, intercen* periods during 1946-1966

Country	Period	Crude activity rate	Standardized activity rates, ages 10 & over Males	Females	Refined activity rates, ages 10 & over Males	Females	Female shares employment FS_{ag}	FS_{non}
			2. Arab countries					
United Arab Rep.	1947-60	-.51	-.66	-.29	-.76	-.29	-.45	+.2€
			3. Other Moslem countries[a]					
Iran	1956-66	-.18	-.46	+.30	-.69	+.33	+.21	+.25
Turkey	1955-60	-.73	-.51	-1.23	-.65	-1.34	-.32	-.03
	1960-65	-.74	-.36	-1.61	-.56	-1.63	-.41	-.05
			4. South and East Asia					
Ceylon	1946-53	-.35	-.60	+.28	-.47	+.27	+.32	+.35
	1953-63	-.42	-.08	-.69	-.35	-.66	-.29	-.46
Japan	1950-55	+.21	-.29	+.07	-.20	+.05	+.23	+.52
	1955-60	+.44	-.11	+.07	-.21	-.03	+.35	+.30
	1960-65	+.38	-.27	-.20	+.24	+.11	-.06	+.37
Malaysia								
W. Malaysia	1947-57	-.44	-	-	-.22	-.07	+.42	-.04
Sabah	1951-60	-.45	-	-	+.01	-.10	-.18	+.49
Sarawak	1947-60	-.92	-	-	-.72	-1.10	-.07	+.30
Mauritius	1952-62	-.52	-.36	-.36	-.86	-.44	-.42	+.05
Nepal	1953-61	-.01	-	-	-.01	+.04	-.01	-.53
Ryukyu Islands	1950-55	-.09	-.39	+.44	+.06	+.63	+.22	+.48
	1955-60	-.24	-.44	-.22	-.80	+.60	+.04	+.32
Thailand	1947-54	+.49	-	-	+.30	+1.05	+.20	-.77
	1954-60	-.63	-.31	-.43	-.34	-.68	-.07	+.89
			5. Latin America, Spain and Portugal					
Argentina	1947-60	-.23	-	-	-.43	-.02	+.04	+.05
Brazil	1950-60	-.07	-.32	+.34	-.37	+.29	+.26	+.09
Chile	1952-60	-.49	-.32	-.49	-.47	-.55	-.36	-.40
Colombia	1951-63	-.32	-.36	.00	-.53	-.03	+.01	-.08
Costa Rica	1950-62	-.33	-.37	+.03	-.53	-.02	-.11	+.17
Ecuador	1950-62	-.51	+.13	-1.37	+.06	-1.35	-.74	-.85
El Salvador	1950-61	-.28	-.26	+.06	-.37	+.03	-.03	+.14
Guatemala	1950-64	-.25	-.18	-.06	-.30	-.08	-.01	-.17
Mexico	1950-60	-.17	-.59	+.39	-.72	+.38	-	-
Nicaragua	1950-63	-.21	-.49	+.52	-.62	+.47	+.21	+.30
Panama	1950-60	-.17	-.28	+.12	-.43	+.07	-.25	+.28
Paraguay	1950-62	-.10	-.02	+.04	-.10	.00	-.06	+.07
Portugal	1950-60	-.11	+.32	-.46	+.28	-.50	-.79	-.36
Puerto Rico	1950-60	-.19	-.21	-.01	-.54	-.14	-.01	-.52
Spain	1950-60	-.05	-.29	+.30	-.31	+.22	-	-
Venezuela	1950-61	-.24	-.20	.00	-.29	-.03	-.14	-.05
			6. Eastern Europe					
Albania	1955-60	-1.68	-	-	-1.37	-2.03	-	-
Bulgaria	1956-65	-.29	-.76	+.02	-.97	-.21	+.47	+.50
Czechoslovakia	1947-61	-.07	-	-	-.57	+.44	+.03	+.82
Hungary	1949-60	+.35	+.03	+.88	-.03	+.89	+.71	+.49
Poland	1950-60	-.38	-	-	-.44	-.11	-	-
Rumania	1956-66	-.74	-1.38	-.93	-1.42	-.99	+.37	+.28
Yugoslavia	1953-61	-.17	-	-	-.53	-.08	+.16	+.68

168

Table A.3. (continued)

Country	Period	Crude activity rate	Standardized activity rates, ages 10 & over		Refined activity rates, ages 10 & over		Female shares in employment	
			Males	Females	Males	Females	FS_{ag}	FS_{nonag}
7. Middle Europe								
Austria	1951-61	-.08	-	-	-.34	+.11	+.04	+.46
Finland	1950-60	-.35	-.41	-.34	-.75	-.59	-.52	+.07
France	1954-62	-.33	-.20	-.08	-.69	-.37	-.29	.00
Germany, West	1950-61	+.15	+.03	+.33	+.14	+.24	.00	+.35
Italy	1951-61	-.37	-.75	-.26	-.73	-.30	+.17	-.12
Switzerland	1950-60	-.05	-.06	-.07	-.23	-.18	-.63	-.09
8. Northwestern Europe, Northern America, and Oceania								
Australia	1947-54	-.14	+.06	+.30	-.05	+.13	+.23	-.08
	1954-61	-.14	-.29	+.19	-.62	+.23	+.31	+.25
Belgium	1947-61	-.21	-.23	+.26	-.39	+.11	+.13	+.19
Canada	1951-61	-.21	-.48	+.47	-.74	+.42	+.66	+.33
Denmark	1950-60	-.25	-.15	-.63	-.38	-.63	-1.40	-.17
Iceland	1951-61	-.40	-.36	-.12	-.57	-.23	-.25	+.07
Netherlands	1947-60	-.29	-	-	-.45	-.34	-1.04	-.19
New Zealand	1951-56	-.12	+.05	+.11	-.10	+.13	-.03	+.01
	1956-61	-.12	-.13	+.20	-.53	+.25	+.17	+.21
Norway	1950-60	-.31	-.39	-.23	-.65	-.26	-.28	-.20
Sweden	1950-60	-.02	-.37	+.24	-.66	+.19	+.02	+.21
	1960-65	+.26	-.55	+.69	-.37	+.95	-[b]	+.38
United Kingdom	1951-61	+.02	-.14	+.15	-.29	+.19	-.13	+.15
United States	1950-60	-.07	+.06	+.50	-.34	+.43	+.10	+.33
9. Miscellaneous								
Guyana	1946-60	-.62	-.24	-.50	-.49	-.57	-.59	-.33
Hong Kong	1961-66	+.11	-	-	-.79	+.79	+.87	+.88
Jamaica	1953-60	-.64	-.51	-.26	-.54	-.48	-1.19	-.22
Singapore	1947-57	-.57	-	-	-.30	+.28	+1.90	+.34
	1957-66	-.37	-.44	+.22	-1.36	+.06	-1.16	+.58
South Africa	1946-60	-.69	-.62	-.85	-.66	-.91	-1.17	-.11
Trinidad & Tobago	1946-60	-.40	-.32	-.02	-.65	-.13	+.13	+.02

See also Albania (Eastern Europe).

The data as recorded indicate an annual increase in FS_{ag} of 2.80 percent, which is due to improved enumeration in the 1965 census.

169

Table A.4. Annual changes in principal measures of participation in the labor force for rural and urban par of countries, intercensal periods during 1946-1966

Country	Period	Rural Crude activity rate	Rural Standardized activity rates, 10+ Males	Rural Standardized activity rates, 10+ Females	Rural Refined activity rates, 10+ Males	Rural Refined activity rates, 10+ Females	Urban Crude activity rate	Urban Standardized activity rates, 10+ Males	Urban Standardized activity rates, 10+ Females	Urban Refined activity rates, 10+ Males	Urban Refined activity rates, 10+ Female
2. Arab countries											
United Arab Rep.	1947-60	-.40	-	-	-.40	-.39	-.34	-	-	-.46	+.02
3. Other Moslem countries											
Iran	1956-66	-.06	-.20	+.47	-.41	+.51	-.35	-.63	+.05	-.93	+.06
Turkey	1955-60	-.39	-.23	-.39	-.38	-.53	-1.12	-.71	-1.60	-.99	-1.66
	1960-65	-.65	-.21	-1.51	-.36	-1.53	-.42	-.30	-.02	-.67	-.04
4. South and East Asia											
Japan	1950-55	+.15	-.33	+.24	-.21	-.22	+.78	+.20	+1.41	-.06	+1.30
	1955-60	+.29	-.24	+.15	-.46	-.02	+.62	+.06	+.37	-.04	+.30
	1960-65	+.11	-.41	-.73	-.18	-.53	+.55	-.17	+.24	+.41	+.56
5. Latin America, Spain, and Portugal											
Argentina	1947-60	-.10	-	-	-.08	-.02	-.33	-	-	-.54	-.12
Chile	1952-60	-.33	-.09	-.65	-.18	-.64	-.61	-.29	-.60	-.53	-.71
Colombia	1951-64	-.22	-.05	-.14	-.15	-.15	-.43	-.54	-.08	-.79	-.14
Costa Rica	1950-63	-.32	-.31	-.01	-.44	-.03	-.38	-.46	+.05	+.34	-.06
El Salvador	1950-61	-.26	-.14	-.07	-.22	-.08	-.33	-.38	+.17	-.57	+.12
Guatemala	1950-64	-.21	-.11	-.15	-.20	-.15	-.40	-.15	-.24	-.36	-.31
Nicaragua	1950-63	-.24	-.30	+.32	-.37	+.29	-.16	-.65	+.65	-.88	+.57
Panama	1950-60	-.15	-.12	-.22	-.18	-.24	-.27	-.27	+.25	-.68	+.12
Puerto Rico	1950-60	-.35	-.43	-.19	-.82	-.30	-.01	+.11	+.11	-.15	-.02
8. Northwestern Europe, Northern America, and Oceania											
New Zealand	1951-56	-.22	-	-	-.08	+.03	-.04	-	-	-.11	+.20
	1956-61	-.20	-	-	-.50	+.03	-.09	-	-	-.35	+.17
Sweden	1960-65	+.37	-.54	-.a	-.76	-.a	-.12	-.37	-.09	-.32	+.09
United States	1950-60	+.03	-.16	+.66	-.44	+.62	-.18	+.19	+.36	-.32	+.27
9. Miscellaneous											
Guyana	1946-60	-.63	-	-	-.49	-.73	-.45	-	-	-.45	-.25

a
Recorded data indicate an annual increase of .87, due to improved enumeration in the 1965 census.

170

Table A.5. Indices of effects of population structure upon crude activity rates for countries, censuses of 1946-1966[a]

Country	Census year	Absolute indices							Relative indices	
		ASI	ASI'	AI$_c$	AI$_m$	AI$_f$	SI	Residual	ASI	ASI'

1. Tropical Africa[b]

Country	Census year	ASI	ASI'	AI$_c$	AI$_m$	AI$_f$	SI	Residual	ASI	ASI'
Botswana	1964	-	-4.00	-3.95	-	-	-0.05	-	-	-8.4
Central African Rep.	1960	+0.52	-4.97	-4.94	+1.52	+4.01	-0.03	-0.04	+0.9	-8.9
Dahomey	1961	-	-9.23	-9.15	-	-	-0.08	-	-	-17.3
Ghana	1960	-6.07	-5.35	-5.52	-0.25	-0.45	+0.18	-0.02	-14.8	-13.1
Guinea	1954/55	-4.60	-6.59	-6.33	0.00	+2.03	-0.25	-0.04	-8.9	-12.7
Liberia	1962	-0.62	-2.22	-2.08	+0.96	+0.65	-0.14	-0.02	-1.5	-5.5
Namibia	1960	-1.58	-1.49	-1.83	-0.01	-0.05	+0.34	-0.02	-4.1	-3.9
Nigeria	1963	-4.46	-3.19	-3.44	-0.84	-0.42	+0.25	-0.01	-13.1	-9.4
Senegal	1960/61	-	-5.93	-5.72	-	-	-0.20	-	-	-13.5
Sierra Leone	1963	-	-2.85	-2.68	-	-	-0.17	-	-	-6.8
Togo	1950/60	-	-10.94	-10.24	-	-	-0.69	-	-	-24.3
Zaire	1955/57	-	-2.99	-3.00	-	-	0.00	-	-	-5.8

1a. Portuguese Africa

Country	Census year	ASI	ASI'	AI$_c$	AI$_m$	AI$_f$	SI	Residual	ASI	ASI'
Angola	1960	-	-2.05	-2.66	-	-	+0.61	-	-	-7.0
Mozambique	1950	-4.16	-3.48	-1.77	-0.89	+0.22	-1.72	0.00	-14.3	-12.0
Portuguese Guinea	1950	-1.43	-	-0.62	-0.11	-0.04	-0.69	-0.01	-4.8	-4.3

2. Arab countries

Country	Census year	ASI	ASI'	AI$_c$	AI$_m$	AI$_f$	SI	Residual	ASI	ASI'
Algeria	1966	-	-3.64	-3.05	-	-	-0.59	0.00	-	-16.8
Iraq	1957	-4.31	-4.01	-3.86	-0.30	0.00	-0.15	-	-15.3	-14.2
Jordan	1961	-4.71	-2.30	-2.46	-2.42	0.00	+0.17	0.00	-20.7	-10.1
Libya	1964	-2.07	-1.68	-2.87	+0.38	-0.02	+1.19	0.00	-8.0	-6.5
Morocco	1960	-4.20	-3.95	-4.03	-0.14	-0.10	+0.08	0.00	-15.0	-14.1
Sudan	1956	-	-4.44	-4.38	-	-	-0.06	-	-	-9.9
Syria	1960	-4.71	-3.51	-3.83	-1.20	+0.01	+0.31	0.00	-18.2	-13.6
Tunisia	1966	-5.06	-2.48	-2.93	-	-	+0.45	-0.02	-16.7	-10.3
United Arab Rep.	1947	-0.72	-0.55	-0.29	-0.18	+0.02	-0.27	0.00	-2.0	-1.6
	1960	-2.76	-2.14	-2.10	-0.64	+0.03	-0.05	-0.01	-9.5	-7.4

3. Other Moslem countries[c]

Country	Census year	ASI	ASI'	AI$_c$	AI$_m$	AI$_f$	SI	Residual	ASI	ASI'
Iran	1956	-2.46	-2.51	-3.18	+0.06	-0.01	+0.67	-0.01	-7.7	-7.8
	1966	-3.68	-3.01	-3.82	-0.74	+0.08	+0.82	-0.01	-12.2	-9.9
Turkey	1955	-2.80	-2.90	-3.00	-0.05	+0.18	+0.10	-0.04	-5.0	-5.2
	1960	-3.21	-2.87	-3.04	-0.29	-0.02	+0.17	-0.03	-6.1	-5.5
	1965	-3.26	-2.52	-2.72	-0.65	-0.07	+0.20	-0.02	-6.7	-5.2

4. South and East Asia

Country	Census year	ASI	ASI'	AI$_c$	AI$_m$	AI$_f$	SI	Residual	ASI	ASI'
Ceylon	1946	+1.44	+1.82	+0.29	-0.20	-0.17	+1.53	-0.01	+3.7	+4.6
	1953	-0.15	-0.10	-1.32	+0.15	-0.19	+1.21	-0.02	-0.4	-0.3
	1963	-1.43	-0.51	-1.47	-0.84	-0.07	+0.96	-0.02	-4.4	-1.6
India	1961	-1.86	-1.87	-2.47	-0.13	+0.16	+0.60	-0.02	-4.3	-4.4
Indonesia	1961	-4.12	-4.53	-4.26	+0.47	-0.05	-0.26	-0.01	-11.5	-12.6
Japan	1950	+0.16	+0.09	+0.42	-0.08	+0.18	-0.34	-0.02	+0.4	+0.2
	1955	+1.61	+1.40	+1.70	+0.08	+0.16	-0.30	-0.02	+3.6	+3.1
	1960	+3.86	+4.04	+4.32	-0.12	-0.06	-0.27	-0.02	+8.2	+8.6
	1965	+6.62	+5.12	+5.38	+0.91	+0.61	-0.26	-0.02	+13.5	+10.4
Khmer Republic	1962	-4.06	-3.10	-3.10	-1.02	+0.10	0.00	-0.03	-9.3	-7.1
Korea, South	1960	-3.46	-2.54	-2.00	-0.91	-0.01	-0.53	-0.01	-11.2	-8.2
Malaysia:										
West Malaysia	1947	-	+0.28	-1.09	-	-	+1.37	-	-	+0.7
	1957	-3.32	-3.01	-3.72	-0.33	+0.03	+0.71	-0.01	-9.6	-8.7
Sabah	1951	-	-0.63	-1.19	-	-	+0.56	-	-	-1.4
	1960	-3.31	-4.23	-5.00	+0.51	+0.43	+0.77	-0.02	-7.8	-10.0
Sarawak	1947	-	-2.18	-2.53	-	-	+0.34	-	-	-3.9
	1960	-5.06	-5.31	-5.42	-0.14	+0.41	+0.12	-0.03	-11.4	-12.0
Mauritius	1952	-1.24	-1.90	-2.05	+0.71	-0.04	+0.16	-0.01	-3.8	-5.8
	1962	-3.81	-2.46	-2.56	-1.02	-0.32	+0.10	-0.01	-13.9	-9.0

171

Country	Census year	Absolute indices							Relative indices	
		ASI	ASI'	AI_c	AI_m	AI_f	SI	Residual	ASI	ASI'

4. South and East Asia (continued)

Country	Census year	ASI	ASI'	AI_c	AI_m	AI_f	SI	Residual	ASI	ASI'
Nepal	1952/54	-	-1.19	-0.97	-	-	-0.22	-	-	-2.
	1961	-1.94	-2.21	-2.01	-0.20	+0.48	-0.20	-0.02	-4.0	-4.
Pakistan	1961	-2.96	-2.96	-4.63	-0.03	+0.04	+1.67	-0.01	-8.8	-8.
Philippines	1960	-5.10	-3.56	-3.60	-1.38	-0.15	+0.05	-0.02	-15.9	-11.
Ryukyu Islands	1950	-3.94	-2.14	-1.30	-1.48	-0.30	-0.84	-0.03	-9.3	-5.
	1955	-4.48	-3.81	-3.24	-0.72	+0.07	-0.56	-0.02	-10.6	-9.
	1960	-4.44	-2.42	-1.94	-1.36	-0.65	-0.48	-0.03	-10.9	-5.
Taiwan	1956	-2.40	-3.75	-4.10	+0.85	+0.52	+0.35	-0.01	-7.2	-11.
Thailand	1947	-	-2.76	-2.76	-	-	0.00	-	-	-5.
	1954	-2.40	-2.84	-2.84	-0.27	+0.75	-0.01	-0.03	-4.2	-5.
	1960	-4.54	-4.39	-4.40	-0.33	+0.22	0.00	-0.04	-8.5	-8.

5. Latin America, Spain, and Portugal

Country	Census year	ASI	ASI'	AI_c	AI_m	AI_f	SI	Residual	ASI	ASI'
Argentina	1947	-	+3.07	+2.34	-	-	+0.73	-	-	+7.
	1960	+2.52	+2.22	+2.22	+0.51	-0.20	0.00	0.00	+6.7	+5.
Bolivia	1950	-3.32	-3.22	-2.92	-0.30	+0.23	-0.29	-0.03	-6.6	-6.
Brazil	1950	-2.20	-2.04	-1.86	-0.42	+0.27	-0.17	-0.01	-6.7	-6.
	1960	-2.90	-2.41	-2.26	-0.59	+0.10	-0.14	-0.01	-9.0	-7.
Chile	1952	-0.84	-0.80	-0.34	-0.16	+0.14	-0.45	-0.02	-2.3	-2.
	1960	-2.32	-1.73	-1.22	-0.56	-0.03	-0.51	-0.01	-7.2	-5.
Colombia	1951	-3.43	-2.74	-2.46	-0.76	+0.08	-0.29	-0.01	-10.2	-8.
	1964	-5.80	-4.31	-3.80	-1.41	-0.06	-0.50	-0.01	-19.6	-14.
Costa Rica	1950	-3.11	-2.57	-2.44	-0.70	+0.20	-0.14	-0.04	-9.1	-7.
	1963	-5.84	-4.47	-4.40	-1.33	-0.04	-0.07	-0.01	-19.6	-15.
Cuba	1953	+1.06	+1.06	+1.06	-0.05	+0.07	+0.67	-0.01	+2.9	+2.
Dominican Republic	1960	-5.25	-3.67	-3.89	-1.45	-0.11	+0.22	-0.01	-18.7	-13.
Ecuador	1950	-4.03	-3.17	-3.00	-0.75	-0.09	-0.18	-0.02	-10.3	-8.
	1962	-4.64	-3.61	-3.50	-0.99	-0.03	-0.11	-0.01	-14.1	-11.
El Salvador	1950	-2.70	-2.11	-1.72	-0.69	+0.11	-0.39	-0.01	-7.7	-6.
	1961	-4.98	-3.91	-3.40	-1.06	0.00	-0.52	-0.01	-15.5	-12.
Guatemala	1950	-2.59	-2.13	-2.37	-0.50	+0.05	+0.24	-0.01	-7.6	-6.
	1964	-4.78	-3.72	-3.64	-1.03	-0.02	-0.08	0.00	-15.6	-12.
Honduras	1961	-5.74	-4.88	-4.64	-0.91	-0.06	-0.24	-0.01	-19.0	-16.
Mexico	1950	-3.50	-2.52	-1.93	-0.92	-0.05	-0.59	-0.01	-10.8	-7.
	1960	-4.48	-3.06	-2.88	-1.33	-0.09	-0.18	0.00	-14.6	-10.
Nicaragua	1950	-4.08	-3.24	-2.50	-0.81	-0.02	-0.74	-0.01	-12.1	-9.
	1963	-7.00	-5.48	-4.96	-1.28	-0.23	-0.53	-0.01	-22.6	-17.
Panama	1950	-1.94	-1.75	-2.29	-0.30	+0.11	+0.54	0.00	-5.6	-5.0
	1960	-3.10	-2.17	-2.63	-0.85	-0.07	+0.46	-0.01	-9.3	-6.
Paraguay	1950	-5.08	-3.63	-2.83	-1.33	-0.09	-0.80	-0.02	-15.2	-10.
	1962	-6.36	-4.51	-3.84	-1.61	-0.23	-0.67	-0.01	-19.7	-14.
Peru	1961	-4.23	-3.03	-2.88	-1.17	-0.02	-0.15	-0.01	-13.4	-9.
Portugal	1950	+1.83	+1.72	+2.88	+0.30	-0.18	-1.16	-0.01	+4.6	+4.
	1960	+1.28	+1.50	+2.99	+0.12	-0.34	-1.49	-0.01	+3.3	+3.9
Puerto Rico	1950	-3.21	-2.08	-2.17	-1.10	-0.01	+0.08	-0.02	-11.8	-7.
	1960	-4.26	-1.53	-1.30	-2.24	-0.48	-0.24	0.00	-16.8	-6.0
Spain	1950	+3.50	+2.37	+3.68	+1.02	+0.10	-1.30	0.00	+9.1	+6.
	1960	+2.96	+2.29	+3.28	+0.91	-0.22	-0.99	-0.01	+7.8	+6.0
Uruguay	1963	+2.88	+3.02	+3.16	+0.19	-0.32	-0.13	-0.01	+7.4	+7.7
Venezuela	1950	-2.38	-2.06	-2.35	-0.40	+0.08	+0.29	-0.01	-7.0	-6.
	1961	-4.20	-3.45	-3.83	-0.71	-0.03	+0.38	-0.01	-13.5	-11.0

6. Eastern Europe

Country	Census year	ASI	ASI'	AI_c	AI_m	AI_f	SI	Residual	ASI	ASI'
Albania	1955	-	-1.58	-1.76	-	-	+0.18	-	-	-3.0
	1960	-	-3.70	-3.94	-	-	+0.24	-	-	-8.2
Bulgaria	1956	+7.53	+4.62	+4.65	+2.04	+0.91	-0.03	-0.03	+13.8	+8.5
	1965	+7.37	+5.98	+5.99	+1.33	+0.08	-0.01	-0.02	+14.2	+11.5
Czechoslovakia	1947	-	+4.46	+5.01	-	-	-0.54	-	-	+9.3
	1961	+3.56	+4.34	+4.62	+0.17	-0.91	-0.28	-0.03	+7.6	+9.2

Country	Census year	Absolute indices							Relative indices	
		ASI	ASI'	AI_c	AI_m	AI_f	SI	Residual	ASI	ASI'

6. Eastern Europe (continued)

Country	Census year	ASI	ASI'	AI_c	AI_m	AI_f	SI	Residual	ASI	ASI'
ermany, East	1964	-	+4.38	+5.59	-	-	-1.21	-	-	+8.9
ungary	1949	+4.85	+3.84	+4.77	+1.24	-0.22	-0.93	-0.02	+10.7	+8.5
	1960	+4.91	+4.15	+4.85	+0.97	-0.19	-0.70	-0.02	+10.0	+8.5
oland	1950	-	+2.60	+3.48	-	-	-0.87	-	-	+4.9
	1960	-	+0.83	+1.41	-	-	-0.58	-	-	+1.7
omania	1956	+5.62	+4.07	+4.35	+1.03	+0.55	-0.28	-0.03	+9.1	+6.6
	1966	+6.78	+5.57	+5.74	+0.94	+0.29	-0.16	-0.03	+12.5	+10.3
.S.S.R.	1959	-	+1.68	+2.33	-	-	-0.65	-	-	+3.2
ugoslavia	1953	+2.36	+2.08	+2.77	+0.32	-0.04	-0.69	-0.01	+5.1	+4.5
	1961	-	+2.03	+2.54	-	-	-0.51	-	-	+4.5

7. Middle Europe

Country	Census year	ASI	ASI'	AI_c	AI_m	AI_f	SI	Residual	ASI	ASI'
ustria	1951	-	+4.78	+6.07	-	-	-1.30	-	-	+9.9
	1961	+2.34	+5.50	+6.43	-0.61	-2.52	-0.94	-0.02	+4.9	+11.5
inland	1950	+3.50	+1.70	+2.38	+1.22	+0.60	-0.68	-0.02	+7.1	+3.4
	1960	+2.84	+3.30	+3.83	-0.01	-0.42	-0.54	-0.02	+6.2	+7.2
rance	1954	+5.04	+3.95	+4.71	+1.25	-0.15	-0.76	-0.02	+11.1	+8.7
	1962	+3.21	+4.69	+5.20	-0.30	-1.16	-0.51	-0.01	+7.5	+11.0
ermany, West	1950	+3.36	+5.34	+6.53	-0.26	-1.70	-1.20	-0.02	+7.3	+11.5
	1961	+3.50	+5.43	+6.42	+0.21	-2.13	-0.98	-0.02	+7.3	+11.3
reece	1961	+3.72	+3.70	+4.26	+0.56	-0.51	-0.56	-0.02	+8.3	+8.2
taly	1951	+3.50	+3.94	+4.53	+0.15	-0.58	-0.59	-0.01	+8.0	+9.0
	1961	+3.58	+4.13	+4.66	+0.24	-0.78	-0.53	-0.02	+9.0	+10.4
witzerland	1950	+5.87	+4.45	+5.10	+1.95	-0.51	-0.65	-0.02	+11.8	+9.0
	1960	+5.84	+5.51	+5.85	+1.31	-0.96	-0.34	-0.02	+11.8	+11.2

8. Northwestern Europe, Northern America, and Oceania

Country	Census year	ASI	ASI'	AI_c	AI_m	AI_f	SI	Residual	ASI	ASI'
ustralia	1947	+4.51	+3.92	+3.59	+1.43	-0.82	+0.03	-0.02	+10.7	+9.3
	1954	+2.62	+2.78	+2.54	+1.09	-1.24	+0.24	-0.02	+6.4	+6.8
	1961	+1.88	+2.87	+2.66	+0.16	-1.14	+0.21	-0.02	+4.7	+7.1
elgium	1947	+5.59	+5.41	+5.71	+0.94	-0.76	-0.31	-0.01	+13.6	+13.1
	1961	+2.42	+4.09	+4.56	0.00	-1.65	-0.47	-0.02	+6.3	+10.7
anada	1951	+2.57	+1.88	+1.64	+0.94	-0.23	+0.24	-0.02	+6.8	+4.9
	1961	+0.53	+1.08	+0.92	-0.09	-0.45	+0.16	-0.01	+1.5	+3.0
enmark	1950	+3.53	+3.86	+4.04	+0.83	-1.14	-0.17	-0.02	+7.3	+8.0
	1960	+3.90	+5.21	+5.40	-0.09	-1.20	-0.20	-0.01	+8.6	+11.4
reland	1951	+2.54	+3.50	+3.12	+0.18	-1.11	+0.38	-0.02	+5.8	+8.0
	1961	+0.38	+2.63	+2.55	-0.66	-1.58	+0.08	-0.01	+1.0	+6.6
etherlands	1947	-	+2.24	+2.43	-	-	-0.18	-	-	+5.6
	1960	+0.50	+2.33	+2.50	-0.57	-1.26	-0.17	0.00	+1.4	+6.4
ew Zealand	1951	+1.30	+2.16	+2.10	+0.36	-1.20	+0.06	-0.01	+3.4	+5.7
	1956	+0.39	+1.49	+1.41	+0.07	-1.15	+0.08	-0.01	+1.0	+4.0
	1961	-0.21	+1.44	+1.38	-0.56	-1.08	+0.06	-0.01	-0.6	+3.9
orway	1950	+4.50	+3.76	+4.03	+1.67	-0.93	-0.26	-0.01	+10.5	+8.8
	1960	+3.66	+4.09	+4.21	+0.63	-1.04	-0.12	-0.02	+9.2	+10.3
weden	1950	+5.05	+4.42	+4.54	+1.63	-0.97	-0.13	-0.02	+11.4	+10.0
	1960	+5.34	+6.06	+6.13	+0.48	-1.19	-0.07	-0.02	+12.2	+13.8
	1965	+6.38	+6.17	+6.20	+0.85	-0.62	-0.03	-0.02	+14.1	+13.6
United Kingdom	1951	+3.91	+4.72	+5.55	+1.12	-1.93	-0.83	-0.01	+8.4	+10.2
	1961	+4.11	+5.33	+5.96	+0.56	-1.77	-0.63	-0.01	+8.8	+11.4
United States	1950	+4.57	+2.61	+2.88	+1.72	+0.27	-0.28	-0.02	+11.5	+6.5
	1960	+1.80	+1.67	+1.99	+0.16	-0.01	-0.32	-0.01	+4.6	+4.3

9. Miscellaneous

Country	Census year	ASI	ASI'	AI_c	AI_m	AI_f	SI	Residual	ASI	ASI'
Cyprus	1960	-	-0.02	+0.39	-	-	-0.41	-	-	0.0
Guyana	1946	-0.82	-0.78	-0.53	-0.01	-0.02	-0.25	-0.02	-2.1	-2.0
	1960	-5.63	-4.14	-4.00	-1.13	-0.34	-0.14	-0.02	-18.0	-13.3

173

Table A.5. (continued)

Country		ASI	ASI'	Absolute indices AI_c	AI_m	AI_f	SI	Resid- ual	Relative indic ASI	ASI
9. Miscellaneous (continued)										
Haiti	1950	-0.74	+0.38	+0.52	-0.79	-0.30	-0.14	-0.04	-1.2	+0.
Hong Kong	1961	-0.90	-1.68	-2.08	+1.12	-0.32	+0.40	-0.02	-2.3	-4.
	1966	-	-1.14	-1.28	-	-	+0.14	-	-	-2.
Israel	1961	-	+0.75	+0.49	-	-	+0.26	-	-	+2.
Jamaica	1953	-1.52	-1.55	-0.92	-0.43	+0.48	-0.63	-0.02	-3.6	-3.
	1960	-3.96	-3.37	-2.65	-0.47	-0.10	-0.72	-0.02	-10.3	-8.
Singapore	1947	-	+3.42	+0.46	-	-	+2.96	-	-	+8.
	1957	-1.03	-2.26	-3.55	+1.10	+0.14	+1.29	-0.01	-3.1	-6.
	1966	-3.64	-1.43	-1.68	-1.86	-0.34	+0.25	-0.01	-12.2	-4.
South Africa	1946	+0.46	+0.31	-0.21	-0.12	+0.30	+0.52	-0.02	+1.0	+0.
	1960	-1.57	-1.19	-1.43	-0.32	-0.05	+0.24	-0.01	-4.4	-3.
Trinidad & Tobago	1946	+0.16	-0.64	-0.72	+0.67	+0.15	+0.08	-0.02	+0.4	-1.
	1960	-3.71	-2.34	-2.22	-0.98	-0.38	-0.12	-0.02	-11.0	-7.

a
The meaning of the indices is explained in Chapter 4, sections 4.2 and 4.3. For explanation of the deriva-
tion of the measures, see Appendix E.
b
See also Portuguese Africa.
c
See also Guinea and Senegal (Tropical Africa), Indonesia and Pakistan (South and East Asia), Albania (Eastern
Europe).

174

Country	Census year	Area	Absolute indices ASI	ASI'	AI_c	AI_m	AI_f	SI	Residual	Relative indices ASI	ASI'
1. Tropical Africa											
entral African Rep.	1960	R	-0.08	-5.46	-5.43	+1.40	+4.02	-0.03	-0.03	-0.1	-9.8
		U	+2.30	-3.36	-3.32	+1.88	+3.82	-0.03	-0.04	+4.2	-6.1
uinea	1954/55	R	-4.81	-6.86	-6.66	-0.05	+2.15	-0.20	-0.04	-9.1	-13.0
		U	-2.70	-3.46	-3.27	+0.38	+0.40	-0.19	-0.02	-6.7	-8.6
hana	1960	R	-6.89	-6.02	-6.05	-0.50	-0.34	+0.04	-0.03	-17.1	-14.9
		U	-2.60	-2.59	-3.28	+0.99	-0.97	+0.69	-0.03	-6.0	-5.9
iberia	1962	R	-1.20	-2.94	-2.53	+1.04	+0.73	-0.41	-0.03	-2.9	-7.1
		U	+5.34	+5.03	+1.12	+0.49	-0.17	+3.91	-0.01	+16.3	+15.4
2. Arab countries											
lgeria	1966	R	-	-3.71	-3.04	-	-	-0.68	-	-	-17.4
		U	-	-3.54	-3.08	-	-	-0.46	-	-	-16.1
orocco	1960	R	-5.08	-4.60	-4.79	-0.35	-0.14	+0.18	0.00	-18.3	-16.6
		U	-2.20	-2.76	-2.82	+0.62	-0.05	+0.06	-0.01	-7.9	-9.9
unisia	1966	R	-6.58	-4.72	-4.84	-1.53	-0.32	+0.13	-0.02	-20.6	-14.7
		U	-3.19	-1.78	-2.52	-1.28	-0.12	+0.74	-0.01	-11.6	-6.5
nited Arab Rep.	1947	R	-	-0.86	-0.38	-	-	-0.48	-	-	-2.5
		U	-	+0.88	+0.15	-	-	+0.73	-	-	+2.7
	1960	R	-	-2.24	-2.02	-	-	-0.22	-	-	-7.6
		U	-	-1.50	-2.01	-	-	+0.51	-	-	-5.4
3. Other Moslem countries[b]											
ran	1956	R	-3.46	-3.41	-3.92	-0.03	-0.01	+0.51	0.00	-10.8	-10.6
		U	-0.76	-0.75	-1.75	+0.01	-0.02	+1.00	0.00	-2.4	-2.4
	1966	R	-5.08	-4.44	-5.05	-0.72	+0.09	+0.60	-0.01	-16.1	-14.1
		U	-2.16	-1.10	-2.22	-1.05	+0.01	+1.11	-0.01	-7.6	-3.9
urkey	1955	R	-5.39	-5.25	-5.19	-0.24	+0.13	-0.06	-0.04	-8.9	-8.7
		U	+5.92	+4.39	+1.58	+1.44	+0.10	+2.82	-0.01	+14.4	+10.7
urkey	1960	R	-6.18	-5.53	-5.47	-0.48	-0.12	-0.06	-0.04	-10.6	-9.4
		U	+4.60	+3.78	+0.92	+0.84	-0.01	+2.85	-0.01	+12.9	+10.6
	1965	R	-6.20	-5.29	-5.19	-0.73	-0.16	-0.10	-0.03	-11.2	-9.6
		U	+3.12	+3.12	+0.71	+0.03	-0.03	+2.41	-0.01	+9.3	+9.3
4. South and East Asia											
eylon	1963	R	-2.34	-1.22	-1.90	-1.03	-0.08	+0.68	0.00	-7.2	-3.8
		U	+2.34	+2.44	+0.14	-0.04	-0.04	+2.30	-0.02	+7.1	+7.4
ndia	1961	R	-2.66	-2.59	-2.94	-0.25	+0.20	+0.35	-0.03	-5.9	-5.8
		U	+1.93	+1.41	-0.82	+0.56	-0.04	+4.23	-0.01	+5.6	+4.1
ndonesia	1961	R	-4.60	-4.99	-4.68	+0.46	-0.06	-0.31	-0.01	-12.6	-13.7
		U	-1.91	-2.24	-2.23	+0.34	+0.01	-0.01	-0.02	-5.8	-6.8
Japan	1950	R	-0.96	-0.15	+0.14	-0.59	-0.20	-0.29	-0.02	-2.0	-0.3
		U	+1.88	+0.39	+0.76	+0.91	+0.60	-0.38	-0.02	+4.8	+1.0
	1955	R	-0.04	+0.61	+0.86	-0.38	-0.24	-0.25	-0.03	-0.1	+1.3
		U	+2.76	+1.92	+2.23	+0.45	+0.41	-0.31	-0.01	+6.4	+4.5
	1960	R	+1.60	+3.06	+3.33	-0.82	-0.61	-0.27	-0.03	+3.2	+6.2
		U	+5.08	+4.54	+4.79	+0.29	+0.27	-0.24	-0.02	+11.0	+9.8
	1965	R	+4.28	+4.89	+5.23	-0.39	-0.20	-0.34	-0.02	+8.6	+9.8
		U	+7.69	+5.24	+5.44	+1.50	+0.96	-0.20	-0.01	+15.7	+10.7
Korea, South	1960	R	-4.12	-2.90	-2.40	-1.12	-0.07	-0.50	-0.02	-12.6	-8.9
		U	-1.80	-1.74	-1.13	-0.34	+0.29	-0.61	-0.01	-6.7	-6.4
Pakistan	1961	R	-3.86	-3.86	-5.15	-0.04	+0.05	+1.29	-0.01	-11.4	-11.4
		U	+2.17	+2.08	-1.94	+0.16	-0.07	+4.02	0.00	+7.0	+6.7
Thailand	1954	R	-2.54	-3.03	-3.02	-0.28	+0.80	-0.01	-0.04	-4.3	-5.1
		U	-0.48	-0.74	-1.23	+0.07	+0.21	+0.48	-0.01	-1.3	-2.1

175

Country	Census year	Area	Absolute indices							Relative index	
			ASI	ASI'	AI$_c$	AI$_m$	AI$_f$	SI	Residual	ASI	ASI

5. Latin America, Spain, and Portugal

Country	Census year	Area	ASI	ASI'	AI$_c$	AI$_m$	AI$_f$	SI	Residual	Rel ASI	Rel ASI
Argentina	1947	R	-	+2.35	-0.59	-	-	+2.95	-	-	+6.
		U	-	+3.74	+4.11	-	-	-0.36	-	-	+8.
	1960	R	+1.17	+1.60	-0.60	-0.38	-0.03	+2.20	-0.02	+3.2	+4.
		U	+3.26	+2.66	+3.21	+0.87	-0.26	-0.55	-0.02	+8.5	+6.
Chile	1952	R	-1.04	-0.08	-1.86	-0.83	-0.13	+1.78	0.00	-3.0	-0.
		U	+0.22	-0.67	+0.72	+0.42	+0.48	-1.39	-0.01	+0.6	-1.
	1960	R	-1.48	-0.30	-2.51	-1.08	-0.09	+2.20	0.00	-4.6	-1.
		U	-2.02	-1.87	-0.56	-0.24	+0.11	-1.31	-0.02	-6.2	-5.
Colombia	1951	R	-3.08	-2.04	-3.33	-0.91	-0.12	+1.29	-0.01	-9.3	-6.
		U	-3.19	-3.11	-1.02	-0.49	+0.42	-2.09	-0.01	-9.2	-9.
	1964	R	-5.08	-3.57	-4.72	-1.32	-0.18	+1.15	0.00	-1.68	-11.
		U	-5.78	-4.36	-2.88	-1.49	+0.09	-1.48	-0.01	-19.9	-15.
Costa Rica	1950	R	-2.92	-2.18	-3.39	-0.82	+0.12	+1.22	-0.05	-8.9	-6.
		U	-2.04	+1.12	+3.23	-5.19	+0.60	-2.12	+1.43	-5.6	+3.
	1963	R	-5.54	-4.20	-5.41	-1.36	+0.02	+1.21	0.00	-19.4	-14.
		U	-4.97	-3.71	-2.14	-1.23	-0.01	-1.57	-0.02	-15.6	-11.
Cuba	1953	R	-0.09	+0.63	-2.14	-0.69	-0.02	+2.77	-0.01	-0.2	+1.
		U	+2.70	+1.73	+2.26	+0.70	+0.28	-0.53	0.00	+7.2	+4.
Ecuador	1962	R	-4.06	-3.15	-3.93	-0.83	-0.07	+0.78	0.00	-12.2	-9.
		U	-5.22	-3.90	-2.72	-1.33	+0.03	-1.18	-0.02	-16.3	-12.
El Salvador	1950	R	-2.38	-1.71	-2.58	-0.74	+0.07	+0.87	-0.01	-7.0	-5.
		U	-2.12	-1.92	-0.04	-0.49	+0.31	-1.88	-0.02	-5.7	-5.
	1961	R	-4.39	-3.42	-4.02	-0.98	+0.03	+0.60	-0.01	-14.1	-11.
		U	-4.82	-3.77	-2.21	-1.13	+0.08	-1.56	-0.01	-14.3	-11.
Guatemala	1950	R	-2.62	-2.07	-2.89	-0.57	+0.02	+0.82	-0.01	-8.0	-6.
		U	-1.32	-1.50	-0.56	-0.15	+0.34	-0.94	-0.02	-3.5	-4.
	1964	R	-4.28	-3.30	-4.14	-0.98	0.00	+0.84	0.00	-14.3	-11.
		U	-4.86	-3.77	-2.47	-1.06	-0.01	-1.30	-0.02	-15.2	-11.
Mexico	1960	R	-4.21	-2.56	-3.21	-1.47	-0.17	+0.64	-0.01	-14.2	-8.
		U	-4.53	-3.35	-2.51	-1.16	-0.01	-0.84	-0.01	-14.3	-10.
Nicaragua	1950	R	-2.62	-1.79	-3.13	-0.73	-0.08	+1.33	-0.02	-7.6	-5.
		U	-5.52	-4.74	-1.22	-0.91	+0.14	-3.51	-0.01	-17.1	-14.
	1963	R	-5.80	-4.60	-5.65	-0.98	-0.21	+1.05	-0.01	-18.4	-14.
		U	-7.60	-5.59	-3.80	-1.73	-0.26	-1.79	-0.02	-25.2	-18.
Panama	1950	R	-2.67	-1.81	-3.60	-0.89	+0.04	+1.79	-0.01	-8.2	-5.
		U	+1.07	-0.56	+0.10	+1.03	+0.61	-0.66	-0.01	+2.8	-1.
	1960	R	-2.93	-1.79	-3.95	-1.13	0.00	+2.16	-0.01	-9.4	-5.
		U	-1.61	-1.29	-0.62	-0.40	+0.10	-0.67	-0.01	-4.5	-3.
Peru	1961	R	-5.44	-4.03	-3.80	-1.31	-0.09	-0.23	-0.01	-18.1	-13.4
		U	-2.84	-1.91	-1.83	-1.02	+0.10	-0.08	-0.01	-8.6	-5.
Portugal	1960	R	+0.81	+1.14	+2.28	-0.11	-0.21	-1.14	-0.01	+2.2	+3.0
		U	+3.88	+3.38	+5.49	+1.30	-0.78	-2.11	-0.02	+9.1	+7.9
Puerto Rico	1950	R	-4.22	-2.35	-2.33	-1.81	-0.06	+0.88	0.00	-16.3	-9.1
		U	-1.18	-1.25	-0.55	-0.14	-0.22	-0.70	-0.01	-4.0	-4.3
	1960	R	-5.48	-1.85	-2.17	-3.18	-0.43	+0.32	-0.01	-24.5	-8.3
		U	-2.10	-0.73	0.00	-1.05	-0.32	-0.72	-0.02	-7.2	-2.5
Spain	1950	R	+3.52	+2.55	+3.20	+0.83	+0.15	-0.65	-0.01	+9.2	+6.7
		U	+3.92	+2.30	+4.44	+1.50	+0.12	-2.14	-0.01	+10.0	+5.9

6. Eastern Europe

Country	Census year	Area	ASI	ASI'	AI$_c$	AI$_m$	AI$_f$	SI	Residual	Rel ASI	Rel ASI
Bulgaria	1956	R	+7.28	+4.94	+4.96	+1.72	+0.66	-0.02	-0.04	+12.2	+8.3
		U	+7.28	+3.94	+3.97	+2.44	+0.92	-0.03	-0.01	+16.4	+8.9

7. Middle Europe

Country	Census year	Area	ASI	ASI'	AI$_c$	AI$_m$	AI$_f$	SI	Residual	Rel ASI	Rel ASI
Finland	1960	R	+1.69	+3.01	+3.14	-0.61	-0.69	-0.12	-0.02	+3.8	+6.8
		U	+5.11	+3.90	+4.89	+1.07	+0.16	-1.00	-0.02	+10.7	+8.2
Greece	1961	R	+2.15	+2.86	+3.39	+0.01	-0.70	-0.53	-0.02	+4.4	+5.8
		U	+5.28	+4.36	+4.92	+1.38	-0.45	-0.56	0.00	+13.3	+11.0

Table A.6. (continued)

Country	Census year	Area	Absolute indices							Relative indices	
			ASI	ASI'	AI_c	AI_m	AI_f	SI	Residual	ASI	ASI'
8. Northwestern Europe, Northern America, and Oceania											
nada	1961	R	-0.68	+1.12	-0.19	-1.28	-0.50	+1.31	-0.01	-2.2	+3.5
		U	+1.34	+1.22	+1.44	+0.50	-0.36	-0.22	-0.01	+3.5	+3.2
w Zealand	1951	R	-	+1.82	+0.47	-	-	+1.34	-	-	+5.0
		U	-	+2.58	+3.36	-	-	-0.78	-	-	+6.5
	1956	R	-	+0.80	-0.39	-	-	+1.19	-	-	+2.3
		U	-	+2.21	+2.85	-	-	-0.64	-	-	+5.6
	1961	R	-	+0.66	-0.41	-	-	+1.08	-	-	+1.9
		U	-	+2.08	+2.57	-	-	-0.49	-	-	+5.3
rway	1960	R	+3.16	+3.97	+3.41	+0.22	-1.03	+0.56	0.00	+8.3	+10.4
		U	+5.46	+4.82	+5.94	+1.54	-0.89	-1.12	-0.02	+12.6	+11.1
eden	1960	R	+4.56	+6.38	+5.65	-0.29	-1.51	+0.73	-0.01	+11.1	+15.5
		U	+6.48	+5.95	+6.53	+1.23	-0.69	-0.58	-0.02	+13.9	+12.8
	1965	R	+5.80	+8.10	+6.84	-0.82	-1.47	+1.26	-0.01	+13.5	+18.8
		U	+6.72	+5.64	+5.97	+1.36	-0.26	-0.32	-0.02	+14.7	+12.3
ited States	1950	R	+2.12	+2.02	+1.47	+0.20	-0.08	+0.55	-0.01	+6.0	+5.8
		U	+6.28	+3.11	+3.71	+2.66	+0.53	-0.60	-0.02	+14.8	+7.3
	1960	R	+0.54	+1.72	+1.34	-0.90	-0.26	+0.38	-0.02	+1.5	+4.9
		U	+2.46	+1.72	+2.28	+0.62	+0.13	-0.57	-0.01	+6.0	+4.2
9. Miscellaneous											
yprus	1960	R	-	-0.58	-0.12	-	-	-0.46	-	-	-1.3
		U	-	+0.91	+1.06	-	-	-0.15	-	-	+2.5
uyana	1946	R	-	-1.60	-2.27	-	-	+0.67	-	-	-4.2
		U	-	-0.51	+1.64	-	-	-2.15	-	-	-1.2
	1960	R	-5.88	-4.21	-4.71	-1.25	-0.41	+0.50	-0.01	-19.8	-14.2
		U	-4.32	-3.22	-1.97	-0.86	-0.22	-1.25	-0.02	-12.4	-9.2
srael	1961	R	-	-2.28	-2.76	-	-	+0.48	-	-	-7.1
		U	-	+1.56	+1.39	-	-	+0.17	-	-	+4.5

The meaning of the indices is explained in Chapter 4, sections 4.2 and 4.3. For explanation of the derivation of the measures, see Appendix E.

See also Guinea (Tropical Africa), Indonesia and Pakistan (South and East Asia).

Table A.7. Age-specific activity rates of males, censuses of 1946-1966

Country and census year	GYAL[a]	15-19	20-29	30-44	45-64	65+	20-24
1. Tropical Africa							
1 Central African Rep. 1960	53.6	64.1	93.6	96.9	90.0	55.0	91.4
2 Ghana 1960	57.3	61.0	93.7	97.5	94.1	73.6	90.9
3 Guinea 1954/55	54.7	83.5	96.2	97.4	90.8	46.6	95.0
4 Liberia 1962	53.1	46.4	81.0	93.8	89.6	63.8	74.8
5 Namibia 1960	61.4	80.0*	97.5	99.2	97.8	80.2	95.4*
6 Nigeria 1963	60.5	56.1	90.9	97.3	97.3	91.6	85.7
1a. Portuguese Africa							
7 Mozambique 1950	59.6	98.3	99.3	98.9	96.9	68.8	99.3
8 Portuguese Guinea 1950	57.2	99.0	98.5	98.3	95.5	52.7	98.4
2. Arab countries							
9 Iraq 1957	59.8	73.1	92.8	97.0	93.8	72.6	89.6
10 Jordan 1961	48.8	51.9	91.9	94.6	80.9	41.8	89.2
11 Libya 1964	51.5	39.6	87.2	95.0	88.8	54.6	80.6
12 Morocco 1960	56.3	61.0	90.6	95.5	92.5	67.8	87.3
13 Syria 1960	51.6	64.4	92.0	96.8	86.7	44.0	88.1
14 Tunisia 1966	50.9	51.4	93.5	96.6	87.1	45.2	91.0
15 United Arab Rep. 1947	62.6	85.6	94.1	97.5	95.3	81.7	92.4
16 1960	56.6	68.5	91.4	98.0	93.5	61.1	86.8
3. Other Moslem countries[b]							
17 Iran 1956	60.1	80.7	96.0	98.8	95.6	73.3	94.1
18 1966	53.4	68.0	93.7	97.7	86.9	45.4	90.8
19 Turkey 1955	63.9	88.0	96.9	98.5	96.7	86.2	96.1
20 1960	62.8	78.8	95.8	98.2	96.6	84.8	94.2
21 1965	61.4	74.0	94.8	98.5	95.9	79.6	92.2
4. South and East Asia							
22 Ceylon 1946	57.4	59.2	89.1	98.9	91.8	77.4	83.3
23 1953	54.2	46.5	88.0	95.4	91.1	67.1	81.3
24 1963	51.4	46.3	89.7	96.4	88.1	50.8	84.2
25 India 1961	58.0	71.4	95.1	97.6	93.8	66.6	93.0
26 NSS[c]	53.8	75.0	93.7	96.1	85.3	49.9	92.0
27 Indonesia 1961	57.4	66.7	90.2	96.4	92.7	72.6	87.2
28 Japan 1950	53.1	61.7*	93.0	97.3	90.2	51.6	90.5
29 1955	52.8	54.3	92.2	97.2	91.5	52.4	88.1
30 1960	52.4	51.6	92.4	97.7	91.5	50.8	87.9
31 1965	52.1	39.1	92.7	98.0	93.0	50.7	87.4

Table A.7. (continued)

25-29	30-34	35-39	40-44	45-49	50-54	55-59	60-64	65-69	70-74	75+	
				1. Tropical Africa							
95.7	96.9	97.0	96.8	95.9	93.5	89.4	81.1*	71.5*	59.1*	34.5*	1
96.5	97.5	97.6	97.4	96.8	95.8	94.2	89.4	84.4	76.4	59.9	2
97.4	97.1	97.9	97.2	97.4	94.8	91.7	79.5	68.4	50.4*	20.8*	3
87.3	93.0	94.4	93.9	93.8	92.1	91.1	81.5	75.7	63.0	52.8	4
99.5*	99.1*	99.3*	99.3*	99.2*	99.0*	98.1*	94.8*	88.2*	82.1*	70.3*	5
96.1	96.8*	97.3*	97.7*	98.0*	97.9	96.6	96.6	95.7*	93.6*	85.6*	6
				1a. Portuguese Africa							
99.3	99.2	98.9	98.6	98.2	96.9	96.5	95.9	96.3	57.5	52.7	7
98.5	97.8	98.6	98.4	98.5	97.5	96.6	89.5	80.1	58.9	19.0	8
				2. Arab countries							
96.0	97.1	96.8	97.1	97.0	95.8	93.3	89.1	83.3	75.6*	58.7*	9
94.5	95.3*	94.6	93.8	91.9	86.6	78.2	67.1	55.1	44.0	26.4	10
93.9	95.3	95.4*	94.3*	94.4*	92.2*	87.3*	81.3*	72.7*	57.7*	33.3*	11
94.0*	95.6*	95.6*	95.3*	95.2*	93.7*	92.4*	88.6*	77.0*	70.2*	56.1*	12
95.9	97.1	97.0	96.1	94.6	91.2	86.2	74.8	60.6	45.0	26.3	13
96.1	96.8	96.7	96.2	95.1	92.5	86.8	74.2	61.4	44.2	29.9	14
95.9	97.2	97.7	97.6	97.6	95.7	94.8	92.9	89.8*	84.4*	71.0*	15
96.1	97.8	98.2	98.0	97.8	96.4	94.5	85.2	74.3	63.5	45.6	16
				3. Other Moslem countries[b]							
97.9	98.7	98.9*	98.9*	98.3*	97.2*	95.5*	91.5*	85.4*	75.9*	58.6*	17
96.6*	97.7*	97.9	97.5	95.9	91.1	86.4	74.1	64.0	43.8	28.5	18
97.7	98.3	98.5	98.5	98.5	97.9	96.4	93.8	91.0*	88.3*	79.4*	19
97.3	98.1	98.3	98.2	98.2	97.8	96.7	93.9	89.1*	86.0*	79.3*	20
97.4	98.4	98.6	98.5	98.1	97.2	95.7	92.6	85.9*	81.0*	72.0*	21
				4. South and East Asia							
95.0	99.3	98.4	99.0	97.5	92.5*	88.7*	88.7*	88.1*	81.5*	62.5*	22
94.7	95.1	95.8	95.3	95.4	93.8	91.2	84.2	77.7*	70.3*	53.3*	23
95.2	96.5	96.6	96.0	95.6	92.8	87.7	76.4	67.9	51.7	32.8	24
97.2	97.5	97.8	97.6	97.4	96.6	93.8	87.5	80.6	69.5	49.5	25
95.4	96.8	96.4	95.0	92.5	89.1	83.7	75.7	63.6	50.8	35.4	26
93.2	95.8	96.9*	96.6*	96.3*	94.8*	92.4*	87.2*	81.7*	74.3	61.7	27
95.5	96.5*	97.8*	97.6*	96.3*	93.9*	90.4*	80.3	69.6	52.2	33.0	28
96.2	97.0	97.3	97.4	97.0	95.5	91.1	82.4	70.8*	52.9*	33.4*	29
96.9	97.8	97.7	97.7	97.1	96.0	90.5	82.5	70.2	52.3	30.0	30
98.0	97.9	97.9	98.0	97.9	97.0	92.8	84.5	71.1*	52.0*	28.9*	31

	Country and census year		GYAL[a]	15-19	20-29	30-44	45-64	65+	20-24

4. South and East Asia (continued)

	Country and census year		GYAL[a]	15-19	20-29	30-44	45-64	65+	20-24
32	Khmer Republic	1962	53.0	58.0	92.7	98.8	91.0	46.0	87.9
33	Korea, South	1960	47.9	45.2	83.3	96.3	86.7	35.3	75.9
34	Malaysia:								
35	West Malaysia	1957	54.4	60.0	95.1	97.5	89.9	58.4	92.7
36	Sabah	1960	56.7	69.0	96.4	98.8	92.7	55.1	94.2
37	Sarawak	1960	56.0	70.9	95.7	98.2	90.3	50.5	93.6
38	Mauritius	1952	49.3	59.1	90.4	95.7	88.1	32.0	87.4
39		1962	46.9	43.2	90.6	97.2	83.5	28.3	84.9
40	Nepal	1961	56.9	91.6	97.4	98.4	92.4	51.1	96.5
41	Pakistan	1961	60.7	76.7	92.6	95.6	93.9	80.1	89.8
42	Philippines	1960	55.4	59.3	86.1	95.1	91.7	68.3	80.8
43	Ryukyu Islands	1950	53.8	67.5	93.8	95.6	89.7	54.9	92.6
44		1955	54.5	50.8	91.7	95.1	94.4	61.4	88.4
45		1960	52.4	46.3	91.1	95.5	89.9	56.4	87.8
46	Taiwan	1956	46.6	77.5	93.7	96.3	72.4	14.4	91.2
47	Thailand	1954	57.2	73.9	90.9	98.1	93.7	58.7	85.7
48		1960	54.9	76.8	92.1	97.7	92.2	47.7	88.2

5. Latin America, Spain, and Portugal

49	Argentina	1960	49.0	72.1	93.4	97.4	77.5	36.4	90.2
50	Bolivia	1950	60.9	78.3	94.8	97.1	94.7	78.9	92.9
51	Brazil	1950	57.5	80.6	94.9	96.9	91.4	63.8	93.4
52		1960	55.1	72.3	94.4	97.1	88.5	57.4	92.3
53	Chile	1952	56.0	66.1	93.9	97.0	90.6	68.3	91.5
54		1960	51.9	61.7	94.3	96.8	85.5	49.3	91.6
55	Colombia	1951	59.2	84.8	96.4	97.9	94.8	71.1	95.4
56		1964	55.5	66.3	92.8	97.3	92.8	58.4	89.8
57	Costa Rica	1950	60.8	91.1	97.4	98.6	96.1	72.3	96.7
58		1963	57.0	77.8	96.0	98.3	95.2	57.8	94.1
59	Cuba	1953	54.8	76.6	92.8	94.9	89.5	54.5	91.5
60	Dominican Rep.	1960	58.5	70.1	96.4	98.6	96.9	69.5	95.0
61	Ecuador	1950	61.7	80.5	94.7	97.2	96.2	86.4	93.0
62		1962	62.4	79.4	96.3	99.0	97.5	85.4	94.2
63	El Salvador	1950	62.2	88.9	96.2	97.4	96.4	82.2	95.5
64		1961	60.7	78.0	95.6	97.8	96.0	79.1	94.1
65	Guatemala	1950	60.9	90.6	97.1	97.9	95.9	72.3	96.6
66		1964	60.0	81.1	96.2	98.0	94.9	73.2	95.2
67	Honduras	1961	58.9	87.5	97.2	98.3	94.8	61.9	96.4
68	Mexico	1950	63.6	79.0	95.3	98.7	98.2	96.2	93.3
69		1960	58.7	67.8	92.7	95.8	93.9	81.1	91.3

Table A.7. (continued)

25-29	30-34	35-39	40-44	45-49	50-54	55-59	60-64	65-69	70-74	75+	
				4. South and East Asia (continued)							
97.4	98.4	99.1	98.8	98.3	96.5	91.0	78.1	61.8	45.1	31.1	32
90.8	95.6	96.3	96.9	96.3	91.1	88.4	71.0	50.7	36.4*	18.9*	33
											34
97.5	97.8	97.7	97.1	96.2	93.7	88.4	81.3	69.9*	57.5*	47.8*	35
98.6	98.7	98.9	98.6	98.1	96.0	93.4	83.3	71.3	56.0	38.0	36
97.8	98.4	98.3	97.8	97.1	95.0	90.1	78.9	67.9	49.5	34.1	37
93.5	95.0	96.1*	95.9*	95.0*	92.2*	87.9*	77.4*	49.5*	29.1*	17.6*	38
96.4*	97.9*	97.5	96.1	94.6	90.0	83.1	66.4	41.6	25.5	17.8	39
98.2	98.3	98.7	98.3	98.0	97.5	94.9	79.1	63.2	48.8	41.3	40
95.4*	95.6*	95.6*	95.6*	95.9*	95.7*	93.2	90.8*	86.9*	81.7*	71.6*	41
91.3	94.5	95.5	95.4	95.1	93.6	91.7	86.4	79.2*	71.5*	54.2*	42
94.9	95.6	95.6	95.5	94.5	92.6	89.5	82.3	71.5	59.1*	34.2*	43
95.1	95.9	94.5	95.0	98.6	98.9	87.5	92.5	82.0	63.9	38.2	44
94.3	95.3	95.6	95.5	94.8	93.5	88.6	82.7	74.2	58.6	36.2	45
96.1	96.4	96.8	95.9	93.6	84.4	67.9	43.6	25.4	12.5	5.3	46
96.1	97.8	98.3	98.3	97.8	97.1*	93.7*	86.3*	74.1*	60.5*	41.5*	47
96.0	97.5	97.8	97.8*	97.3*	96.1*	92.5*	82.9*	67.8*	49.0*	26.2*	48
				5. Latin America, Spain and Portugal							
96.7	97.8	97.8	96.5	94.6	87.1	71.4	56.9	46.7	37.2	25.3	49
96.7	97.3	97.3	96.8	96.6	95.5	94.6	92.2	88.3	81.3	67.0	50
96.4	97.0*	97.2*	96.6*	95.9*	94.2*	90.7*	85.0*	78.2*	67.9*	45.3*	51
96.5	97.2*	97.3*	96.9*	94.9*	92.2	87.6	79.2	69.0	59.4*	43.8*	52
96.3	97.1	97.2	96.6	94.8	91.9	89.8	85.8	80.8	70.7	53.5	53
97.0	97.5	97.0	95.7	93.4	88.0	83.7	76.8	66.0*	50.9*	31.0*	54
97.3	97.9	98.0	97.7	97.3	96.4	94.8	90.5	85.6	74.0	53.8	55
95.9	97.0	97.6	97.4	96.9	95.1	92.5	86.8	72.0	61.9	41.3	56
98.2*	98.6*	98.7*	98.6*	97.9*	97.2*	96.1*	93.4*	90.9*	71.7	54.5	57
97.8	98.3	98.4	98.2	98.0	96.8	95.4	90.4	72.1	61.8	39.5	58
94.1	94.8	95.0	94.8	94.3	92.4	89.2	82.1	70.8*	53.1*	39.6*	59
97.8	98.6	98.6	98.5	98.2	97.9	96.7	95.1	81.8	73.0	53.9	60
96.4*	96.9*	97.2*	97.4*	97.2*	96.6*	96.0*	94.9*	92.7*	89.1*	77.6	61
98.5	99.0	99.1	98.9	98.8	98.1	97.1	95.9	92.9	88.7	74.8	62
96.9*	97.4*	97.5*	97.5*	97.5*	97.4*	96.4*	94.5*	91.4*	85.9*	69.4	63
97.1	97.9	97.8	97.7	97.6	97.1	95.7	93.7	90.9	82.6	63.9	64
97.7	97.9	98.0	97.8	97.7	96.7	96.3	92.9	87.9	78.1	50.8	65
97.3	97.9	98.1	97.9	97.3	96.6	95.0	90.8	85.6	76.9	57.0	66
98.0	98.3	98.4	98.1	98.0	96.1	94.8	90.1	82.7	64.8	38.2	67
97.3	98.5	98.8	98.7	98.6	98.3	98.1	97.8	97.1	97.0	94.3	68
94.1	95.4	96.0	96.1	95.7	94.9	93.5	91.3	88.3	84.0	70.9	69

	Country and census year	GYAL[a]	15-19	20-29	30-44	45-64	65+	20-24

5. Latin America, Spain, and Portugal (continued)

	Country and census year	GYAL[a]	15-19	20-29	30-44	45-64	65+	20-24
70	Nicaragua	1950	64.1	89.6	97.6	98.6	97.9	86.6	96.9
71		1963	59.5	75.5	95.4	97.8	94.9	72.6	93.6
72	Panama	1950	57.6	68.3	96.2	98.1	93.1	68.9	94.8
73		1960	54.7	63.2	94.4	97.1	91.4	56.8	92.3
74	Paraguay	1950	59.8	82.7	97.4	98.3	96.9	72.9	96.6
75		1962	59.8	81.7	97.0	98.7	96.3	74.1	95.7
76	Peru	1961	56.9	54.9	94.5	98.8	96.1	69.2	91.6
77	Portugal	1950	56.8	75.5	90.4	95.8	89.8	65.8	87.2
78		1960	57.7	86.5	96.5	97.9	90.2	61.6	95.0
79	Puerto Rico	1950	46.1	39.5*	78.3	87.5	82.1	43.8	78.2
80		1960	43.0	27.7	80.6	89.5	80.6	26.3	76.0
81	Spain	1950	57.6	79.9	94.9	98.7	94.8	63.8	92.7
82		1960	55.1	74.0	93.1	97.8	94.2	53.6	90.4
83	Uruguay	1963	46.6	69.3	95.2	97.4	76.4	21.3	93.5
84	Venezuela	1950	58.0	79.2	94.2	96.0	92.6	71.1	93.1
85		1961	57.3	62.1	94.8	98.0	94.0	69.0	92.2

6. Eastern Europe

	Country and census year	GYAL[a]	15-19	20-29	30-44	45-64	65+	20-24
86	Bulgaria	1956	53.7	53.7	89.1	97.6	92.7	58.7	82.1
87		1965	44.8	35.6	86.9	97.7	82.1	21.4	78.0
88	Czechoslovakia	1961	46.3	46.8	95.8	97.9	81.2	23.0	93.4
89	Hungary	1949	55.4	77.7	94.8	97.9	89.7	59.9	92.6
90		1960	55.1	78.9	97.1	98.8	89.4	56.1	95.3
91	Rumania	1956	59.7	88.1	96.3	98.5	94.3	68.7	94.8
92		1966	49.5	48.5	94.0	98.1	87.0	36.9	90.8
93	Yugoslavia	1953	55.8	81.5	95.0	98.0	88.6	58.7	93.7

7. Middle Europe

	Country and census year	GYAL[a]	15-19	20-29	30-44	45-64	65+	20-24
94	Austria	1961	47.7	81.5	93.5	97.6	85.8	14.4	90.2
95	Finland	1950	54.4	74.2	92.5	97.6	93.3	53.3	90.4
96		1960	50.2	58.3	90.5	97.3	90.1	37.0	86.1
97	France	1954	49.9	65.5*	93.7	97.0	86.5	35.6	91.2*
98		1962	47.4	59.6*	93.4	94.9	84.7	24.5	90.5*
99	Germany, West	1950	49.7	84.3	93.8	96.9	87.8	24.7	93.2
100		1961	49.4	81.3	93.7	97.7	87.7	21.8	91.1
101	Greece	1961	52.1	66.5*	93.1	96.6	87.0	43.8	90.3*
102	Italy	1951	53.6	83.0	93.1	97.5	87.4	42.7	90.5
103		1961	47.3	68.9	92.3	96.3	80.5	23.2	88.8
104	Switzerland	1950	54.1	73.9*	93.5	98.6	94.5	49.0	90.8*
105		1960	53.3	69.6*	94.3	98.9	95.5	42.7	91.4*

182

25-29	30-34	35-39	40-44	45-49	50-54	55-59	60-64	65-69	70-74	75+	

5. Latin America, Spain, and Portugal (continued)

25-29	30-34	35-39	40-44	45-49	50-54	55-59	60-64	65-69	70-74	75+	
98.3	98.5	98.7	98.6	98.6	98.3	97.8	96.8	94.7	88.4	76.6	70
97.3	97.6	97.9*	97.7*	97.3*	96.2*	94.7*	91.5*	85.4*	76.2*	56.1*	71
97.7	97.9	98.1	98.4	97.8	96.3	93.4	85.2	77.3	71.6	57.9	72
96.5	97.0	97.1	97.1	96.4	95.0	92.4	81.8	68.9	57.8	43.8	73
98.1*	98.4*	98.4*	98.2*	98.0*	97.7*	96.8*	95.0*	87.7*	76.0*	55.1*	74
98.2	98.7*	98.8*	98.5*	98.0*	97.1*	96.0*	94.1*	89.1*	77.3*	55.8	75
97.5	98.7	98.8	98.7	98.5	97.7	96.1	91.9	85.3	70.7	51.7	76
93.5	95.6	96.0	95.7	94.6	92.3	88.2	84.3	78.1	69.0	50.3	77
98.0	98.4	98.1	97.2	96.2	93.5	89.4	81.8	72.9	63.4	48.4	78
78.3	83.3	89.0	90.1	89.7	86.3	81.2	71.2	60.4	45.7	25.5	79
85.2	89.0	89.9	89.7	89.3	86.5	81.7	64.8	40.0	25.4	13.5	80
97.1	99.0	98.7	98.5	98.2	97.5	94.7	89.0	80.0	66.0	45.3	81
95.8*	97.9*	97.8*	97.6*	97.3*	96.0*	94.0*	89.4*	74.3*	55.5*	31.0*	82
96.8	97.8*	97.6*	96.8*	93.4*	87.0	72.8	52.4	32.0*	21.0*	10.9*	83
95.3*	95.9*	96.2*	95.8*	95.6*	94.1*	92.1*	88.4*	82.2*	74.6*	56.5	84
97.3	98.1	98.1	97.9	97.6	96.2	94.5	87.8	79.6	72.8	54.6	85

6. Eastern Europe

25-29	30-34	35-39	40-44	45-49	50-54	55-59	60-64	65-69	70-74	75+	
96.2	97.4	97.6	97.7	97.5	96.3	92.6	84.5	74.9	58.2	42.9	86
95.8	98.0	97.7	97.4	96.5	93.1	83.6	55.1	35.8	21.4	7.0	87
98.2	98.4	98.0	97.3	96.0	92.9	84.8	51.1	37.9	22.8	8.3	88
96.9	98.4	97.8	97.5	96.1	93.6	88.4	80.7	72.8	63.0	44.1	89
98.9	99.0	98.8	98.5	97.9	96.7	93.3	69.6	65.5	58.8	44.1	90
97.8	98.4*	98.6*	98.5*	97.6*	96.7	94.2	88.8*	80.0*	70.5*	55.5*	91
97.2	98.3	98.4	97.8	96.7	94.0	89.6	67.5	50.6	37.4	22.6	92
96.2	97.8	98.2	98.0	97.0	94.1	84.9	78.3	71.2	62.5	42.3	93

7. Middle Europe

25-29	30-34	35-39	40-44	45-49	50-54	55-59	60-64	65-69	70-74	75+	
96.9	98.4	97.5	97.0	96.2	93.9	87.0	66.0	24.4	15.0	3.8	94
94.7*	97.5*	97.8*	97.7*	97.2*	95.9*	93.4	86.6	73.7*	54.0*	32.3*	95
94.9	97.4	97.3	97.2	96.4	94.5	90.3	79.0	53.7	36.4*	21.0*	96
96.3*	97.3	96.7	97.1	96.4	94.0	83.8	71.7	52.8*	35.0*	19.0*	97
96.4*	97.3*	97.1*	90.2*	95.1*	92.3*	83.6*	67.8*	36.6*	23.4*	13.5*	98
94.3	96.4	97.3	97.2	96.7	93.5	87.6	73.5	39.6	26.7	7.8	99
96.2	98.3	97.8*	97.1	96.1*	93.8*	88.7*	72.3*	32.6*	21.4*	11.3	100
95.9*	97.3*	96.6	95.8	94.9	91.5	85.6	76.1	61.5	40.9	29.1	101
95.8	97.5	97.9	97.2	96.3	93.9	88.4	71.2	55.8	42.8	29.7	102
95.8	97.2	96.5	95.2	94.0	90.8	83.7	53.6	35.0*	22.5*	12.2*	103
96.2*	98.4*	98.7*	98.6*	98.2*	97.1*	94.9*	87.9*	66.1*	46.5*	34.4*	104
97.1*	98.8*	99.1*	98.9*	98.7*	97.9*	96.0*	89.2*	60.6*	39.6*	27.8*	105

Table A.7. (continued)

Country and census year		GYAL[a]	15-19	20-29	30-44	45-64	65+	20-24

8. Northwestern Europe, Northern America and Oceania

	Country and census year		GYAL	15-19	20-29	30-44	45-64	65+	20-24
106	Australia	1947	51.4	81.1	95.3	98.0	90.6	32.0	93.8
107		1954	51.4	79.7	97.5	98.3	91.1	30.7	96.6
108		1961	50.0	69.6	96.5	98.4	91.4	25.2	94.9
109	Belgium	1947	47.8	71.1	90.2	96.1	84.9	23.5	84.9
110		1961	44.9	50.3	92.4	96.7	85.2	9.6	87.6
111	Canada	1951	50.5	58.5	94.1	96.8	90.0	35.6	92.4
112		1961	47.1	41.4	90.4	94.4	86.6	28.2	87.2
113	Denmark	1950	52.6	84.2	94.3	98.3	93.8	34.0	92.0
114		1960	52.1	74.9	93.9	98.6	94.3	33.4	91.3
115	Ireland	1951	56.1	78.9*	96.8	97.5	92.6	58.1	96.3
116		1961	53.9	62.8*	93.1	97.4	92.6	51.8	90.0
117	Netherlands	1960	48.8	63.1	94.1	98.6	92.3	19.0	91.1
118	New Zealand	1951	48.7	71.3	96.8	97.7	85.3	24.8	95.9
119		1956	49.1	68.0	97.2	98.3	87.8	24.6	96.0
120		1961	48.8	65.3	96.4	98.4	88.8	22.4	94.5
121	Norway	1950	53.0	72.7	91.9	97.8	94.3	41.4	89.4
122		1960	50.8	53.7	88.1	98.1	94.4	35.9	81.9
123	Sweden	1950	51.3	74.4	93.1	98.1	91.2	34.8	90.0
124		1960	48.6	59.2	89.1	96.6	91.5	26.1	85.1*
125		1965	47.0	50.7	85.1	95.5	91.1	22.7	79.6
126	United Kingdom	1951	52.1	83.9	96.2	98.5	94.5	29.8	94.9
127		1961	51.1	74.8	95.6	98.8	96.3	23.7	93.3
128	United States	1950	48.6	44.6	86.1	94.3	87.5	39.1	81.9
129		1960	47.8	43.1	90.0	95.7	88.0	29.3	86.1

9. Miscellaneous

	Country and census year		GYAL	15-19	20-29	30-44	45-64	65+	20-24
130	Guyana	1946	56.5	78.4	98.3	98.5	92.5	59.6	97.8
131		1960	52.3	78.2	96.9	97.6	89.1	40.5	96.8
132	Haiti	1950	63.2	83.5	96.9	98.8	97.8	87.0	95.5
133	Hong Kong	1961	51.2	54.3	93.4	98.2	90.4	40.4	89.3
134	Jamaica	1953	56.8	65.3*	93.7	96.4	92.9	65.6	91.9
135		1960	54.0	57.2	93.7	97.5	91.4	55.2	90.3
136	Singapore	1957	49.6	59.4	95.1	98.4	85.6	32.7	92.3
137		1966	46.8	44.1	94.6	98.4	81.3	26.9	91.7
138	South Africa	1946	60.2	74.6	97.1	98.9	95.8	68.8	95.6
139		1960	55.1	50.4	97.6	98.8	96.5	53.0	96.1
140	Trinidad & Tobago	1946	55.1	75.5	98.3	98.4	92.1	53.7	97.7
141		1960	51.4	53.2*	97.9	99.4	91.4	38.3	96.1*

*Estimated by interpolation or extrapolation.

[a]Gross years of active life of males in ages 10 and over. See Appendix D for explanation.

184

Table A.7. (continued)

25-29	30-34	35-39	40-44	45-49	50-54	55-59	60-64	65-69	70-74	75+	

8. Northwestern Europe, Northern America, and Oceania

25-29	30-34	35-39	40-44	45-49	50-54	55-59	60-64	65-69	70-74	75+	
96.8	98.1	98.1	97.7	96.7	94.3	91.3	79.9	49.7	28.7	17.6	106
98.4	98.5	98.3	98.0	97.3	95.7	91.5	79.8	48.8	29.0	14.4	107
98.2	98.6	98.5	98.0	97.4	96.0	92.7	79.6	40.1	23.8	11.8	108
95.6	96.6	96.3	95.5	93.8	89.6	82.9	73.4	33.5*	25.0*	12.0*	109
97.2	97.8	96.6	95.6	94.0	91.1	85.1	70.8	14.7	9.2*	4.8*	110
95.9*	97.1*	96.8*	96.5*	95.5*	93.4*	89.6	81.4	60.1	31.3	15.5	111
93.6	94.6	94.6	94.0	92.9	90.7	86.8	75.8	47.6*	25.2*	11.9*	112
96.5*	98.1*	98.5*	98.3*	97.7*	96.7*	94.7	85.9	57.5	29.4	15.1	113
96.6	98.6	98.7	98.5	98.0	97.0	94.7	87.5	58.4	28.1	13.6	114
97.3	97.7	97.5	97.3	96.4*	94.6*	92.4*	86.9*	73.7*	58.2*	42.5	115
96.3	97.4	97.5	97.3	97.0*	95.8*	93.5*	83.9*	69.6	50.4	35.3	116
97.1	98.6	98.8	98.5	98.1	96.8	93.4	80.8	33.2	17.5	6.5	117
97.7	97.8	97.8	97.5	97.0	93.8	86.6	63.9	40.0	23.3	11.1	118
98.5	98.6	98.3	98.1	97.6	96.0	90.1	67.5	41.6	22.6	9.6	119
98.2*	98.7*	98.5*	98.0*	97.9*	96.6*	91.6*	69.0*	39.1*	20.7*	7.4	120
94.4	97.5*	98.0*	97.8*	97.4*	97.0*	94.3*	88.6	73.4	32.9*	17.9*	121
94.3	97.9	98.2	98.1	97.7	96.9	95.0	88.0	70.5	26.7	10.5	122
96.1	98.1	98.3	97.9	97.0	95.5	92.5	79.7	56.4	30.4	17.6	123
93.1*	96.3*	96.8*	96.8*	96.2	95.1	92.3	82.5	50.6	20.3	7.3	124
90.6	95.1	95.8	95.8	95.6	94.5	91.9	82.4	45.7	16.8	5.7	125
97.6	98.3	98.5	98.6	98.3	97.1	95.0	87.7	47.9	28.2	13.2	126
97.9	98.7	98.7	98.9	98.8	96.4	97.1	91.0	39.9	21.4	9.9	127
90.3	93.9	94.6	94.3	93.2	90.6	86.7	79.4	59.8	38.7	18.6	128
93.9	95.8	95.8	95.4	94.4	92.2	87.7	77.6	43.9	28.7	15.5	129

9. Miscellaneous

25-29	30-34	35-39	40-44	45-49	50-54	55-59	60-64	65-69	70-74	75+	
98.7	98.9	98.8	97.8	97.4	95.4	91.3	85.9	71.5	62.0	45.4	130
97.0	97.6	97.8	97.5	96.7	94.6	89.4	75.9	53.5	42.0	25.9	131
98.3	98.7	98.9	98.8	98.7	98.3	97.6	96.4	94.5	90.2	76.3	132
97.6*	98.0*	98.2*	98.4*	97.7*	95.7*	89.9*	78.1*	61.3*	41.4*	18.5*	133
95.4	96.3	96.8	96.3	95.9	97.5	93.0	85.4	80.3	67.3*	49.1*	134
96.9*	97.5*	97.7*	97.3*	97.0*	94.1*	89.9*	84.4*	73.6*	57.1*	34.9*	135
98.0	98.6	98.5	98.0	96.9	93.5	85.1	66.9	49.8	30.9	17.4	136
97.5	98.9	98.7	97.7	95.8	91.9	79.0	58.5	39.4	23.2	18.0	137
98.6	98.9	98.9	98.8	98.6	97.8	96.2	90.6	82.5	67.8	56.1	138
99.1*	99.5*	99.1*	97.6*	98.8*	97.9*	96.2*	93.3*	69.3*	50.0*	39.8*	139
98.8	98.5	98.4	98.2	97.0	95.3	92.3	83.9	70.7	58.1	32.3	140
99.6*	99.8*	99.7*	98.8*	97.0*	95.8*	90.2*	82.4*	61.5*	32.3*	21.0*	141

[b]See also Guinea (Tropical Africa), Indonesia and Pakistan (South and East Asia).
[c]Averages of rates indicated by results of National Sample Survey round 14 (1958-1959) and 15 (1959-1960).

185

Table A.8. Age-specific activity rates of females, censuses of 1946-1966

Country and census year		GYAL[a]	15-19	20-29	30-44	45-64	65+	20-24
		1. Tropical Africa						
1	Central African Rep. 1960	47.3	83.3	93.9	96.6	75.5	23.8	92.2
2	Ghana 1960	37.5	53.3	52.2	60.9	67.9	45.5	52.7
3	Guinea 1954/55	42.9	76.8	88.8	91.7	64.1	12.2	88.2
4	Liberia 1962	26.1	34.9	42.7	49.6	43.3	20.2	41.2
5	Namibia 1960	15.9	36.1*	27.8	17.5	22.1	20.2	33.7*
6	Nigeria 1963	20.2	19.2	27.4	31.5	34.3	30.9	25.5
		1a. Portuguese Africa						
7	Mozambique 1950	4.2	5.3	8.8	9.8	6.8	1.3	8.4
8	Portuguese Guinea 1950	0.9	2.0	0.7	0.7	1.1	2.3	0.8
		2. Arab countries						
9	Iraq 1957	2.0	3.3	3.2	2.7	2.8	2.2	3.5
10	Jordan 1961	2.3	4.8	5.8	4.2	3.0	1.4	6.9
11	Libya 1964	2.9	5.0	4.6	5.0	4.9	1.8	4.9
12	Morocco 1960	6.4	9.9	7.3	9.2	11.0	6.7	7.6
13	Syria 1960	4.4	11.4	9.6	8.1	5.2	1.4	10.0
14	Tunisia 1966	15.5	30.7	25.6	27.2	26.1	12.9	27.6
15	United Arab Rep. 1947	6.6	12.1	8.4	9.7	10.2	7.7	8.7
16	1960	3.3	8.6	6.1	4.7	3.9	1.8	7.3
		3. Other Moslem countries[b]						
17	Iran 1956	6.1	12.1	8.9	9.4	9.4	5.8	9.3
18	1966	7.3	15.5	13.5	12.3	9.8	4.4	14.2
19	Turkey 1955	48.2	74.3	72.9	72.4	71.0	63.3	73.4
20	1960	44.2	66.2	66.1	65.6	65.4	59.8	65.7
21	1965	34.3	60.6	60.7	59.9	60.0	13.7	61.1
		4. South and East Asia						
22	Ceylon 1946	18.1	24.3	25.1	31.2	30.0	20.7	23.8
23	1953	19.8	27.7	28.6	32.3	33.9	23.1	28.7
24	1963	12.7	21.7	28.6	25.8	19.2	5.9	29.4
25	India 1961	25.5	40.7	44.0	48.6	40.8	16.3	43.3
26	NSS[c]	20.4	30.1	36.0	42.6	31.3	10.6	34.0
27	Indonesia 1961	21.9	30.6	27.0	31.7	39.6	27.8	27.4
28	Japan 1950	28.7	54.8*	56.1	51.3	46.5	20.7	64.0
29	1955	29.0	50.1	60.0	52.8	47.4	20.0	68.2
30	1960	29.5	49.7	59.7	54.4	48.5	20.6	69.4
31	1965	29.2	38.1	58.1	56.0	52.3	17.1	69.5

186

Table A.8. (continued)

25-29	30-34	35-39	40-44	45-49	50-54	55-59	60-64	65-69	70-74	75+	
				1.	Tropical Africa						
95.6	96.4	97.1	96.3	93.1	87.2	70.3	51.6*	36.5*	24.2*	10.7*	1
51.6	57.3	59.6	65.6	66.7	70.1	70.5	64.3	59.5	49.1	28.0	2
89.3	91.6	91.9	91.6	86.7	73.5	59.5	36.9	22.8	10.7*	3.1*	3
44.3	47.9	49.8	51.0	49.9	46.9	44.3	32.0	26.3	19.7	14.5	4
21.9*	17.0*	16.6*	18.9*	21.9*	22.5*	22.9*	21.3*	21.0*	20.2*	19.3*	5
29.2	30.3*	31.5*	32.6*	33.9*	35.0	34.2	34.2	33.5*	31.7*	27.5*	6
				1a.	Portuguese Africa						
9.1	9.4	10.0	10.0	9.7	8.7	6.5	2.3	1.8	1.3	0.7	7
0.7	0.6	0.8	0.7	0.9	1.1	1.1	1.2	1.2	2.0	3.8	8
				2.	Arab countries						
3.0	2.7	2.6	2.9	2.7	3.0	2.8	2.7	2.3	2.3	2.0	9
4.7	4.3*	4.2*	4.2*	3.9*	3.3*	2.6*	2.1*	1.8*	1.5*	0.8*	10
4.4	4.5	4.8	5.6	5.9	5.7	4.6	3.4	2.6	1.7	1.1	11
7.0	8.0	9.4	10.3	11.7	11.2	11.9	9.4	9.4	6.4	4.3	12
9.1	8.5	7.9	8.0	6.8	5.8	4.6	3.4	2.3	1.2	0.6	13
23.6	24.9	27.8	28.8	30.4	27.7	23.6	22.5	18.6	11.6	8.4	14
8.1	8.8	9.5	10.7	10.3	11.2	9.4	9.8	9.9*	8.1*	5.1*	15
4.8	4.5	4.4	5.3	4.4	4.7	3.4	3.2	2.3	2.0	1.3	16
				3.	Other Moslem countries[b]						
8.6*	8.7*	9.4*	10.1*	10.3*	10.0*	9.3*	7.9*	6.9*	5.8*	4.6*	17
12.8	12.1	12.3	12.5	12.1	10.8	8.8	7.6	5.7	4.8	2.8	18
72.5	72.0	71.8	73.5	71.4	73.8	67.7	71.1	64.5*	65.2*	60.3*	19
66.5	65.1	63.3	68.4	64.4	68.1	62.5	66.8	61.5*	62.9*	55.0*	20
60.3	60.3	58.2	61.0	60.3	62.3	57.4	59.9	19.4*	15.1*	6.5*	21
				4.	South and East Asia						
26.3	28.8	31.1	33.7	33.4	31.2*	28.7*	26.8*	24.8*	21.7*	15.6*	22
28.5	30.1	32.2	34.5	35.6	35.8	34.1	30.1	28.1*	24.0*	17.4*	23
27.8	25.1	26.0	26.2	26.3	21.1	17.9	11.3	7.8	5.6	4.1	24
44.8	46.7	49.1	50.1	49.3	45.0	39.2	29.7	23.8	15.3	9.7	25
38.1	41.4	43.3	43.2	39.3	34.5	28.6	22.9	17.7	11.4	2.8	26
26.6*	28.2*	31.5*	35.5*	39.1*	40.6*	40.3*	38.4*	34.2*	28.9	20.3	27
48.3	48.5*	51.6*	53.7*	52.5*	51.0*	44.8*	37.9	29.0	22.2	10.9	28
51.8	49.6	53.4	55.5	54.4	51.3	45.7	38.4	29.5*	20.6*	10.0*	29
50.1	51.3	55.1	56.7	56.8	51.7	46.7	39.1	30.6	21.1	10.2	30
46.8	48.3	57.6	62.2	61.9	57.8	50.0	39.6	27.5*	17.1*	6.8*	31

Table A.8. (continued)

Country and census year		GYAL[a]	15-19	20-29	30-44	45-64	65+	20-24

4. South and East Asia (continued)

	Country	Year	GYAL	15-19	20-29	30-44	45-64	65+	20-24
32	Khmer Republic	1962	32.4	66.9	61.1	61.3	50.3	14.9	63.7
33	Korea, South	1960	16.2	25.5	28.6	32.2	28.5	8.4	30.7
34	Malaysia:								
35	West Malaysia	1957	17.5	27.9	29.4	33.3	30.4	11.3	31.2
36	Sabah	1960	25.2	46.7	43.3	47.9	39.8	12.8	43.7
37	Sarawak	1960	30.4	58.4	56.0	58.0	45.3	14.8	55.7
38	Mauritius	1952	13.5	14.0	18.9	25.3	29.3	7.0	18.4
39		1962	10.9	8.4	16.7	22.4	22.0	6.5	16.5
40	Nepal	1961	32.4	77.2	66.8	58.8	46.1	17.5	69.1
41	Pakistan	1961	9.4	12.6	14.8	15.8	14.9	9.8	14.2
42	Philippines	1960	17.6	29.6	27.5	27.0	27.9	21.4	28.9
43	Ryukyu Islands	1950	32.8	59.1	56.8	62.1	55.5	22.1	60.2
44		1955	35.3	51.2	62.6	64.5	62.8	26.2	64.7
45		1960	35.1	45.1	64.9	63.8	60.9	29.1	70.9
46	Taiwan	1956	9.0	40.9	21.6	14.3	6.3	0.7	26.8
47	Thailand	1954	48.6	84.5	85.8	86.3	78.0	27.5	86.6
48		1960	47.4	84.6	85.8	86.7	77.4	25.7	86.6

5. Latin America, Spain, and Portugal

	Country	Year	GYAL	15-19	20-29	30-44	45-64	65+	20-24
49	Argentina	1960	12.4	33.8	34.5	22.8	14.0	5.0	39.6
50	Bolivia	1950	35.9	66.7	64.5	66.4	51.2	22.0	64.8
51	Brazil	1950	7.6	23.4	16.2	11.2	9.3	5.5	18.9
52		1960	10.3	23.4	20.6	17.1	14.2	8.5	22.5
53	Chile	1952	15.6	28.4	32.7	27.7	23.3	13.1	35.1
54		1960	12.5	23.5	30.2	22.8	17.8	7.8	32.4
55	Colombia	1951	11.5	23.6	22.0	19.1	16.8	10.4	23.9
56		1964	11.4	21.8	23.9	19.8	17.1	8.4	26.3
57	Costa Rica	1950	8.8	22.5	22.4	15.7	11.1	5.5	22.6
58		1963	9.0	19.7	22.3	17.7	11.7	4.1	24.4
59	Cuba	1953	11.1	17.2	22.2	21.1	16.5	8.3	22.3
60	Dominican Republic	1960	6.5	9.0	12.2	12.4	10.9	4.6	12.2
61	Ecuador	1950	22.8	33.9	34.0	35.3	35.8	28.7	34.9
62		1962	10.8	20.2	19.4	16.4	15.9	12.2	21.2
63	El Salvador	1950	10.5	20.7	19.4	17.1	14.7	10.7	20.9
64		1961	10.8	19.9	22.4	18.6	15.3	9.6	23.3
65	Guatemala	1950	8.4	15.8	13.9	13.6	12.9	8.8	14.9
66		1964	7.8	15.5	13.6	12.2	12.1	7.4	14.4
67	Honduras	1961	7.3	16.6	16.4	12.2	10.4	4.5	18.5
68	Mexico	1950	9.0	15.2	12.2	13.5	13.7	13.2	11.2
69		1960	11.4	20.7	19.9	17.1	17.8	13.3	22.9

25-29	30-34	35-39	40-44	45-49	50-54	55-59	60-64	65-69	70-74	75+	
			4.	South	and East	Asia	(continued)				
58.4	61.3	61.3	61.3	61.3	58.0	49.5	32.4	22.7	14.3	7.8	32
26.6	29.0	32.9	34.8	35.2	32.8	29.3	16.8	12.0	7.9*	5.4*	33
											34
27.7	30.4	34.1	35.3	36.3	33.7	29.3	22.3	15.6	11.4*	6.8*	35
43.0	44.5	49.4	49.9	50.6	43.5	37.8	27.1	21.0	10.9	6.6	36
56.2	56.6	59.1	58.3	56.0	50.3	43.4	31.6	22.5	14.2	7.8	37
19.4	21.7	25.2	29.0	31.3	30.7	29.7	25.3	9.3	6.3	5.2	38
17.0	19.3	22.1	25.7	26.3	25.8	23.5	12.4	8.0*	6.2*	5.4*	39
64.6	61.4	59.0	55.9	53.9	51.3	45.9	33.4	25.5	16.0	10.9	40
15.4*	15.6*	15.8*	16.1*	16.8*	16.3*	14.0*	12.6*	11.4*	9.9*	8.2*	41
26.1	26.3	26.8	27.9	28.9	29.0	28.3	25.5	23.7*	21.5*	19.1*	42
53.5	58.9	62.8	64.6	64.5	59.7	53.8	43.9	32.5	22.7*	11.2*	43
60.5	59.7	65.7	68.2	72.5	67.9	63.3	47.6	43.3	24.3	10.8	44
58.8	58.3	64.5	68.7	68.7	64.5	59.0	51.6	44.1	30.7	12.6	45
16.4	14.9	14.8	13.3	10.7	7.3	4.7	2.5	1.5	0.6	0.2	46
85.0	85.6	86.6	86.7	87.8	84.6*	77.4*	62.1*	42.9*	26.9*	12.8*	47
84.9	85.2	86.6	88.3*	86.7*	83.6*	77.5*	61.8*	42.6*	26.6*	8.0*	48
			5.	Latin	America,	Spain and	Portugal				
29.4	24.4	22.5	21.5	19.4	15.5	12.0	9.0	6.9	4.9	3.2	49
64.2	66.3	64.6	68.3	65.3	66.7	43.3	29.7	26.2	22.8	17.2	50
13.5*	11.5*	11.3*	10.9*	10.4*	9.8*	8.9*	8.0*	7.2*	5.6*	3.8*	51
18.8	17.4*	17.2*	16.8*	16.0*	15.1	13.4	12.1	10.1	8.7*	6.8*	52
30.4	28.0	27.5	27.6	26.5	24.6	22.4	19.5	16.8	13.5	9.1	53
27.9	23.8	22.5	22.2	21.3	19.4	16.8	13.7	11.0*	7.8*	4.5*	54
20.2	19.0	19.1	19.1	18.2	17.7	15.9	15.5	12.9	11.2	7.3	55
21.6	19.8	19.7	19.8	19.3	18.3	16.5	14.2	11.0	9.0	5.3	56
18.2*	15.9*	16.2*	15.0*	14.1*	12.3*	10.1*	8.0*	7.1*	5.6	3.7	57
20.3	18.8	18.0	16.5	14.9	12.7	10.5	8.6	6.0	4.0	2.3	58
22.1	21.3	21.1	20.9	19.6	18.2	15.5	12.9	10.5*	8.7*	5.8*	59
12.3	12.2	12.4	12.6	12.9	10.3	11.1	9.3	7.2	4.5	2.2	60
33.2*	34.6*	35.3*	36.1*	36.6*	36.5*	35.9*	34.0*	32.3*	29.9*	23.9	61
17.6	16.6	16.1	16.6	16.2	16.4	15.6	15.2	13.3	13.6	9.6	62
17.9*	16.8*	17.1*	17.5*	16.6*	15.0*	14.0*	13.1*	11.9*	10.9*	9.3	63
21.4	19.7	18.5	17.7	17.4	16.1	14.6	13.1	11.7	9.8	7.3	64
12.9	13.3	14.1	13.6	14.1	12.8	13.1	11.4	11.7	9.2	5.6	65
12.8	12.3	11.9	12.4	13.3	12.9	11.7	10.5	8.9	8.7	4.6	66
14.4	12.6	11.9	12.1	12.0	11.3	10.1	8.3	6.8	4.4	2.3	67
13.3	13.4	13.6	13.7	13.8	13.7	13.9	13.5	13.8	13.3	12.5	68
16.9	16.0	17.0	18.3	18.0	18.0	17.7	17.3	15.8	14.4	9.8	69

Table A.8. (continued)

Country and census year		GYAL[a]	15-19	20-29	30-44	45-64	65+	20-24

5. Latin America, Spain, and Portugal (continued)

70	Nicaragua	1950	8.7	15.0	15.5	14.3	13.4	9.1	16.3
71		1963	13.3	20.0	23.4	24.1	21.7	12.1	23.9
72	Panama	1950	12.6	23.4	27.4	24.7	17.7	8.1	29.6
73		1960	13.3	23.5	29.8	27.3	19.5	6.6	31.2
74	Paraguay	1950	14.3	25.8	26.5	25.0	22.4	12.3	27.7
75		1962	14.2	24.0	29.6	26.1	22.6	9.3	31.2
76	Peru	1961	13.1	27.1	25.4	20.7	19.8	12.1	28.0
77	Portugal	1950	13.4	34.4	27.1	19.2	17.9	12.1	31.2
78		1960	10.3	27.3	23.2	15.6	13.3	7.8	26.5
79	Puerto Rico	1950	11.3	19.6	27.6	25.0	14.9	4.8	29.1
80		1960	11.5	10.6	31.1	26.2	16.5	4.0	31.9
81	Spain	1950	9.3	19.6	19.6	12.8	13.7	10.5	21.3
82		1960	11.0	27.1	23.8	14.7	16.5	10.2	28.2
83	Uruguay	1963	14.6	29.8	38.8	35.1	18.4	3.5	40.3
84	Venezuela	1950	11.4	22.0	22.0	19.7	16.7	10.3	23.5
85		1961	11.1	17.9	24.8	22.0	15.6	7.3	25.8

6. Eastern Europe

86	Bulgaria	1956	35.8	47.1	69.1	75.9	58.4	22.4	69.0
87		1965	33.5	32.7	77.9	87.1	50.8	5.4	72.1
88	Czechoslovakia	1961	29.9	55.0	63.5	64.5	50.0	7.2	69.2
89	Hungary	1949	19.6	55.5	39.4	29.1	26.2	19.0	45.0
90		1960	26.3	52.5	52.0	50.5	38.2	20.4	55.3
91	Rumania	1956	43.5	80.7	76.2	74.3	68.9	36.4	78.1
92		1966	37.4	50.8	76.4	78.4	61.7	20.3	74.3
93	Yugoslavia	1953	22.1	65.9	53.6	38.5	24.7	11.3	60.0

7. Middle Europe

94	Austria	1961	27.9	76.5	67.0	54.4	39.5	7.0	75.2
95	Finland	1950	31.3	53.4	61.0	58.7	53.5	19.7	64.4
96		1960	28.4	41.7	58.8	57.5	50.8	11.1	60.7
97	France	1954	23.8	42.9	49.8	40.5	42.6	13.5	57.0
98		1962	23.1	35.5*	53.4	39.8	41.6	11.4	61.5
99	Germany, West	1950	23.2	77.1	60.5	37.8	30.5	8.8	70.4
100		1961	2.52	78.2	61.3	45.4	33.5	7.7	71.9
101	Greece	1961	21.0	46.8	47.9	37.6	29.3	10.2	52.2
102	Italy	1951	15.9	39.4	36.7	28.3	20.4	6.8	40.5
103		1961	14.5	39.3	35.3	27.0	19.2	5.0	40.6
104	Switzerland	1950	26.0	68.9*	61.4	41.3	39.8	15.1	77.3*
105		1960	25.4	66.3*	61.9	41.1	38.4	13.2	77.2*

190

25-29	30-34	35-39	40-44	45-49	50-54	55-59	60-64	65-69	70-74	75+	

5. Latin America, Spain and Portugal (continued)

25-29	30-34	35-39	40-44	45-49	50-54	55-59	60-64	65-69	70-74	75+	
14.7	14.3	14.5	14.1	13.9	13.4	13.7	12.5	11.6	9.3	6.6	70
22.9	24.2	24.1*	23.9*	24.4*	23.3*	21.2*	18.0*	15.1*	12.4*	8.6*	71
25.2	25.1	25.1	24.0	21.9	19.5	16.6	13.0	11.4	8.1	4.9	72
28.3	27.7	27.1	27.0	26.1	21.8	17.4	12.9	9.6	6.7	3.5	73
25.2*	24.0*	25.2*	25.8*	25.3*	24.4*	21.8*	17.8*	14.3*	12.3*	10.2*	74
28.0	26.1*	26.1*	26.1*	24.8*	24.1*	22.5*	19.0*	14.0*	8.9*	4.9	75
22.8	21.2	20.3	20.7	20.7	20.6	19.6	18.4	16.3	11.3	8.6	76
23.0	20.0	19.1	18.5	18.8	18.5	17.8	16.6	14.9	12.4	9.0	77
19.8	16.6	15.3	14.7	14.2	13.6	13.3	12.1	10.2	7.9	5.5	78
26.1	25.7	25.3	24.0	21.3	16.4	12.6	9.2	6.7	4.5	3.2	79
30.4	28.8	25.8	24.0	20.7	19.1	15.1	10.9	6.1	4.0	1.7	80
17.9	14.4	12.1	11.8	13.3	14.1	14.0	13.3	12.5	10.6	8.3	81
19.4*	13.7*	14.2*	16.2*	17.2*	16.9*	16.5*	15.3*	13.1*	10.3*	7.2*	82
37.3	34.1*	30.9*	29.8*	27.6*	20.4	16.5	9.1	5.5*	3.3*	1.6*	83
20.5*	19.8*	19.7*	19.6*	18.9*	17.4*	16.1*	14.4*	12.8*	11.0*	7.2	84
23.8	22.9	22.0	21.0	19.3	17.1	14.6	11.6	9.1	8.0	4.9	85

6. Eastern Europe

25-29	30-34	35-39	40-44	45-49	50-54	55-59	60-64	65-69	70-74	75+	
69.3	73.2	76.9	77.7	73.4	64.6	54.0	41.6	32.2	19.9	15.2	86
83.8	86.4	88.0	86.9	81.1	68.8	35.3	18.3	9.7	5.0	1.6	87
57.9	59.6	65.9	68.1	66.6	60.0	43.1	30.3	14.1	5.7	1.9	88
33.8	30.9	28.6	27.6	27.0	25.4	26.7	25.8	22.7	19.5	14.7	89
48.7	49.1	50.7	51.8	49.7	46.3	30.6	26.1	24.1	20.8	16.4	90
74.3	73.0*	74.5*	75.4*	75.4*	72.6	67.7	59.7*	51.0*	37.9*	20.4*	91
78.5	78.4	78.7	78.1	75.2	71.3	58.8	41.5	29.9	20.4	10.5	92
47.3	42.0	37.8	35.8	31.5	26.4	22.1	18.8	15.6	11.6	6.6	93

7. Middle Europe

25-29	30-34	35-39	40-44	45-49	50-54	55-59	60-64	65-69	70-74	75+	
58.7	54.9	55.3	53.1	50.9	47.2	40.1	19.8	11.2	6.8	2.9	94
57.6*	56.2*	59.0*	60.8*	61.0*	58.6*	52.6	42.0	30.0*	20.1*	9.1*	95
56.9	55.6	57.3	59.5	59.7	56.9	50.6	36.0	19.0*	9.8*	4.4*	96
42.6	38.4	39.1	43.9	46.6	46.3	42.4	34.9	21.7*	12.6*	6.1*	97
45.3	38.7	39.6	41.2	45.0	45.3	42.2	33.9	19.2	10.3	4.8	98
50.5	40.5	36.9	36.1	36.6	34.6	29.8	20.8	13.8	8.7	3.9	99
50.7	44.6	46.3	45.4	42.3	38.1	32.8	20.9	12.2	7.4	3.5	100
43.6	38.6	37.5	36.7	36.3*	32.6*	27.1*	21.3*	15.2*	9.9*	5.4	101
32.9	29.5	28.5	26.8	25.9	23.7	18.8	13.1	10.3	6.7	3.5	102
30.1	27.5	27.3	26.1	24.6	22.7	16.8	12.8	8.5*	4.8*	1.8*	103
45.4*	43.3*	39.7*	40.9*	42.6*	41.8*	41.1*	33.6*	23.0*	14.3*	8.2*	104
46.7*	42.2*	39.7*	41.4*	41.8*	40.7*	39.5*	31.5*	21.1*	11.4*	7.2*	105

Country and census year		GYAL[a]	15-19	20-29	30-44	45-64	65+	20-24
	8. Northwestern Europe, Northern America, and Oceania							
106 Australia	1947	13.7	66.4	36.7	18.5	15.4	4.8	49.0
107	1954	15.2	68.2	37.5	22.2	19.3	4.7	48.7
108	1961	16.3	64.4	38.9	26.4	22.4	4.4	50.8
109 Belgium	1947	13.9	41.8	35.0	24.9	18.1	5.2	40.5
110	1961	15.9	40.6	44.4	30.4	20.8	3.7	52.2
111 Canada	1951	13.1	37.9	36.2	22.2	17.4	4.9	46.9
112	1961	17.1	34.2	40.5	30.0	28.8	6.8	49.5
113 Denmark	1950	24.8	83.2	54.4	41.6	36.7	8.0	64.2
114	1960	21.5	66.7	48.8	36.0	33.0	7.3	58.9
115 Ireland	1951	19.0	58.0*	53.2	22.8	21.5	17.0	64.8
116	1961	18.3	55.0*	52.9	20.8	21.8	15.3	67.2
117 Netherlands	1960	12.4	59.3	37.6	15.6	14.1	2.5	52.8
118 New Zealand	1951	14.0	64.5	39.1	20.4	16.5	3.1	52.8
119	1956	14.7	63.7	37.3	21.8	19.9	3.5	50.6
120	1961	15.5	63.9	35.9	23.6	23.0	3.4	49.8
121 Norway	1950	16.1	48.1	41.3	20.4	24.2	8.8	51.3
122	1960	15.0	42.5	36.6	19.1	24.4	7.6	47.7
123 Sweden	1950	18.0	54.3	47.3	27.3	26.4	7.6	57.3
124	1960	19.7	46.6	49.6	35.8	31.5	4.5	57.3*
125	1965	22.7	40.8	50.4	45.2	40.4	5.0	56.3
126 United Kingdom	1951	20.9	78.7	53.0	34.5	27.7	5.2	65.4
127	1961	22.8	70.7	51.0	40.3	35.8	5.7	62.5
128 United States	1950	16.9	26.3	37.9	33.7	28.0	7.3	43.1
129	1960	21.1	27.6	40.0	40.3	40.6	10.1	44.8
	9. Miscellaneous							
130 Guyana	1946	20.8	28.5	34.5	37.4	38.0	16.1	34.8
131	1960	15.7	25.4	24.8	29.1	30.2	9.3	25.0
132 Haiti	1950	52.8	81.1	85.5	86.3	83.8	59.8	85.8
133 Hong Kong	1961	20.7	47.9	41.9	37.1	34.8	8.5	51.1
134 Jamaica	1953	27.5	34.4*	52.9	54.1	46.9	18.5	52.9
135	1960	25.7	32.0	53.1	52.0	42.6	15.5	51.8
136 Singapore	1957	12.5	23.4	19.7	21.4	25.2	5.7	22.9
137	1966	13.1	25.5	33.4	20.7	21.6	6.7	40.9
138 South Africa	1946	20.2	61.9*	41.9	26.1	22.7	15.7	50.4
139	1960	15.1	29.8	32.7	26.2	23.6	9.4	37.4
140 Trinidad & Tobago	1946	18.0	33.0	32.2	31.5	31.9	12.3	32.5
141	1960	18.0	18.9	36.5	35.3	33.7	9.2	35.5

*Estimated by interpolation or extrapolation.

[a]Gross years of active life of males in ages 10 and over. See Appendix D for explanation.

Table A.8. (continued)

25-29	30-34	35-39	40-44	45-49	50-54	55-59	60-64	65-69	70-74	75+	

8. Northwestern Europe, Northern America, and Oceania

24.4	18.3	18.3	19.1	19.1	17.1	15.1	10.4	6.9	4.1*	3.3*	106
26.4	21.7	21.6	23.4	24.4	22.4	18.4	11.9	7.0	4.5	2.6	107
27.0	24.2	27.0	28.1	28.0	26.2	22.3	13.3	7.0	3.9	2.2	108
29.4	25.6	25.1	24.0	22.0	19.8	17.3	13.3	8.3*	5.3*	1.9*	109
36.5	31.2	29.9	30.0	28.4	25.3	20.1	9.4	5.3	3.5*	2.2*	110
25.4*	22.9*	22.0*	21.6*	21.1*	19.7*	16.3	12.4	8.5	4.6	1.5	111
31.5	27.8	30.0	32.3	34.0	32.8	27.9	20.3	12.0*	6.8*	1.7*	112
44.6*	38.5*	42.0*	44.3*	44.1*	42.6*	36.5	23.6	13.0	6.9	4.2	113
38.7	34.4	35.8	37.7	37.9	37.4	34.3	22.7	12.1	6.3	3.4	114
41.5	27.0	21.2	20.2	20.6*	21.9*	22.7*	20.9*	19.6*	17.6*	13.9	115
38.7	24.0	19.1	19.2	20.5*	21.7*	23.2*	21.9*	18.9	15.0	11.8	116
22.5	15.6	15.3	16.1	16.8	16.3	13.9	9.5	4.3	2.3	1.0	117
25.3	19.6	19.9	21.5	22.4	19.5	15.2	8.9	5.2	2.7	1.5	118
24.1	19.8	21.5	24.2	25.7	23.9	18.9	11.0	6.0	3.1	1.4	119
22.0*	19.9*	23.9*	27.1*	29.6*	27.7*	22.1*	12.7*	6.5*	2.8*	1.0	120
31.3	20.4*	19.4*	21.4*	24.5*	25.9*	24.7*	21.9	16.5	6.9*	2.8*	121
25.6	18.8	18.7	19.9	22.5	24.9	27.0	23.1	16.1	4.8	1.8	122
37.2	27.3	26.2	28.5	30.8	29.7	26.3	18.9	11.8	6.4	4.6	123
42.0	35.6	35.4	36.5	37.0	35.8	31.8	21.4	9.7	2.9	1.0	124
44.5	40.9	45.7	49.0	49.3	45.8	39.5	27.0	10.9	3.3	0.9	125
40.5	33.4	34.2	35.8	35.1	33.3	27.5	14.9	8.8	4.7	2.0	126
39.6	36.5	40.7	43.8	43.8	42.4	36.8	20.3	10.3	4.9	1.8	127
32.6	30.9	33.9	36.2	34.8	30.8	25.9	20.5	12.8	6.6	2.6	128
35.1	35.5	40.2	45.3	47.4	45.8	39.6	29.5	16.6	9.6	4.2	129

9. Miscellaneous

34.1	35.3	37.3	39.5	40.4	40.2	38.5	32.8	22.5	16.8	9.0	130
24.6	26.3	28.8	32.3	33.3	33.1	31.0	23.4	14.4	9.3	4.2	131
85.2	85.6	86.2	87.0	87.0	85.0	83.4	79.8	73.9	63.2	42.2	132
32.6*	35.1*	37.0*	39.1*	43.6*	40.2*	32.0*	23.5*	15.8*	8.0*	1.7*	133
52.8	52.8	54.7	54.9	51.5	49.7	47.8	38.5	32.0	20.8*	2.8*	134
54.4*	52.4*	52.0*	51.5*	49.6*	46.9*	41.3*	32.8*	25.4*	19.2*	2.0*	135
16.4	17.3	20.8	26.3	30.1	28.8	24.7	17.1	10.5	4.7	2.0	136
25.9	21.0	19.2	21.9	20.4	24.4	23.2	18.5	11.7	6.4	1.9	137
33.4	27.6	25.4	25.2	24.9	23.7	21.8	20.6	18.5	15.7	12.8	138
28.0	26.5	26.2*	25.8*	25.6*	25.0*	23.3*	20.7*	15.8*	8.7*	3.8*	139
31.9	28.7	30.1	35.8	35.1	33.1	31.2	28.1	19.8	13.3	3.6	140
37.4	32.5	34.1	39.1*	40.2*	36.1*	32.4*	26.1*	15.4*	9.7*	2.4*	141

[b]See also Guinea (Tropical Africa), Indonesia and Pakistan (South and East Asia).
[c]Averages of rates indicated by results of National Sample Survey round 14 (1958-1959) and 15 (1959-1960).

Table A.9. Rural and urban age-specific activity rates of males, censuses of 1946-1966

Country and census year			GYAL[a]	15-19	20-29	30-44	45-64	65+	20-24
			1. Tropical Africa						
1	Central African Rep. 1960	Rural	53.6	68.9	94.8	97.2	90.0	52.0	93.0
2		Urban	52.8	49.8	89.3	96.0	92.1	55.8	86.4
3	Ghana 1960	Rural	57.8	62.8	94.2	97.7	94.5	74.7	91.5
4		Urban	54.5	54.7	92.4	96.6	91.5	64.0	89.3
5	Guinea 1954/55	Rural	54.8	84.9	96.8	97.6	90.8	46.3	95.7
6		Urban	54.2	70.7	91.6	95.6	91.7	52.1	89.2
7	Liberia 1962	Rural	53.9	48.9	82.2	94.7	90.4	64.4	76.3
8		Urban	44.4	34.6	76.1	86.3	75.7	45.1	68.8
			2. Arab countries						
9	Morocco 1960	Rural	58.7	70.7	91.0	95.8	94.3	75.0	88.3
10		Urban	49.2	43.0	89.9	94.5	87.6	40.0	85.4
11	Tunisia 1966	Rural	52.6	64.8	95.4	96.9	88.3	48.5	94.3
12		Urban	48.6	36.8	91.5	96.1	85.3	40.1	87.6
			3. Other Moslem countries[b]						
13	Iran 1956	Rural	61.5	92.0	98.1	99.1	96.3	75.2	97.7
14		Urban	57.1	61.9	92.8	98.4	94.0	67.6	89.1
15	1966	Rural	55.9	84.7	97.0	98.2	89.1	46.2	96.0
16		Urban	50.2	48.6	90.3	96.9	83.4	44.3	85.9
17	Turkey 1955	Rural	66.5	94.1	98.6	99.1	96.4	94.3	98.2
18		Urban	56.0	69.8	93.8	96.6	90.4	62.9	92.9
19	1960	Rural	66.3	89.7	98.2	99.1	98.9	95.4	97.4
20		Urban	54.0	56.3	92.3	96.2	90.2	58.6	90.5
21	1965	Rural	65.3	86.7	97.9	99.3	98.6	91.1	96.8
22		Urban	52.5	52.9	91.2	97.1	88.8	51.9	87.7
			4. South and East Asia						
23	Ceylon 1963	Rural	52.0	47.8	90.6	96.7	89.2	52.1	85.5
24		Urban	48.9	40.8	86.8	95.2	83.6	44.7	80.3
25	India 1961	Rural	59.5	78.2	96.4	97.7	95.6	69.8	95.4
26		Urban	50.7	45.7	90.9	97.4	84.9	47.8	85.0
27	Indonesia 1961	Rural	58.5	71.6	91.3	96.6	93.9	75.2	89.2
28		Urban	50.3	45.8	85.6	95.6	84.2	52.8	79.4
29	Japan 1950	Rural	54.9	66.3*	95.4	97.5	92.4	56.9	94.5
30		Urban	49.0	54.1*	89.5	97.1	86.1	36.7	84.8
31	1955	Rural	54.6	56.0	95.6	97.5	93.5	57.6	94.2
32		Urban	51.2	53.1	89.9	97.0	89.8	46.5	84.4
33	1960	Rural	53.9	49.9	96.4	98.0	92.8	56.4	94.9
34		Urban	51.4	52.3	90.8	97.6	90.6	46.2	85.2
35	1965	Rural	52.9	34.7	96.4	98.2	93.8	53.5	94.0
36		Urban	51.7	40.8	91.7	97.9	92.6	48.7	85.6
37	Korea, South 1960	Rural	49.8	52.5	89.4	96.6	89.2	37.3	85.3
38		Urban	42.1	29.5	69.6	95.5	77.5	24.4	55.4

194

Table A.9. (continued)

25-29	30-34	35-39	40-44	45-49	50-54	55-59	60-64	65-69	70-74	75+	

1. Tropical Africa

25-29	30-34	35-39	40-44	45-49	50-54	55-59	60-64	65-69	70-74	75+	
96.5	97.2	97.4	97.0	95.9	93.8	89.8	80.5*	69.2*	56.2*	30.7*	1
93.3	96.0	95.9	96.2	96.0	92.4	87.7	92.1*	85.5*	76.2*	5.6*	2
96.8*	97.7*	97.8*	97.6*	97.1*	96.2*	94.7*	90.0*	85.3*	77.6*	61.3*	3
95.6*	96.7*	96.8*	96.4*	95.6*	94.1*	91.4*	84.9*	77.8*	68.1*	46.0*	4
97.8	97.3	98.0	97.5	97.3	95.0	91.7	79.1	68.4	50.2	20.3	5
94.0	95.6	97.1	94.1	97.6	91.9	91.9	85.6	69.1	55.9	31.4	6
88.1	94.2	95.3	94.6	94.6	92.7	91.9	82.3	76.5	63.6	53.2	7
83.4	85.8	87.3	85.7	81.7	81.8	76.1	63.2	55.1	43.5	36.7	8

2. Arab countries

25-29	30-34	35-39	40-44	45-49	50-54	55-59	60-64	65-69	70-74	75+	
93.8	95.6	95.9	95.9	96.1	94.7	94.8	91.6	86.3	76.9	61.9	9
94.4	95.5	94.5	93.6	92.9	90.3	87.5	79.6	50.5	41.6	27.9	10
96.6	97.1	97.0	96.6	95.6	93.0	87.7	77.0	64.8	48.2	32.7	11
95.4	96.5	96.3	95.6	94.5	91.6	85.3	69.7	56.2	38.8	25.5	12

3. Other Moslem countries[b]

25-29	30-34	35-39	40-44	45-49	50-54	55-59	60-64	65-69	70-74	75+	
98.5*	99.0*	99.1*	99.1*	98.6*	97.7*	96.4*	92.7*	86.6*	77.2*	61.8*	13
96.6*	98.2*	98.5*	98.4*	97.8*	96.2*	93.3*	88.7*	82.6*	71.4*	48.9*	14
98.0	98.3	98.4	97.9	96.8	93.4	89.1	76.8	68.9*	43.1*	26.5*	15
94.7	96.7	97.2	96.7	94.6	87.6	81.9	69.5	55.3*	45.2*	32.4*	16
99.0	99.1	99.2	99.1	99.2	99.0	98.6	97.7	98.7*	96.2*	87.9*	17
94.7	96.3	96.7	96.9	96.5	94.2	89.9	81.1	71.8*	64.3*	52.6*	18
98.9	99.0	99.2	99.2	99.3	99.1	98.9	98.1	97.3*	95.5*	93.3*	19
94.1	96.1	96.5	96.1	95.6	94.0	90.3	80.9	70.0*	60.5*	45.2*	20
99.0	99.3	99.3	99.3	99.3	99.0	98.6	97.6	95.0*	92.1*	86.2*	21
94.8	96.8	97.3	97.1	95.9	93.1	88.9	77.3	63.5*	52.8*	39.3*	22

4. South and East Asia

25-29	30-34	35-39	40-44	45-49	50-54	55-59	60-64	65-69	70-74	75+	
95.8	96.9	97.0	96.3	96.1	93.3	88.9	78.6	70.3	52.8	33.1	23
93.4	95.2	95.4	95.0	93.8	91.1	82.9	66.7	57.3	46.1	30.8	24
97.3	97.5	97.8	97.8	97.8	95.6	90.7	84.6	73.0	51.8	25
96.8	97.6	97.7	96.8	95.7	92.1	81.5	70.5	58.9	48.9	35.6	26
93.4*	96.0*	97.0*	96.8*	96.5*	95.4*	93.9*	89.9*	84.3*	77.0	64.1	27
91.8*	94.5*	96.1*	96.1*	95.3*	90.8*	82.3*	68.3*	62.1*	53.5	42.7	28
96.4	97.1*	97.7*	97.6*	97.0*	94.8*	92.8*	85.0	76.0	58.9	35.9	29
94.2	95.5*	98.0*	97.7*	95.2*	92.5*	85.9*	70.9	54.8	34.3	20.9	30
97.1	97.4	97.6	97.6	97.5	96.3	93.2	86.9	74.9*	58.1*	39.9*	31
95.5	96.7	97.1	97.2	96.7	94.9	89.4	78.2	66.6*	47.0*	25.7*	32
97.9	98.2	98.0	97.7	97.2	96.1	91.5	86.5	76.1	58.7	34.3	33
96.4	97.5	97.5	97.7	97.1	96.0	89.8	79.7	65.8	47.0	25.9	34
98.7	98.1	98.2	98.2	98.0	97.0	93.3	86.9	74.2*	55.5*	30.7*	35
97.8	97.9	97.8	98.0	97.8	97.0	92.5	83.0	69.1*	49.6*	27.6*	36
93.6	96.2	96.4	97.4	97.1	91.4	91.7	76.7	53.8	38.8*	19.4*	37
83.8	94.5	96.1	95.9	94.4	90.1	76.9	48.5	35.0	22.4*	15.7*	38

Country and census year			GYAL[a]	15-19	20-29	30-44	45-64	65+	20-24
		4. South and East Asia (continued)							
39 Pakistan	1961	Rural	62.1	80.6	93.9	96.2	95.1	83.4	91.9
40		Urban	51.9	58.8	87.2	92.6	85.6	54.5	81.9
41 Thailand	1954	Rural	58.3	78.1	91.8	98.8	94.8	60.9	86.8
42		Urban	44.9	34.7	82.4	92.4	80.8	29.0	76.0
		5. Latin America, Spain, and Portugal							
43 Argentina	1960	Rural	57.3	86.2	96.5	98.0	92.2	63.4	95.1
44		Urban	46.3	65.2	92.2	97.2	73.0	28.1	88.2
45 Chile	1952	Rural	60.2	79.8	97.0	98.3	96.0	79.2	96.0
46		Urban	52.6	54.5	91.9	96.1	86.5	58.1	88.6
47	1960	Rural	57.9	79.8	98.0	98.2	94.7	64.8	97.5
48		Urban	48.5	51.6	92.3	96.1	80.4	40.1	88.4
49 Colombia	1951	Rural	61.1	92.3	98.1	98.4	96.4	76.4	98.0
50		Urban	55.9	71.8	93.6	96.9	91.8	61.7	91.4
51	1964	Rural	59.6	85.4	97.4	98.4	96.0	67.9	96.6
52		Urban	51.1	47.7	88.6	96.3	89.3	47.7	83.3
53 Costa Rica	1950	Rural	62.8	96.9	99.1	99.3	97.8	78.2	98.9
54		Urban	56.8	77.8	94.0	97.2	93.1	62.6	92.0
55	1963	Rural	59.5	89.4	98.3	98.9	96.7	64.7	97.7
56		Urban	52.3	54.3	91.1	97.1	92.3	46.3	86.5
57 Cuba	1953	Rural	58.2	87.8	95.0	95.7	92.4	63.5	94.3
58		Urban	52.1	66.1	91.2	94.3	87.8	48.7	89.2
59 Ecuador	1962	Rural	65.0	92.0	99.0	99.4	98.8	90.9	98.7
60		Urban	57.4	57.6	91.2	98.2	94.9	73.6	85.6
61 El Salvador	1950	Rural	63.7	94.3	98.2	98.5	97.5	84.0	97.9
62		Urban	59.3	78.4	92.7	95.6	94.5	79.3	91.4
63	1961	Rural	62.8	88.7	98.4	98.8	97.2	81.5	97.9
64		Urban	57.2	60.2	91.0	96.2	94.0	75.3	87.9
65 Guatemala	1950	Rural	62.1	94.9	98.5	98.7	96.9	73.7	98.3
66		Urban	57.4	76.9	93.3	95.7	93.0	68.5	92.0
67	1964	Rural	61.8	89.7	97.6	98.2	95.7	76.8	97.3
68		Urban	56.6	63.6	93.5	97.6	93.4	66.9	90.9
69 Mexico	1960	Rural	59.7	74.6	92.4	95.7	94.6	84.0	91.1
70		Urban	57.6	60.6	93.0	95.9	93.0	77.9	91.5
71 Nicaragua	1950	Rural	66.0	96.9	99.2	99.3	98.8	91.0	99.2
72		Urban	60.1	73.6	93.9	97.1	96.1	79.4	92.0
73	1963	Rural	62.9	90.0	98.1	98.9	97.3	79.7	97.6
74		Urban	54.1	51.2	90.7	95.9	91.2	62.7	86.3
75 Panama	1950	Rural	61.0	82.8	97.9	98.4	96.3	79.3	97.5
76		Urban	51.7	39.9	93.6	97.8	88.7	52.0	90.2
77	1960	Rural	60.0	80.7	96.9	98.0	95.4	75.6	96.1
78		Urban	48.2	38.8	90.7	96.0	86.3	35.9	86.8

196

25-29	30-34	35-39	40-44	45-49	50-54	55-59	60-64	65-69	70-74	75+	

4. South and East Asia (continued)

25-29	30-34	35-39	40-44	45-49	50-54	55-59	60-64	65-69	70-74	75+	
96.0*	96.2*	96.2*	96.2*	96.4*	96.4*	94.7	92.7*	89.5*	85.0*	75.8*	39
92.4*	92.6*	92.7*	92.6*	92.6*	90.7*	82.1	77.2*	68.7*	54.9*	40.0*	40
96.9	98.4	98.9	99.0	98.3	97.6*	95.0*	88.5*	76.7*	63.0*	43.0*	41
88.7	92.6	92.6	91.9	93.1	91.6*	79.3*	59.4*	42.1*	25.1*	19.9*	42

5. Latin America, Spain, and Portugal

25-29	30-34	35-39	40-44	45-49	50-54	55-59	60-64	65-69	70-74	75+	
97.9	98.1	98.1	97.7	97.2	95.5	91.2	84.8	76.9	66.2	47.1	43
96.2	97.7	97.7	96.2	93.8	84.5	65.4	48.4	37.4	28.2	18.8	44
97.9	98.4	98.4	98.2	97.6	96.7	96.1	93.5	90.8	82.1	64.7	45
95.3	96.3	96.3	95.6	92.9	88.5	85.2	79.3	72.3	60.2	42.0	46
98.4	98.4	98.3	97.9	97.5	96.0	94.7	90.8	84.0*	67.0*	43.4*	47
96.3	97.1	96.5	94.6	91.3	83.9	77.8	68.7	55.7*	41.4*	23.2*	48
98.3	98.5	98.5	98.3	98.0	97.5	96.7	93.3	90.0	79.3	60.0	49
95.7	97.0	97.0	96.8	96.1	94.4	91.8	85.0	78.3	64.0	42.8	50
98.1	98.3	98.5	98.4	98.1	97.2	96.2	92.4	81.7	71.3	50.6	51
93.8	95.8	96.7	96.3	95.6	92.8	88.6	80.1	61.9	50.7	30.6	52
99.3*	99.3*	99.3*	99.3*	98.9*	98.4*	97.9*	96.0*	95.6*	77.3	61.7	53
96.1*	97.2*	97.4*	97.1*	96.0*	94.8*	92.9*	88.6*	82.9*	62.3	42.4	54
98.9	99.1	99.0	98.8	98.7	97.9	97.0	93.2	78.8	68.8	46.3	55
95.7	96.8	97.4	97.2	96.7	94.9	92.6	84.8	60.9	49.6	28.5	56
95.6	95.7	95.9	95.6	95.6	94.0	92.5	87.7	77.4*	62.9*	50.3*	57
93.1	94.1	94.3	94.3	93.5	91.5	87.3	78.9	66.5*	47.0*	32.8*	58
99.3	99.4	99.5	99.4	99.4	99.1	98.7	98.1	96.8	94.0	81.9	59
96.8	98.3	98.3	98.1	97.7	96.3	94.5	91.0	85.9	76.8	58.0	60
98.5*	98.7*	98.4*	98.3*	98.4*	98.3*	97.6*	95.9*	93.1*	87.7*	71.4	61
94.0*	94.9*	95.7*	96.2*	96.2*	95.6*	94.1*	92.2*	88.3*	83.5*	66.2	62
98.9	98.9	98.8	98.6	98.4	98.1	97.0	95.4	93.3	85.1	66.1	63
94.1	96.3	96.1	96.2	96.3	95.4	93.6	90.7	86.8	78.4	60.8	64
98.7	98.7	98.8	98.5	98.5	97.6	97.3	94.0	89.5	80.6	51.0	65
94.8	95.6	95.8	95.6	95.4	94.0	93.5	89.0	83.7	71.5	50.3	66
97.9	98.3	98.1	98.1	97.8	97.0	95.8	92.3	87.8	81.0	61.5	67
96.1	97.1	98.1	97.6	96.1	96.0	93.7	87.9	81.9	70.5	48.2	68
93.8	95.0	95.9	96.1	96.0	95.5	94.5	92.5	90.0	86.6	75.3	69
94.5	95.7	96.1	96.0	95.4	94.3	92.4	90.0	86.5	81.2	66.0	70
99.2*	99.3*	99.4*	99.2*	99.2*	98.9*	98.8*	98.4*	97.9*	92.0*	83.0*	71
95.9*	96.9*	97.1*	97.4*	97.5*	97.1*	96.1*	93.6*	89.3*	82.3*	66.6*	72
98.7	98.9	99.0*	98.9*	98.7*	98.4*	97.4*	94.8*	90.5*	82.9*	65.8*	73
95.1	95.8	96.1*	95.9*	94.9*	93.0*	90.8*	86.1*	78.5*	66.9*	42.8*	74
98.2	98.1	98.3	98.6	98.4	97.8	96.3	92.8	88.4	81.3*	68.3*	75
97.0	97.6	97.8	98.0	96.3	93.9	89.6	74.7	63.7	54.6*	37.7*	76
97.8	98.0	98.0	98.1	97.8	96.9	95.6	91.3	86.5	79.6	60.6	77
94.7	95.9	96.1	96.0	94.8	92.6	88.1	69.5	49.4	34.5	23.9	78

Table A.9. (continued)

Country and census year			GYAL[a]	15-19	20-29	30-44	45-64	65+	20-24
	5. Latin America, Spain, and Portugal (continued)								
79 Peru	1961	Rural	59.2	63.8	98.1	99.2	97.9	75.5	97.2
80		Urban	54.2	46.3	91.3	98.3	93.9	59.9	86.6
81 Portugal	1960	Rural	59.1	91.3	97.7	97.8	91.3	65.7	97.0
82		Urban	52.3	67.4	92.1	98.1	86.6	44.9	87.7
83 Puerto Rico	1950	Rural	48.6	44.3	83.6	90.1	85.3	48.2	83.4
84		Urban	42.4	31.5	71.5	84.0	77.4	36.8	71.2
85	1960	Rural	43.7	31.5	83.8	89.5	80.6	27.3	80.8
86		Urban	42.2	22.0	77.1	89.6	80.5	25.1	70.5
87 Spain	1950	Rural	59.8	85.1	96.7	99.0	96.7	71.8	95.2
88		Urban	52.8	69.9	91.9	98.3	91.4	44.7	88.6
	6. Eastern Europe								
89 Bulgaria	1956	Rural	56.1	68.8	92.5	98.4	95.1	63.3	87.3
90		Urban	48.4	31.8	82.5	96.1	86.6	45.5	71.1
	7. Middle Europe								
91 Finland	1960	Rural	51.7	63.9	92.2	97.3	91.3	42.1	88.8
92		Urban	47.1	48.0	87.8	97.4	87.9	24.7	81.7
93 Greece	1951	Rural	56.7	76.1	93.9	95.3	93.5	63.7	93.5
94		Urban	52.3	60.2	88.6	94.7	89.0	51.4	86.9
95	1961	Rural	56.4	77.7*	96.5	97.7	93.0	56.1	95.3*
96		Urban	46.1	53.3*	89.9	95.3	79.2	24.2	86.0*
	8. Northwestern Europe, Northern America, and Oceania								
97 Canada	1961	Rural	47.1	44.4	87.7	91.5	84.5	33.5	84.9
98		Urban	46.9	39.7	91.4	95.4	87.5	25.4	88.2
99 Norway	1960	Rural	51.6	57.2	89.7	98.3	95.0	37.4	84.3
100		Urban	49.1	45.0	84.6	97.7	93.3	32.7	76.7
101 Sweden	1960	Rural	49.5	63.4	90.5	96.9	91.8	28.7	86.5
102		Urban	47.6	54.9	87.9	96.3	91.2	22.7	83.9
103	1965	Rural	48.0	58.1	86.4	95.1	90.0	28.0	81.5
104		Urban	46.5	48.2	84.8	95.7	91.5	19.9	79.1
105 United States	1950	Rural	49.4	50.2	89.5	93.7	86.2	42.3	87.7
106		Urban	48.0	40.2	84.3	94.6	88.1	36.9	78.8
107	1960	Rural	47.2	43.0	90.5	94.1	85.4	30.2	88.2
108		Urban	48.0	43.2	89.7	96.3	89.1	28.9	85.2
	9. Miscellaneous								
109 Guyana	1960	Rural	53.1	80.9	98.2	98.2	90.4	41.9	98.5
110		Urban	50.3	71.5	93.5	96.2	86.1	37.2	92.3

*Estimated by interpolation or extrapolation.

[a]Gross years of active life of females in ages 10 and over. See Appendix D for explanation.

[b]See also Guinea (Tropical Africa), Indonesia and Pakistan (South and East Asia).

198

25-29	30-34	35-39	40-44	45-49	50-54	55-59	60-64	65-69	70-74	75+	

5. Latin America, Spain, and Portugal (continued)

99.0	99.2	99.2	99.1	99.1	98.7	98.4	95.4	90.9	77.9	57.7	79
96.0	98.2	98.4	98.3	97.9	96.5	93.7	87.5	78.6	60.6	40.4	80
98.5	98.4	98.0	97.1	96.2	93.9	90.6	84.5	79.3	66.8	51.1	81
96.5	98.3	98.4	97.6	96.0	92.1	85.5	72.7	50.0	49.1	35.7	82
83.8	87.0	91.4	91.9	91.8	89.1	85.2	75.4	64.9	50.8	28.8	83
71.9	78.6	85.6	87.8	86.9	82.4	75.5	64.7	53.2	37.2	19.9	84
86.8	89.5	89.7	89.2	88.7	86.6	82.1	65.0	41.6	26.6	13.7	85
83.6	88.5	90.1	90.3	90.0	86.3	81.2	64.6	38.0	23.9	13.3	86
98.2*	99.2*	99.0*	98.8*	98.6*	98.2*	96.6*	93.4*	88.0*	76.3*	51.3*	87
95.1*	98.6*	98.2*	98.0*	97.4*	96.4*	91.4*	80.5*	62.5*	41.6*	30.0*	88

6. Eastern Europe

| 97.6 | 98.4 | 98.4 | 98.5 | 98.4 | 97.4 | 95.1 | 89.7 | 80.0 | 62.7 | 47.3 | 89 |
| 94.0 | 96.0 | 96.3 | 96.1 | 95.4 | 93.3 | 86.3 | 71.4 | 61.8 | 44.8 | 29.9 | 90 |

7. Middle Europe

95.5	97.4	97.3	97.1	96.6	95.0	91.7	81.9	59.4	42.2*	24.6*	91
93.9	97.4	97.4	97.4	96.2	93.8	88.1	73.5	41.5	22.0*	10.6*	92
94.3	94.8	95.4	95.5	96.1	94.3	92.9	90.8	82.4	67.2	41.4	93
90.3	94.3	95.0	94.7	93.9	92.1	88.4	81.8	67.7	53.0	33.6	94
97.7*	98.2*	97.7*	97.3	97.0*	95.5*	92.4*	87.1*	78.2*	53.6*	36.5	95
93.8*	96.2*	95.4*	94.1	92.4*	86.4*	76.6*	61.5*	37.6*	20.7*	14.4	96

8. Northwestern Europe, Northern America, and Oceania

90.4*	91.4*	91.8*	91.3*	90.4*	88.3*	85.1*	74.4*	50.0*	31.4*	19.1*	97
94.7*	95.7*	95.6*	95.0*	94.0*	91.8*	87.6*	76.5*	46.3*	22.0*	8.0*	98
95.1	98.1	98.4	98.3	97.8	97.1	95.5	89.5	73.0	27.8	11.4	99
92.5	97.5	97.8	97.8	97.6	96.5	94.0	85.2	65.5	24.3	8.3	100
94.5*	96.9*	97.0*	96.8*	96.3	95.1	92.3	83.5	54.7	23.0	8.3	101
92.0*	95.7*	96.5*	96.8*	96.1	95.0	92.3	81.4	45.4	16.8	5.8	102
91.3	94.9	95.3	95.1	94.6	93.5	90.5	81.4	52.0	23.5	8.4	103
90.4	95.1	95.9	96.0	96.0	94.8	92.4	82.9	42.5	13.3	4.1	104
91.3	93.5	94.1	93.6	92.3	89.3	85.1	78.2	61.6	43.2	21.9	105
89.9	94.1	94.9	94.7	93.6	91.3	87.5	80.1	58.7	35.7	16.2	106
92.8	94.4	94.2	93.7	92.7	89.9	85.0	74.0	43.5	30.4	16.7	107
94.3	96.4	96.5	96.1	95.2	93.1	88.9	79.2	44.0	27.8	14.8	108

9. Miscellaneous

| 97.9 | 98.1 | 98.3 | 98.2 | 97.5 | 95.4 | 90.6 | 78.3 | 55.4 | 43.4 | 26.9 | 109 |
| 94.8 | 96.3 | 96.7 | 95.6 | 94.6 | 92.6 | 86.5 | 70.5 | 49.0 | 38.8 | 23.9 | 110 |

Table A.10. Rural and urban age-specific activity rates of females, censuses of 1946-1966

	Country and census year			GYAL[a]	15-19	20-29	30-44	45-64	65+	20-24
	1. Tropical Africa									
1	Central African Rep.	1960	Rural	47.6	87.6	96.5	97.6	75.4	21.6	95.7
2			Urban	46.1	69.2	85.5	93.3	77.4	28.4	81.2
3	Ghana	1960	Rural	37.5	54.0	52.0	60.0	67.8	46.3	52.7
4			Urban	37.5	50.8	53.1	65.2	68.5	40.7	52.7
5	Guinea	1954/55	Rural	44.4	81.5	93.5	94.9	65.4	12.4	93.0
6			Urban	25.3	31.6	39.0	53.4	45.9	10.8	38.5
7	Liberia	1962	Rural	27.3	38.2	46.1	51.6	44.4	20.5	45.0
8			Urban	9.4	5.5	13.1	19.0	18.6	7.8	11.5
	2. Arab countries									
9	Morocco	1960	Rural	5.4	7.5	4.9	6.8	9.2	6.7	4.9
10			Urban	7.6	11.3	9.2	13.1	13.5	6.5	9.4
11	Tunisia	1966	Rural	20.0	36.9	30.3	34.9	34.2	18.9	32.0
12			Urban	9.1	22.3	18.8	15.3	14.1	5.9	21.6
	3. Other Moslem countries[b]									
13	Iran	1956	Rural	5.8	13.3	9.3	9.2	8.5	4.8	9.8
14			Urban	6.7	10.0	8.1	9.8	11.3	8.2	8.2
15		1966	Rural	7.9	19.8	14.8	13.5	9.7	3.8	15.6
16			Urban	6.5	9.8	11.4	10.4	9.9	5.6	12.1
17	Turkey	1955	Rural	59.4	88.5	88.1	88.4	87.7	81.3	88.4
18			Urban	11.1	20.0	17.9	19.6	17.5	10.6	18.0
19		1960	Rural	58.5	86.1	85.6	85.8	86.4	82.5	85.3
20			Urban	5.3	10.7	9.6	10.7	7.9	3.0	10.3
21		1965	Rural	46.9	83.0	82.3	81.9	82.1	18.9	82.9
22			Urban	5.0	10.4	11.0	10.0	7.4	1.9	12.4
	4. South and East Asia									
23	Ceylon	1963	Rural	13.6	24.4	30.5	27.8	20.4	5.9	31.5
24			Urban	8.9	10.6	20.2	16.9	13.7	5.6	20.2
25	India	1961	Rural	28.3	47.3	50.1	53.9	44.6	17.6	49.4
26			Urban	11.1	11.9	16.7	22.6	19.8	8.2	16.1
27	Indonesia	1961	Rural	22.7	32.1	27.4	32.3	41.0	29.6	27.9
28			Urban	16.9	24.1	25.0	28.7	30.2	16.9	25.3
29	Japan	1950	Rural	34.9	58.8*	66.3	63.9	58.0	25.3	71.9
30			Urban	18.4	48.2*	41.7	32.6	26.4	10.1	52.4
31		1955	Rural	36.1	51.4	70.4	68.3	60.6	26.2	75.0
32			Urban	23.5	49.1	53.2	41.9	36.6	13.9	63.7
33		1960	Rural	37.2	48.4	71.1	71.4	63.1	28.5	76.0
34			Urban	24.8	50.3	54.5	45.1	39.4	14.7	66.4
35		1965	Rural	34.8	33.4	65.9	71.0	63.2	21.2	72.8
36			Urban	26.4	40.1	55.4	49.3	46.4	14.5	68.4

25-29	30-34	35-39	40-44	45-49	50-54	55-59	60-64	65-69	70-74	75+	

1. Tropical Africa

25-29	30-34	35-39	40-44	45-49	50-54	55-59	60-64	65-69	70-74	75+	
97.3	98.0	97.9	96.8	93.4	86.7	69.2	52.1*	34.8*	21.4*	8.6*	1
89.8	91.1	94.4	94.5	91.4	89.6	75.1	53.5*	41.9*	26.8*	16.4*	2
51.2*	56.7*	58.4*	65.0*	66.2*	70.0*	70.5*	64.5*	59.8*	49.7*	29.3*	3
53.4*	60.5*	65.9*	69.1*	69.7*	70.9*	70.4*	62.9*	57.5*	44.5*	20.2*	4
94.1	95.2	95.2	94.2	88.6	75.0	60.6	37.3	23.5	10.8	2.9	5
39.6	50.6	51.9	57.7	58.9	52.1	42.0	30.7	14.3	10.0	8.0	6
47.2	50.3	51.8	52.6	51.3	48.3	45.5	32.7	26.8	20.1	14.7	7
14.7	17.1	19.2	20.6	21.7	18.7	19.9	14.1	8.6	5.1	9.5	8

2. Arab countries

25-29	30-34	35-39	40-44	45-49	50-54	55-59	60-64	65-69	70-74	75+	
4.9	5.8	6.6	7.8	8.7	9.4	9.9	8.7	9.4	6.3	4.3	9
9.1	11.1	12.9	15.2	15.3	14.8	12.8	11.2	8.4	6.6	4.3	10
28.7	31.6	35.7	37.4	39.3	36.3	30.5	30.9	26.0	17.4	13.2	11
15.9	14.4	15.3	16.1	16.7	15.1	13.2	11.3	9.1	5.4	3.4	12

3. Other Moslem countries[b]

25-29	30-34	35-39	40-44	45-49	50-54	55-59	60-64	65-69	70-74	75+	
8.9*	8.7*	9.1*	9.7*	9.6*	9.1*	8.4*	6.8*	5.9*	4.8*	3.6*	13
8.0*	8.5*	9.9*	10.8*	11.6*	11.8*	11.4*	10.4*	9.2*	8.3*	7.1*	14
14.0	13.5	13.8	13.3	12.8	10.6	8.9	6.7	4.6*	4.1*	2.7*	15
10.7	9.7	10.1	11.3	11.0	11.0	8.7	9.0	7.8*	6.2*	3.0*	16
87.9	87.8	88.3	89.2	88.9	89.0	86.6	86.1	84.8*	81.2*	77.8*	17
17.8	18.8	19.8	20.2	19.3	19.3	16.6	14.8	13.0*	10.9*	8.0*	18
85.9	85.1	84.8	87.6	86.6	87.5	85.7	86.0	86.6*	83.4*	77.7*	19
8.8	10.0	11.1	11.1	10.3	8.5	7.4	5.6	4.1*	3.1*	1.8*	20
81.7	81.6	81.1	83.1	83.5	83.6	81.4	79.8	27.2*	20.3*	9.3*	21
9.5	8.8	10.3	10.9	10.3	8.2	6.5	4.6	3.1*	2.0*	0.6*	22

4. South and East Asia

25-29	30-34	35-39	40-44	45-49	50-54	55-59	60-64	65-69	70-74	75+	
29.5	26.8	28.1	28.5	28.4	22.6	19.0	11.7	8.1	5.6	4.1	23
20.2	18.0	16.5	16.3	17.0	15.2	13.1	9.7	6.9	5.6	4.2	24
50.8	52.3	54.5	54.9	53.9	49.2	42.9	32.3	25.9	16.4	10.6	25
17.3	20.2	22.5	25.3	24.0	22.3	17.8	15.3	11.4	8.7	4.4	26
26.9*	28.6*	32.0*	36.1*	39.9*	41.7*	41.9*	40.5*	36.3*	30.9	21.7	27
24.7*	25.8*	28.5*	31.8*	33.7*	32.6*	29.5*	25.0*	21.3*	17.3	12.3	28
60.7	61.9*	63.6*	66.3*	65.4*	63.4*	55.5*	47.5	36.0	27.3	12.6	29
31.1	29.7*	33.7*	34.4*	32.2*	30.0*	25.1*	18.6	13.9	10.2	6.4	30
65.8	65.6	68.9	70.5	68.7	65.1	59.2	49.6	38.6*	27.3*	12.6*	31
42.8	38.7	42.3	44.7	43.3	40.5	34.4	28.3	20.9*	13.9*	7.0*	32
66.2	69.0	72.2	72.9	72.1	66.8	61.3	52.1	41.7	29.6	14.1	33
42.5	42.0	45.5	47.6	47.7	42.5	37.3	30.2	22.6	14.5	7.0	34
59.0	64.2	73.0	75.9	74.1	69.1	60.7	49.1	34.8*	21.7*	7.1*	35
42.5	41.8	50.4	55.5	55.6	51.7	44.1	34.1	22.9*	14.0*	6.6*	36

	Country and census year			GYAL[a]	15-19	20-29	30-44	45-64	65+	20-24
		4.	South and East Asia (continued)							
37	Korea, South	1960	Rural	18.3	23.9	31.1	38.8	32.6	9.6	30.1
38			Urban	10.2	28.6	23.2	17.2	15.2	3.8	31.8
39	Pakistan	1961	Rural	10.2	14.3	16.3	17.2	15.9	10.5	15.7
40			Urban	3.8	2.7	4.9	6.3	7.1	4.9	4.3
41	Thailand	1954	Rural	51.0	89.1	90.1	90.9	81.5	28.6	91.0
42			Urban	21.9	32.2	38.7	40.5	34.7	17.0	38.5
		5.	Latin America, Spain, and Portugal							
43	Argentina	1960	Rural	8.2	26.8	19.4	11.8	10.1	5.9	23.2
44			Urban	13.5	36.4	39.2	25.5	14.8	4.8	45.1
45	Chile	1952	Rural	10.0	18.0	16.4	14.7	16.1	12.6	17.8
46			Urban	18.4	34.2	40.1	34.0	26.9	13.4	42.8
47		1960	Rural	6.1	12.2	11.3	8.3	9.4	7.3	12.4
48			Urban	14.7	27.8	36.6	27.6	20.9	7.9	39.4
49	Colombia	1951	Rural	9.1	14.1	13.6	14.0	15.2	11.4	14.0
50			Urban	14.4	34.8	31.8	25.4	18.7	9.5	35.0
51		1964	Rural	7.8	11.2	11.8	12.2	14.0	8.7	12.3
52			Urban	14.0	28.9	32.7	25.9	19.5	8.2	36.2
53	Costa Rica	1950	Rural	4.5	14.1	9.8	6.9	5.7	3.4	11.4
54			Urban	14.9	37.1	36.5	28.9	18.3	7.6	39.5
55		1963	Rural	4.3	12.6	10.8	7.7	5.1	2.2	12.5
56			Urban	15.4	30.1	39.7	32.0	19.9	6.1	42.4
57	Cuba	1953	Rural	7.8	13.1	12.8	12.0	11.7	9.0	13.3
58			Urban	12.7	20.5	27.5	25.5	18.5	8.1	27.7
59	Ecuador	1962	Rural	8.2	13.7	11.7	11.0	12.9	12.2	12.5
60			Urban	14.8	29.4	31.9	25.1	20.5	12.1	35.0
61	El Salvador	1950	Rural	5.9	12.2	9.7	8.6	8.1	6.9	10.5
62			Urban	16.5	33.9	33.3	29.0	22.7	14.3	35.8
63		1961	Rural	5.3	11.7	9.8	8.0	7.3	5.5	10.5
64			Urban	17.6	31.1	39.4	32.8	24.6	13.6	40.7
65	Guatemala	1950	Rural	5.0	9.1	7.3	7.7	7.6	5.4	7.6
66			Urban	16.7	34.5	31.1	28.2	24.6	14.8	34.0
67		1964	Rural	3.6	7.1	5.0	5.1	5.7	4.1	5.2
68			Urban	14.3	29.5	28.8	24.3	21.3	11.3	30.3
69	Mexico	1960	Rural	8.6	12.5	12.8	12.8	14.3	12.0	14.3
70			Urban	13.8	28.3	26.2	20.7	20.6	14.3	30.5
71	Nicaragua	1950	Rural	5.6	7.2	8.3	8.3	8.8	8.0	8.2
72			Urban	12.9	26.8	26.7	22.9	18.7	10.2	28.2
73		1963	Rural	8.7	10.5	11.9	14.2	15.0	10.7	11.9
74			Urban	18.6	31.4	38.2	35.7	28.3	13.0	39.0
75	Panama	1950	Rural	7.2	17.2	13.8	11.4	10.0	6.3	15.5
76			Urban	18.9	31.8	44.5	39.3	26.5	10.1	47.5

202

Table A.10. (continued)

25-29	30-34	35-39	40-44	45-49	50-54	55-59	60-64	65-69	70-74	75+	
				4.	South and East Asia (continued)						
32.1	36.1	39.9	40.5	40.2	37.4	33.8	19.0	13.8	9.0*	6.1*	37
14.6	14.3	17.5	19.7	20.6	18.1	14.1	8.1	5.5	3.7*	2.4*	38
16.8*	17.1*	0.1*	17.4*	17.9*	17.4*	14.9	13.5*	12.2*	10.5*	8.7*	39
5.4*	5.7*	6.2*	7.0*	8.2*	7.8*	6.6	5.9*	5.4*	4.9*	4.3*	40
89.3	90.0	91.1	91.5	91.0	89.1*	81.1*	65.0*	44.8*	27.9*	13.0*	41
38.9	40.9	41.1	39.4	47.8	33.8*	30.7*	26.6*	22.3*	17.8*	11.0*	42
				5.	Latin America, Spain, and Portugal						
15.6	12.5	11.6	11.2	10.9	10.4	10.0	8.9	7.6	6.2	4.0	43
33.3	27.4	25.2	24.0	21.3	16.6	12.5	9.0	6.8	4.7	3.0	44
15.0	14.1	14.4	15.6	15.8	16.5	16.0	16.0	15.0	13.1	9.8	45
37.4	34.4	33.9	33.6	31.8	28.6	25.6	21.4	17.7	13.7	8.7	46
10.2	8.3	8.0	8.7	9.2	9.8	9.5	9.0	8.4*	7.4*	5.9*	47
33.7	28.6	27.5	26.9	25.7	22.9	19.4	15.5	11.9*	8.0*	4.0*	48
13.3	13.2	13.8	14.9	15.0	15.6	14.9	15.3	13.9	12.0	8.4	49
28.7	26.1	25.8	24.4	22.1	20.1	17.0	15.8	11.9	10.2	6.2	50
11.4	11.4	11.9	13.2	13.8	14.6	14.0	13.5	11.0	9.3	5.7	51
29.2	26.3	26.1	25.2	23.8	21.1	18.2	14.8	11.0	8.8	4.9	52
8.1*	6.9*	6.9*	6.7*	6.6*	6.2*	5.4*	4.6*	4.1*	3.3	2.9	53
33.5*	29.7*	29.5*	27.4*	24.6*	20.4*	15.9*	12.3*	10.2*	8.1	4.6	54
9.0	8.4	7.7	6.9	6.2	5.6	4.5	4.0	2.8	2.4	1.2	55
37.1	33.7	32.4	29.8	26.1	21.3	17.8	14.2	9.4	5.6	3.3	56
12.3	11.8	12.0	12.2	12.6	11.9	11.5	10.9	9.9*	9.0*	8.2*	57
27.3	26.0	25.6	24.9	22.7	20.6	16.9	13.6	10.7*	8.5*	5.0*	58
10.9	10.8	10.7	11.6	11.7	13.2	12.8	13.8	12.8	13.9	9.9	59
28.9	25.7	25.0	24.8	23.3	21.6	19.5	17.6	14.0	13.3	9.0	60
8.8*	8.5*	8.8*	8.6*	8.6*	8.4*	7.9*	7.7*	7.5*	7.0*	6.4	61
30.9*	29.4*	29.3*	28.5*	26.5*	23.7*	21.0*	19.5*	16.9*	14.2*	11.9	62
9.1	8.3	7.8	8.0	8.1	7.2	7.0	6.7	6.5	5.7	4.4	63
38.1	35.1	32.4	30.8	28.5	26.7	22.9	20.4	16.8	14.0	9.8	64
7.0	7.3	7.8	7.9	8.1	7.6	7.9	6.9	7.5	5.4	3.5	65
28.3	28.0	28.8	27.8	27.6	25.2	23.9	21.8	18.7	15.8	9.9	66
4.8	4.8	5.0	5.4	5.8	6.3	5.5	5.1	3.5	4.5	4.3	67
27.3	25.7	23.7	23.6	24.4	22.9	20.1	17.7	15.2	13.8	5.0	68
11.3	12.0	12.8	13.6	13.9	14.1	14.5	14.7	14.0	12.8	9.4	69
21.9	19.3	20.7	22.2	21.4	21.2	20.2	19.6	17.2	15.7	10.1	70
8.3*	8.6*	8.3*	8.0*	8.5*	8.6*	9.1*	9.0*	8.9*	8.1*	6.9*	71
25.1*	23.1*	23.0*	22.6*	20.8*	19.1*	18.3*	16.5*	13.9*	10.3*	6.3*	72
11.9	13.5	14.1*	14.9*	15.5*	15.4*	15.2*	14.0*	12.9*	11.3*	8.0*	73
37.3	36.7	35.8*	34.6*	34.0*	31.3*	26.4*	21.7*	16.7*	13.3*	9.0*	74
12.2	11.4	11.2	11.7	10.8	10.8	9.6	8.8	7.6	6.7*	4.6*	75
41.5	39.5	40.3	38.2	35.3	29.2	23.5	17.9	15.2	9.9*	5.2*	76

	Country and census year			GYAL[a]	15-19	20-29	30-44	45-64	65+	20-24

5. Latin America, Spain, and Portugal (continued)

				GYAL[a]	15-19	20-29	30-44	45-64	65+	20-24
77	Panama	1960	Rural	5.7	14.3	11.6	9.1	8.1	4.0	12.8
78			Urban	20.4	32.3	48.2	43.6	29.7	8.6	49.8
79	Peru	1961	Rural	11.5	23.5	18.1	16.1	18.5	13.7	20.0
80			Urban	14.7	30.5	32.7	25.5	21.2	9.8	35.8
81	Portugal	1960	Rural	8.1	21.6	16.7	11.1	10.9	7.7	19.5
82			Urban	16.6	46.8	42.1	27.7	20.0	8.2	47.8
83	Puerto Rico	1950	Rural	8.5	17.8	21.3	18.3	10.2	3.7	23.0
84			Urban	14.4	21.8	34.5	32.5	19.8	5.8	36.0
85		1960	Rural	7.6	7.9	21.7	17.2	10.0	2.8	22.8
86			Urban	15.3	14.2	40.3	34.9	22.5	5.0	41.2
87	Spain	1950	Rural	7.9	14.4	12.0	9.5	12.2	12.5	14.0
88			Urban	11.5	28.4	30.7	17.3	15.9	7.0	32.3

6. Eastern Europe

89	Bulgaria	1956	Rural	42.8	67.0	80.7	87.9	69.2	27.9	80.1
90			Urban	21.6	18.6	50.0	53.4	32.2	8.2	49.2

7. Middle Europe

91	Finland	1960	Rural	27.8	39.1	53.8	55.6	50.6	12.8	55.5
92			Urban	29.2	45.5	64.7	59.8	51.1	8.3	66.8
93	Greece	1951	Rural	8.4	21.1	18.0	13.4	11.9	5.3	20.1
94			Urban	10.8	30.4	28.7	18.4	12.3	4.1	33.0
95		1961	Rural	28.0	57.5	57.0	51.8	42.2	15.1	60.2
96			Urban	12.4	32.4	36.8	22.8	13.3	2.8	41.8

8. Northwestern Europe, Northern America, and Oceania

97	Canada	1961	Rural	12.0	22.5	27.1	21.0	21.3	4.8	33.2
98			Urban	18.9	39.7	44.7	33.1	31.5	7.5	54.6
99	Norway	1960	Rural	11.9	40.3	28.9	13.6	17.7	6.7	38.9
100			Urban	20.3	46.9	50.5	29.9	35.1	9.0	62.2
101	Sweden	1960	Rural	15.2	44.9	40.7	25.9	22.0	3.6	49.1
102			Urban	23.3	48.1	56.2	43.6	39.8	5.4	63.1
103		1965	Rural	19.1	36.8	41.7	38.0	32.6	5.8	47.0
104			Urban	23.6	41.9	51.8	46.8	42.7	4.7	57.8
105	United States	1950	Rural	11.9	18.6	25.2	24.1	19.7	5.6	28.8
106			Urban	19.3	31.3	43.5	38.1	31.7	8.2	49.6
107		1960	Rural	16.8	20.6	31.5	34.0	31.5	7.6	34.9
108			Urban	22.8	30.8	43.1	42.7	44.0	11.1	48.3

25-29	30-34	35-39	40-44	45-49	50-54	55-59	60-64	65-69	70-74	75+	

5. Latin America, Spain, and Portugal (continued)

25-29	30-34	35-39	40-44	45-49	50-54	55-59	60-64	65-69	70-74	75+	
10.3	9.5	8.8	9.1	9.5	8.6	7.5	6.8	5.1	4.4	2.7	77
46.5	44.5	44.0	42.4	40.3	33.6	26.7	18.4	13.2	8.4	4.1	78
16.1	15.7	15.7	17.1	17.8	18.8	18.7	18.8	17.6	12.3	11.1	79
29.6	26.5	25.4	24.7	23.9	22.6	20.5	17.9	14.7	9.9	4.8	80
13.9	11.4	10.8	10.9	10.9	10.8	11.1	10.9	9.9	7.7	5.5	81
36.4	30.4	27.4	25.3	23.3	21.5	19.6	15.6	10.8	8.6	5.3	82
19.7	19.7	18.7	16.6	14.4	10.9	8.9	6.6	4.8	3.5	2.8	83
33.0	32.1	33.1	32.2	28.6	22.3	16.3	11.8	8.6	5.4	3.6	84
20.7	18.9	16.9	15.8	12.3	11.3	9.0	7.3	3.9	3.1	1.3	85
39.5	37.8	34.7	32.4	29.2	26.2	20.3	14.3	8.1	4.8	2.0	86
10.0*	8.7*	9.5*	10.5*	10.8*	11.5*	12.9*	13.4*	13.4*	12.7*	11.5*	87
29.1*	22.3*	15.8*	13.8*	17.1*	18.0*	15.6*	13.1*	11.1*	7.0*	3.0*	88

6. Eastern Europe

25-29	30-34	35-39	40-44	45-49	50-54	55-59	60-64	65-69	70-74	75+	
81.2	86.1	88.9	88.6	84.0	75.4	65.4	52.1	40.2	24.8	18.9	89
50.8	51.6	54.5	54.0	47.9	37.2	26.4	17.4	12.3	7.2	5.1	90

7. Middle Europe

25-29	30-34	35-39	40-44	45-49	50-54	55-59	60-64	65-69	70-74	75+	
52.1	52.6	56.0	58.3	58.9	56.5	50.3	36.6	21.3	11.8*	5.5*	91
62.5	59.4	59.0	61.2	60.7	57.4	51.0	35.2	15.7	6.6*	2.6*	92
15.9	13.2	13.2	13.9	14.3	12.8	11.3	9.2	7.2	5.4	3.3	93
24.4	20.6	17.7	16.8	14.8	13.6	11.8	8.8	5.8	4.0	2.6	94
53.8	51.5	51.9	52.1	51.1*	46.2*	39.8*	31.7*	22.7*	15.0*	7.7	95
31.8	24.9	22.5	21.0	18.7*	15.8*	11.2*	7.5*	4.6*	2.4*	1.5	96

8. Northwestern Europe, Northern America, and Oceania

25-29	30-34	35-39	40-44	45-49	50-54	55-59	60-64	65-69	70-74	75+	
20.9*	18.2*	21.2*	23.6*	25.4*	24.1*	21.1*	14.5*	8.7*	4.6*	1.1*	97
34.8*	31.0*	32.9*	35.4*	37.1*	35.9*	30.5*	22.5*	13.2*	7.6*	1.9*	98
18.9	13.4	13.2	14.2	15.5	18.0	19.3	17.8	13.6	4.6	1.8	99
38.9	29.9	29.4	30.4	34.8	36.1	38.4	31.0	20.0	5.2	1.8	100
32.3	26.4	29.5	25.7	25.6	24.7	22.3	15.4	7.5	2.5	0.9	101
49.3	42.7	43.0	45.1	46.4	45.3	40.4	27.2	11.9	3.3	1.0	102
36.4	35.7	38.4	39.9	39.9	36.7	31.4	22.6	11.4	4.6	1.5	103
45.8	42.0	47.3	51.2	51.8	48.5	42.1	28.6	10.7	2.8	0.7	104
21.6	21.8	24.5	25.9	24.8	21.7	18.1	14.3	9.3	5.2	2.2	105
37.4	35.1	38.3	40.9	39.2	34.8	29.4	23.4	14.4	7.4	2.8	106
28.0	30.1	34.2	37.7	38.4	36.1	30.0	21.5	12.2	7.3	3.3	107
37.8	37.5	42.5	48.1	50.9	49.5	43.3	32.4	18.2	10.4	4.6	108

Table A.10. (continued)

Country and census year			GYAL[a]	15-19	20-29	30-44	45-64	65+	20-24
			9. Miscellaneous						
109 Guyana	1960		Rural	13.3	18.0	16.1	24.7	28.1	8.8	15.1
110			Urban	20.4	43.4	43.0	37.4	33.7	10.0	46.3

25-29	30-34	35-39	40-44	45-49	50-54	55-59	60-64	65-69	70-74	75+
				9. Miscellaneous						
17.0	21.4	24.1	28.4	30.0	30.8	29.1	22.5	13.8	8.7	3.8	109
39.8	35.8	37.3	39.1	39.0	36.8	34.1	25.0	15.5	10.0	4.6	110

*
Estimated by interpolation or extrapolation.
a
Gross years of active life of females in ages 10 and over. See Appendix D for explanation.
b
.See also Guinea (Tropical Africa), Indonesia and Pakistan (South and East Asia).

Selection and Adjustment of Data

B.1. *Censuses not Included in the Data Compilation*

As stated in chapter 1, the aim of the data compilation for this study was to include all censuses providing useable measures of the labor force, taken during the period of 1946 to 1966 inclusive, in countries having an estimated population of 500,000 or more in 1960. Where data of complete censuses were lacking, estimates based on national demographic sample surveys were to be included as substitutes if available. However, some censuses or sample surveys were not included for the reasons stated below.

(a) *Data were obtained too late to be incorporated into the processing and tabulation of statistical material.* The following censuses and surveys were not included for this reason:

Madagascar, 1957	Denmark, 1965
Guyana, 1965	Ireland, 1966
Taiwan, 1966	United Kingdom, 1966
South Korea, 1966	Australia, 1966
West Malaysia, 1962	New Zealand, 1966

(b) *Large components of the population or areas of the country were not covered by the enumerations.* In addition to censuses or surveys limited to nonindigenous minorities in a number of African countries, the following were omitted for this reason:

Israel, 1948: The census was limited to the Jewish population.

Namibia (former South West Africa), 1946, 1951: The enumeration of the indigenous population was limited to residents of the Police Zone, who constituted only a minority of the total indigenous population.

Niger, 1960: Estimates were based on a sample survey that did not cover Niamey City (about 30,000 inhabitants) and nomadic population estimated at 234,000. Labor force figures given in the United Nations, *Demographic Yearbook*, 1964, disagree seriously with those given in the I.L.O. *Year Books of Labour Statistics*.

(c) *A comprehensive and consistent set of tabulations of the population and labor force was not found.* Two censuses were omitted for this reason:

Czechoslovakia, 1951   East Germany, 1946.

Appendix B

(d) *Conditions of the economy and the labor market were abnormal at the time of the census.* For this reason, the following censuses taken during or in the aftermath of war or internal conflict were omitted:

Algeria, 1954   West Germany, 1946
France, 1946   South Korea, 1955

The census of Lesotho, 1966, was omitted because the labor force measures were affected greatly by the absence of a large fraction of the male population, employed outside the country.

(e) *The labor force enumerations were judged to be inconsistent with those of other censuses of the same country;* that is, intercensal changes were indicated that were scarcely if at all credible. It has to be admitted that the credibility of intercensal changes indicated by the data of some of the censuses retained in the compilation could also be challenged, and that the selection of censuses to be retained and those to be discarded was not founded on any clear-cut, objective criteria. However, the reliability of the picture of intercensal changes was improved by eliminating some of the most dubious measures. The censuses rejected for this reason are listed below with brief explanations.

Algeria, 1954; Libya, 1954; Morocco, 1950; Tunisia, 1956
The differences between female activity rates recorded in these censuses and more recent censuses of the same countries were too great to be accepted as plausible measures of actual changes during the intervals. The refined activity rates as recorded are listed in Table B.a.

Table B.a

		Males	Females
Algeria	1954	75.2	37.6
	1966	65.7	2.6
Libya	1954	81.6	7.6
	1964	69.6	4.4
Morocco			
(Moslem pop.)	1952	78.4	34.2
	1960	76.9	9.2
Tunisia	1956	72.5	35.0
	1966	68.1	22.1

Although the rates for females recorded in the earlier censuses may well have been nearer the truth than those recorded

209

Appendix B

in the later censuses, there is little reason for supposing the same to have been true of the activity rates recorded for males. For the purpose of cross-sectional comparisons with the statistics of other countries, it was considered preferable on the whole to retain the more recent data and to discard those of the earlier censuses. In the case of Algeria, this alternative was preferred also for reason (d).

India, 1951; Pakistan, 1951

The following refined activity rates of males and females are indicated by the Indian and Pakistani censuses of 1951 and 1961:

| | India | | Pakistan | |
	Males	Females	Males	Females
1951	72.8	31.8	77.2	5.7
1961	81.1	39.9	84.4	13.8

The increases are contrary to generally declining secular trends in the rates for both sexes indicated by the censuses since 1911, and in the case of males, contrary also to the postwar trend in most of the other countries for which data were obtained. The concepts and definitions applied in the 1951 and 1961 censuses were different. Indian scholars have been divided in their opinions of the reliability of measures of 1951–1961 changes in the labor force derived from the census figures.[1] Preliminary returns of the 1971 Indian census, which show large decreases from 1961 levels of both male and female activity rates, intensify doubt about the validity of the changes indicated between 1951 and 1961.

Philippines, 1948

Another instance of apparent increases in activity rates of both males and females where decreasing secular trends of the rates for both sexes had been indicated previously is found in the comparison between 1948 and 1960 census data for the Philippines. The standardized activity rates are as follows:

[1] J. N. Sinha, "Comparability of 1961 and 1951 Census Economic Data," *Artha Vijnana* (December 1964); comment by P. M. Visaria, and rejoinder, *ibid.* (December 1965); J. P. Ambannavar, "Changes in the Employment Pattern of the Indian Working Force, 1911–1961," *Developing Economies* (Tokyo, March 1970); G. M. Farooq, *Dimensions and Structure of Labor Force and Their Changes in the Process of Economic Development: A Case Study of Pakistan* (Ph.D. dissertation, University of Pennsylvania, 1970).

	Males	Females
1948	68.1	16.2
1960	75.2	24.9

The report of the 1960 census warns that the labor force data of 1948 and 1960 are not comparable. This has been confirmed by detailed examination of the data.[2]

South Korea, 1955

Here, as in the case of Algeria, both reasons (d) and (e) argue for rejection of the data. The standardized activity rates of males and females recorded in the 1955 and 1960 censuses of South Korea were as follows:

	Males	Females
1955	69.7	42.5
1960	68.3	24.4

The results of Yu's study of the 1955 census data for this country show strong reasons for doubting the reliability of the labor force measures and major difficulties in reconciling them with the data of the 1960 census.

Turkey, 1950

The Turkish censuses of 1955, 1960, and 1965 provided a fairly consistent and internally comparable series of labor force measures based on essentially the same definitions and the same system of classification (except that the basis for enumeration of females over age sixty-five in the labor force seems to have been altered in 1965). The 1950 census data do not fit so well into this series, as the definitions and the classification system were different. It was considered preferable, therefore, to omit the 1950 data.

Honduras, 1950

The refined activity rates of males and females indicated by the censuses of 1950 and 1961 in Honduras were as follows:

[2] See Yeun-chung Yu, *The Development of the Economically Active Population in East Asia, 1947–1966* (Ph.D. dissertation, University of Pennsylvania, 1969); also United Nations, *Population Growth and Manpower in the Philippines* (New York, 1958); Virginia M. Moscoso, "Our Economically Active Population," *Philippine Social Security Bulletin* (March 1962).

	Males	Females
1950	74.6	58.3
1961	82.2	11.9

The decrease in the rate for females, from one of the highest in the world to a position far below the world average during only eleven years, is patently incredible. As in the case of the North African countries, it is possible that the rate recorded in the earlier census might have been more nearly accurate than the later one; but the alternative of rejecting the more recent data and retaining those of the 1950 census as a basis for cross-sectional comparisons was still less attractive in the case of Honduras in view of the poverty of the 1950 census tabulations. The tabulation of the labor force by age groups for each sex was not found for 1950, nor was there a classification by sex in the tabulations of occupation and industry groups. Moreover, the male refined activity rate of 1950 appears to be inconsistent with the 1961 rate.

Greece, 1951

The standardized activity rates derived from the Greek censuses of 1951 and 1961 were as follows:

	Males	Females
1951	77.3	16.0
1961	76.2	34.7

The large increase in the rate for females is spurious. It is explained by the information given in the 1961 census report, that female workers in agriculture were greatly underenumerated in 1951 and that the quality of the enumeration was improved in 1961.

Yugoslavia, 1948

The Yugoslavian censuses indicate the following trends of refined activity rates of males and females:

	Males	Females
1948	84.9	73.1
1953	80.9	38.3
1961	76.6	39.0

The statistics of economically active population tabulated in the 1948 census include all persons receiving income regard-

less of employment, and all housewives in agricultural households. In 1953, inactive recipients of income, such as pensioners and social assistance recipients, were excluded, and
farm housewives were included only if they spent one-half
or more of their time in agricultural work. It is stated in the
1948 census report that exclusion of pensioners and social
assistance recipients from the labor force figures would lower
the crude activity rate by only 1.7 percentage points. Thus
the effect of the difference in definitions between the 1948
census and the later censuses seems to have been relatively
small in the case of the males, but the measures of female
labor force are clearly not comparable.

B.2. *Adjustments of Labor Force Measures*

In some cases where the definitions of the labor force applied in
the tabulations of census returns deviated from normal or internationally recommended standards, data that served as a basis for
adjustments to improve comparability were found in the census
reports or elsewhere. Such adjustments are described below.

Austria, 1951
> First-job seekers (7,767 males, 6,025 females), tabulated
> separately in the census reports, were added to the labor force.

Belgium, 1947
> Labor force figures shown in the 1961 census report were ad-
> justed by adding 6,400 males in military service other than
> career military personnel (who were included in the eco-
> nomically active population as tabulated in the 1947 census).

Denmark, 1950, 1960
> Housewives and daughters occupied with domestic duties at
> home were deducted from the labor force. In the census tabu-
> lations of economically active population by occupational
> groups, the numbers of housewives were given as 104,165 for
> 1950 and 56,009 for 1960; and of daughters, 39,694 for
> 1950 and 29,983 for 1960.

France, 1954, 1962
> Corrected age-specific activity rates including males con-
> scripted for military service (*militaires du contingent*), given
> by Alfred Nizard, "La Population active selon les recense-

213

ments depuis 1946," *Population* 26(1) (January-February 1971), Annexe III, were used as a basis for adjusting the census statistics.

West Germany, 1961

The labor force figures are those given in United Nations, *Demographic Yearbook*, 1964, including 294,000 males in military service who were not included in the economically active population as tabulated in the census reports.

Greece, 1961

An estimate of 128,300 males in military service was added to the labor force. This estimate was derived from figures shown in the census tabulations for the combined category of military service and inmates of institutions, not included in the economically active population. In the rural-urban classification of population and labor force, the category of "semiurban" was combined with rural population.

Iraq, 1957

Labor force figures are sums of figures for occupational groups tabulated in the census report, except "persons not related to the economy." These sums differ slightly from figures shown in United Nations, *Demographic Yearbook*, 1964.

Italy, 1951

First-job seekers, tabulated separately in the census reports, were added to the labor force.

South Korea, 1960

A category of "economic activity status not reported," shown in the census tabulations, was not included in the labor force.

Mexico, 1950, 1960

The 1950 census tabulations show the classification of labor force by sex and by age separately but not in combination. Age-specific activity rates by sex are estimates made by the staff of the Colegio de México and kindly made available for use in this study.

The 1960 census tabulations of labor force by sex and age groups were falsified by a tabulation error. On the basis of a sample of the census returns, the staff of the Colegio de México made estimates of age-specific activity rates of each sex in the rural and urban sectors of the country. These are published in J. Morelos, "Entradas a la actividad, salidas y vida media activa en México, 1960–1965," *Demografía y Economía* 4 (1968), 36.

For the present study, labor force totals and activity rates by sex and age for Mexico as a whole in 1960 were derived by applying Morelos' estimated rural and urban age-specific activity rates to the rural and urban population figures by sex and age groups as given by the census tabulations, and summing up the results for country totals.

Pakistan, 1961
Rural and urban population and labor force figures by sex and age groups were taken from Pakistan Planning Division, Manpower Section, *Projections of Labour Force for Pakistan and Provinces, 1960–1990* (Islamabad, 1969).

Poland, 1950, 1960
Estimated numbers of armed forces were added to the labor force: 393,000 males for 1950, 290,000 for 1960, according to Andrew Elias, "Magnitude and distribution of the labor force in Eastern Europe," in *Economic Developments in Eastern Europe*, U.S. Congress, 91st Congress, 2nd Sess., Joint Economic Committee, Subcommittee on Foreign Economic Policy (Washington, D.C., 1970), pp. 156, 213.

Portugal, 1950, 1960
Males and females occupied with domestic duties at home were deducted from the labor force. These persons were tabulated in the census reports as an occupational category of the economically active population.

Portuguese Guinea, 1950
Females in the occupational category, "domesticas rurais," numbering 159,690, were deducted from the labor force.

Sierra Leone, 1963
Armed forces, tabulated separately in the census reports, were added to the labor force.

Sudan, 1956
Labor force measures used in this study, unlike the data shown in the United Nations, *Demographic Yearbook*, 1964, and the I.L.O. *Year Books of Labour Statistics*, are sums of

persons who reported a *gainful occupation* as their primary activity and those who reported such an occupation as a secondary activity only. Data taken from United Nations, *Population Growth and Manpower in the Sudan* (New York, 1964).

Sweden, 1960, 1965

Males on military service not employed as civilians during the four months preceding the census were added to the labor force: 44,330 for 1960, 59,829 for 1965 as given in the census tabulations of categories of persons not included in the economically active population.

Switzerland, 1950, 1960

Persons who reported a gainful occupation as a secondary activity only were added to the labor force: 1,008 males and 190,285 females for 1950, 8,167 males and 154,267 females for 1960, as given in the census tabulations of persons not included in the economically active population.

Syria, 1960

Unemployed persons seeking work were included in the labor force and those not seeking work were excluded, by reference to the classification shown in the census tabulations. Labor force figures shown in the United Nations, *Demographic Yearbook*, 1964, exclude all unemployed.

Togo, 1958/60

Labor force includes 14,130 apprentices and 2,630 unemployed persons not classified by sex in the census tabulations; these were assumed to be all males.

Tunisia, 1966

Labor force includes 250,000 females reported in the census as unpaid family workers but not included in the census tabulations of the labor force by industry groups. Because the industry classification of these workers was not available, female shares in agricultural and nonagricultural employment are not included in the compilation of data for this study.

USSR, 1959

Members of families of collective farmers, workers, and employees working on individual agricultural plots have been added to the labor force: 913,903 males and 8,950,898 females, as tabulated separately in the report of the census.

United Arab Republic, 1947, 1960:
  Labor force figures are taken from Abdel-Fattah Nassef, *The Egyptian Labor Force: Its Dimensions and Changing Structure, 1907–1960* (University of Pennsylvania, Population Studies Center, Philadelphia, 1970). These figures were adjusted by Nassef for comparability between censuses by deducting the category of "ill-defined activities" from the totals of the economically active population as tabulated in the census reports, and deducting housewives and students from the tabulated totals for 1947.

Adjustment of Age Limits and Classifications

C.1. *Adjustment to Age Reference of Ten Years and Over*

The labor force enumerations in some censuses have no stated age limits; apparently all persons reporting an economic activity are counted, including children irrespective of age. In most censuses, however, some minimal age limit is imposed. Such limits varied from five to fifteen years in the censuses that were included in the data compilation for this study. To eliminate effects of variations in this respect, the numbers of the labor force on which crude, standardized, and refined activity rates were based were adjusted wherever possible to an age reference of ten years and over. This adjustment was, of course, not necessary where a ten-year limit was imposed in the census, and it posed no problem wherever an age classification of the labor force was given with a break at ten years. Otherwise the necessary adjustment was estimated, if possible, on the basis of whatever relevant data could be found in each case. In some cases, estimates were based on data for other countries in circumstances similar to those of the country in question.

The alternative of adjusting the data to a standard age reference of fifteen years and over was considered and rejected. Measures on that basis would have understated the size of the labor force appreciably in many less-developed countries. Moreover, difficulties would have been encountered in the case of censuses in which lower age limits were adopted and classifications of the labor force by age groups were not available.

For the measures of female shares in agricultural and nonagricultural employment, adjustments to a uniform age reference were not undertaken. The varying minimal age limits have less effect on FS_{ag} and FS_{nonag} than they have on the labor force totals, and adjustments of FS_{ag} and FS_{nonag} would have run into greater difficulties.

Various methods were used to estimate adjustments of the male and female labor force totals, according to the types of data available in each case. A few examples will illustrate some of the methods used most frequently.

Example of Colombia: In many cases, estimates were made by interpolation or extrapolation in the series of specific activity rates

218

of each sex by age groupings found in the census tabulations. For example, in the censuses of Colombia (1951 and 1964), where the labor force enumeration referred to the age group of 12 years and over, activity rates for ages 10 and 11 were estimated by extrapolation from the recorded rates for 12 to 14 and 15 to 19, as shown in Table C.a.

Table C.a

	1951		1964	
	Males	Females	Males	Females
Recorded rates: 15–19	84.78	23.62	66.29	21.85
12–14	28.82	10.34	26.87	7.29
Estimated rate: 10–11	8.00	1.81	7.57	1.21

To estimate the rates for ages 10 and 11, those for the higher age groups were charted and their curves extrapolated downward to an assumed level of zero at age 5, taking into account the forms of age curves of male and female rates for single years of age between 5 and 15 provided by tabulations of the 1961 census of Peru. The estimated rates for 10 and 11 were applied to the population figures for that age group[1] to derive estimated numbers of persons aged 10 and 11 in the labor force, which were added to the recorded numbers for ages 12 and over (Table C.b).

Table C.b

	1951		1964	
	Males	Females	Males	Females
Recorded labor force:				
12 and over	3,054,420	701,189	4,102,063	1,032,062
12–14	115,287	40,758	179,534	48,087
Estimated labor force:				
10–11	23,371	4,759	36,383	5,587
10 and over	3,077,791	705,948	4,138,446	1,037,649
10–14	138,658	45,517	215,917	53,674

Although the estimates for the age group 10 to 14 might be considerably in error, the labor force totals for 10 years and over and

[1] In the available tabulations of population by age groups, no subdivision of the group 10 to 14 years was found. The numbers of ages 10 to 11 and 12 to 14 were estimated approximately by interpolation.

Appendix C

the corresponding refined activity rates for each sex would not be affected seriously. This can be demonstrated by comparing the estimated rates with those which would obtain on two extreme assumptions with regard to the age group 10 and 11: (a) that its activity rates were zero for both sexes, and (b) that its activity rates were the same as those recorded for age group 12 to 14. The figures are shown in Table C.c.

Table C.c

	1951		1964	
	Males	Females	Males	Females
Specific activity rates, ages 10–14:				
As estimated	20.3	6.9	18.8	4.8
Assumption (a)	16.8	6.2	15.6	4.3
Assumption (b)	28.8	10.3	26.9	7.3
Refined activity rates, ages 10 and over:				
As estimated	80.3	17.8	73.5	17.4
Assumption (a)	79.7	17.7	72.8	17.3
Assumption (b)	81.7	18.4	75.1	17.9

Example of the United States: This example illustrates the use of data from earlier censuses of the same country as a basis for the estimated adjustments—a method that was applicable in a number of cases. The labor force enumerations in the United States censuses of 1940, 1950, and 1960 referred to the age group of 14 years and over, but data for 10 years and over were given by the censuses of 1930 and earlier years. Lee, Miller, Brainerd, and Easterlin made estimates for age group 10 to 13 in 1940 and 1950 by assuming that the trends since 1930 in activity rates of this age group in each state would have paralleled the trends of the rates for 14 and 15 years.[2] On this basis, the estimated activity rates of age group 10 to 13 as of 1950 were 3.5 percent for males and 1.0 percent for females in the coterminous United States. In view of the fact that the activity rates recorded for age 14 in the 1960 census were slightly higher than those of 1950, the estimated rates for 10 to 13 in 1950 were assumed to remain at the same levels in 1960. As in the case of Colombia, the resulting estimates for the

[2] *Population Redistribution and Economic Growth, United States 1870–1950* I (Philadelphia, American Philosophical Society, 1957), 366–67.

age group 10 to 14 could be rather wide of the mark, but the refined rates in the population ten years and over would not be much affected. With calculations assuming (a) zero activity rates for age group 10 to 13, and (b) the same rates for 10 to 13 as for age 14, indications of extreme limits of possible errors were obtained (Table C.d).

Table C.d

	1950		1960	
	Males	*Females*	*Males*	*Females*
Specific activity rates, ages 10–14:				
As estimated	5.3	1.6	5.2	1.8
Assumption (a)	2.5	0.8	2.3	0.9
Assumption (b)	13.2	4.1	13.9	5.7
Refined activity rates, ages 10 and over:				
As estimated	73.1	27.0	69.7	31.3
Assumption (a)	72.8	26.9	69.7	31.3
Assumption (b)	73.8	27.2	71.1	31.8

Example of Guinea: Wider error margins must be admitted in some cases, especially of little-developed countries where the age limits for the labor force enumerations were relatively high and no firm basis could be found for estimating activity rates of children below the specified age limits. The example of Guinea (1954/55) will serve as an illustration. The labor force enumeration in this case was limited to the age group 14 years and over and no data on the extent of participation by children of ages 10 to 13 were available. For ages 14 to 19, activity rates of 85.9 percent for males and 84.9 percent for females were recorded. In view of these high rates for ages 14 to 19 and the varied levels of rates for ages 10 to 14 recorded in other African and Asian countries, the activity rates for 10 to 14 in Guinea were placed by conjecture at 23.5 percent for males and 32.0 percent for females. Considerably higher or lower rates for either sex might be assumed with almost equal plausibility, and the resulting variation in estimates of the refined activity rates for ages 10 and over would be appreciable, although not very large in any event. To illustrate, if the rates for ages 10 to 14 of both sexes were put at 15 percent as assumption (a) and 50 percent as assumption (b), the corresponding range of estimates of the refined rates for ages 10 and over would be as shown in Table C.e.

Table C.e

	Males	Females
As estimated	80.7	76.5
Assumption (a)	79.5	74.5
Assumption (b)	84.7	78.0

Because of the uncertainty of the estimates for age group 10 to 14 in many cases, activity rates for this age group are not shown in the tables although they are included in the totals for 10 years and over.

C.2. Adjustment to Standard Age Classification in Five-Year Groups

For the purposes of this study, the varied age groupings found in the census tabulations of the labor force were converted to a standard classification by five-year age groups from 10 to 74 years, 75 years and over. Where a category of age not reported was found in the census tabulations, it was eliminated by pro rata distribution among the age groups from 10 years up. (Unreported categories in age tabulations of the population, as well as the labor force, were dealt with in the same way.)

The conversion to the standard classification in five-year groups was done by interpolation and extrapolation of the specific activity rates for each sex in the age groups given by the census tabulations. Such interpolations and extrapolations were aided in many cases by using as models the rates for other countries where age classifications in the desired standard form were given. The results were adjusted to force agreement with the labor force numbers shown by the census tabulations for given age groups.

Conversion to the standard classification was ordinarily not attempted unless the census age classification of the labor force was given at least in five-year groups up to the age of 25 and ten-year groups between 25 and 65 years. Where only classifications in broader age groupings were available, simply the totals for 10 years and over by sex were used for the analyses in this study.

In Tables A.7 to A.10, Appendix A, age-specific activity rates that were estimated by interpolation and extrapolation are marked with an asterisk. The estimated rates for age groups under 65 years are seldom likely to be affected by significant errors. There is less reliability, on the whole, in estimated rates for the age groups 65 to 69, 70 to 74, and 75 years and over, which were often derived by uncertain extrapolations from data for the combined age group of 65 years and over.

Standardized and Refined Activity Rates

Levels of participation by males and females in the labor force of each country are measured in this study by standardized activity rates in the male and female population ten years of age and over (Stand$_m$ and Stand$_f$). These rates have been calculated by weighting the age-specific activity rates of each sex according to the proportions of the age groups within the total of ten years and over, for each sex, in a model population having approximately the same age structure as estimated for the world population as of 1960. The model was derived from the Coale-Demeny series of stable populations, "model West," mortality level 14 (female expectation of life at birth equal to 50 years), interpolated for an annual growth rate of 17.5 per 1,000.[1] Table D.1 shows the age composition of the model for each sex.

Table D.1. Model age structure of male and female population for calculation of standardized activity rates and related measures

Age	Males	Females
All ages	10,000	10,000
0-4	1,385	1,358
5-9	1,208	1,186
10-14	1,089	1,068
15-19	981	961
20-24	878	860
25-29	780	767
30-34	692	680
35-39	610	601
40-44	533	529
45-49	460	463
50-54	390	400
55-59	320	338
60-64	253	276
65-69	186	213
70-74	124	150
75 and over	111	150

Where age classifications of population and labor force were lacking or not in satisfactory form for calculating standardized

[1] Ansley J. Coale and Paul Demeny, *Regional Model Life Tables and Stable Populations* (Princeton, 1966).

rates, refined activity rates have been used as substitutes: that is, simple percentages of labor force members among the male and female population ten years of age and over (RAR_m and RAR_f). As a test of the reliability of refined rates as substitutes for standardized rates, Table D.2 shows the results of a comparison be-

Table D.2. Comparison of levels of refined activity rates (RAR_m and RAR_f) with standardized rates ($Stand_m$ and $Stand_f$) for regional groups of countries, cross-sectional censuses

Regional groups	No. of countries Total	Both RAR & Stand given	Frequency distribution of RAR/Stand Above 1.05	1.02- 1.05	1.00- 1.02	0.98- 1.00	0.95- 0.98	Below 0.95
Males								
All countries	100	84	1	9	19	22	24	9
1. Tropical Africa	15	8	1	1	3	2	1	-
2. Arab countries	9	7	-	-	-	3	2	2
3. Other Moslem countries	7	5	-	-	2	2	1	-
4. South and East Asia	16	16	-	1	2	7	4	2
5. Latin America, etc.	22	22	-	1	3	2	12	4
6. Eastern Europe	9	4	-	3	1	-	-	-
7. Middle Europe	7	7	-	1	5	1	-	-
8. Northwestern Europe, etc.	11	11	-	1	5	4	1	-
9. Miscellaneous	9	7	-	1	-	2	3	1
Females								
All countries	100	84	4	5	20	19	19	17
1. Tropical Africa	15	8	3	1	-	1	2	1
2. Arab countries	9	7	-	-	4	-	3	-
3. Other Moslem countries	7	5	1	-	2	2	-	-
4. South and East Asia	16	16	1	3	6	3	2	1
5. Latin America, etc.	22	22	-	-	6	9	6	1
6. Eastern Europe	9	4	-	-	2	1	1	-
7. Middle Europe	7	7	-	-	-	-	2	5
8. Northwestern Europe, etc.	11	11	-	-	1	1	-	9
9. Miscellaneous	9	7	-	1	-	3	3	-

tween the two for countries where both types of rates could be calculated as of the cross-sectional census dates.

In the case of males, with few exceptions, the refined activity rates do not differ greatly from standardized rates. Differences of less than 2 percent (ratios of $RAR_m/Stand_m$ between 0.98 and 1.02) are found in forty-one of the eighty-four countries, and differences exceeding 5 percent in only ten countries. A downward bias of refined rates for males predominates in the regional group of Latin America, Spain, and Portugal, where the ratio of $RAR_m/Stand_m$ falls below 0.98 in sixteen of the twenty-two countries. The use of refined rates as substitutes for standardized rates was, fortunately, not required for any countries in this region as of the cross-sectional census dates.

The opposite bias in male refined activity rates prevails among the Eastern European countries, where RAR_m exceeds $Stand_m$

in all of the four countries for which both types of rates could be calculated. In the five Eastern European countries where refined rates had to be used as substitutes for standardized rates, the effect may have been to overstate somewhat the levels of participation by males in the labor force.

In the case of females, considerable differences between refined and standardized activity rates occur more frequently. In seventeen of the eighty-four countries, the ratio of $RAR_f/Stand_f$ falls below 0.95. This downward bias of RAR_f occurs most frequently in the regional groups of middle Europe (five out of seven countries) and northwestern Europe, northern America, and Oceania (nine out of eleven countries). Substitution of RAR_f instead of $Stand_f$ was not, however, required for any countries in these two regional groups as of cross-sectional census dates. In four countries, the ratio of $RAR_f/Stand_f$ exceeds 1.05, but in two of these cases (Central African Republic and Guinea), the high ratio is patently due to gross errors in the age structure of the population shown by the census statistics.

Another measure of overall level of participation in the labor force by either sex is the gross years of active life (GYAL), shown in Tables A.7 to A.10. In the calculation of gross years of active life, the activity rates of all age groups are weighted equally instead of being weighted according to the structure of the model population. Designating the age-specific rates for either sex as $R(a)$, the measure is derived as follows:

$$ \text{GYAL} = \frac{5}{100} \sum_{a=10-14}^{a=75+} R(a) $$

The result is the average number of years in the labor force for a cohort of males or females having the activity rates at each age as recorded in the census, if no working years were lost by mortality. Its potential maximum, calculated according to the formula given above, would be seventy years in a population having activity rates of 100 percent in all ages from ten years up. (The group of seventy-five years and over is treated as a five-year age group like the others, as if all the population in this group were between seventy-five and eighty years of age.)

Since the measure of gross years of active life gives equal weight to the activity rates for all age groups, it serves better than the standardized activity rate to represent the average level of age-

226

specific rates. On the other hand, the levels of the rates for different age groups are not equally important for their effects on the relative size of the labor force; in this respect, the rates for ages 15 to 19, for example, are more important than those for ages 65 to 69. Standardized activity rates take account of the relative importance of age groups; and for this reason they are used in the present study to measure over-all levels of participation by males and females in the labor force. Gross years of active life are also useful supplementary measures in certain contexts.

Measures of Population Structure Effects

Effects upon crude activity rates of variations in the sex-age structure of population in different countries, as compared with the model used for calculating standardized activity rates, are measured by the indices discussed in chapter 4 and tabulated for each country in Appendix A, Table A.5 and A.6.

The net effect on the crude activity rate of all differences between the structure of the given population and that of the model is measured by the age-sex index (ASI). This is decomposed as follows into measures of effects of differences in particular features of the population structure:

$$ASI = AI_c + AI_m + AI_f + SI + RES$$

where AI_c represents the effect of difference between the given population and the model in the proportions of age groups under and over ten years in the population; AI_m and AI_f represent the effects of differences in age structure of the male and the female population ten years of age and over; SI represents the effect of difference in the sex ratio of population ten years of age and over; and RES is a residual due to interactions.

A method of standardization is used to calculate these indices, involving several standardized activity rates. In addition to the standardized rates for males and females ten years of age and over ($Stand_m$ and $Stand_f$), calculated as explained in Appendix D, a standardized rate for both sexes together in the population ten years of age and over ($Stand_t$) and one for both sexes in the total population of all ages ($Stand'_t$) are used. The latter rates are derived from $Stand_m$ and $Stand_f$ by the following equations:

$Stand_t = .4983516\ Stand_m + .5016484\ Stand_f$

$Stand'_t = .74315\ Stand_t$

The constants, .4983516 and .5016484, are the proportions of males and females in population ten years of age and over of the model (Table D.1), and .74315 is the ratio of the total of both sexes, ten years and over, to the total of all ages in the model population.

The age-sex index, ASI, is given by:

$ASI = CAR - Stand'_t$

that is, the difference between the crude activity rate in the given population and the corresponding rate which would obtain if the sex-age structure were the same as that of the model, with the age-specific activity rates of each sex as recorded in the given population.

For example, in the case of Bulgaria (1965), with CAR $=$ 51.87, $\text{Stand}_m = 66.04$, and $\text{Stand}_f = 53.69$,

$$\text{Stand}_t = (.4983516 \times 66.04) + (.5016484 \times 53.69) = 59.84$$
$$\text{Stand}'_t = .74315 \times 59.84 = 44.47$$
$$\text{ASI} = 51.87 - 44.47 = +7.40$$

AI_c, the component of ASI due to the proportions of population under ten and ten years of age and over, is given by:

$$\text{AI}_c = \text{Stand}_t \ (P_{10+}/P - .74315)$$

P_{10+}/P being the ratio of the age group ten years and over to the total in the given population and .74315 the corresponding ratio in the model. In the example of Bulgaria (1965), with $P_{10+}/P = .84335$, we have:

$$\text{AI}_c = 59.84 \times (+.10020) = +6.00^1$$

AI_m and AI_f, the components of ASI due to age structure of the male and female population ten years of age and over, are measured by differences between standardized and unstandardized (refined) activity rates of each sex, ten years and over, weighted with the proportions of males and females ten years and over to the total population:

$$\text{AI}_m = (\text{RAR}_m - \text{Stand}_m) \ \frac{P_{10+m}}{P}$$

$$\text{AI}_f = (\text{RAR}_f - \text{Stand}_f) \ \frac{P_{10+f}}{P}$$

In the example of Bulgaria (1965), with $\text{RAR}_m = 69.20$, $\text{Stand}_m = 66.04$, $\text{RAR}_f = 53.88$, $\text{Stand}_f = 53.69$, $P_{10+m}/P = .41972$, and $P_{10+f}/P = .42362$, we have:

[1] In calculating the indices shown in Appendix A, Tables A.5 and A.6, instead of P_{10+}/P, the ratio of CAR/RAR was substituted because the values of P had inadvertently been omitted from the punched cards. Slight errors due to rounding were introduced by this substitution: AI_c of $+5.99$ instead of $+6.00$ was obtained in the example of Bulgaria (1965). Analogous substitutions were made in the equations of the other indices defined below.

Appendix E

$$AI_m = +3.16 \times .41972 = +1.33$$
$$AI_f = +0.19 \times .42362 = +0.08$$

SI, the component of ASI due to the sex ratio in the population ten years and over, is measured by calculating differences between the proportions of males and females in the given population and the model, ten years of age and over, and weighting these differences by the standardized activity rates of males and females ten years and over:

$$SI = \frac{P_{10+}}{P} \left[\left(\frac{P_{10+m}}{P_{10+}} - .4983516 \right) Stand_m + \left(\frac{P_{10+f}}{P_{10+}} - .5016484 \right) Stand_f \right]$$

For Bulgaria (1965), with $\frac{P_{10+}}{P} = .84335$, $\frac{P_{10+m}}{P_{10+}} = .49769$,

$\frac{P_{10+f}}{P_{10+}} = .50231$, $Stand_m = 66.04$, and $Stand_f = 53.69$, we have:

$$SI = .84335 \left[(-.00066 \times 66.04) + (+.00067 \times 53.69) \right]$$
$$= -.0069$$

RES, the residual due to interaction, is obtained as the difference between ASI and the sum of $AI_c + AI_m + AI_f + SI$. This residual is small in all cases considered in this study, ranging from 0.00 to −0.04.

Where the necessary classifications of population and labor force by age groups for calculation of standardized activity rates were lacking, it was not possible to calculate AI_m and AI_f, but approximations to AI_c and SI were obtained by substituting the refined activity rate (RAR) instead of $Stand_t$ in the formula above for AI_c, and the refined rates for the two sexes (RAR_m and RAR_f) instead of the $Stand_m$ and $Stand_f$ in the formula for SI. An approximation to ASI was then obtained by assuming the sum of the missing components, AI_m and AI_f, to be negligible. Thus,

$$ASI' = AI_c + SI$$

That ASI' ordinarily provides a fairly close approximation to ASI is verified by Table E.1, which shows the frequency distribu-

230

Table E.1. Comparison of levels of ASI and ASI' for regional groups of countries, cross-sectional censuses

Regional groups	No. of countries		Frequency distribution of ASI' - ASI			
	Total	Both ASI and ASI' given	Above +2.0	0.0 to +2.0	-2.0 to 0.0	Below -2.0
All countries	100	84	5	59	18	2
1. Tropical Africa	15	8	-	5	2	1
2. Arab countries	9	7	1	5	-	1
3. Other Moslem countries	7	5	-	3	2	-
4. South and East Asia	16	16	1	8	7	-
5. Latin America, etc.	22	22	1	19	2	-
6. Eastern Europe	9	4	-	1	3	-
7. Middle Europe	7	7	1	4	2	-
8. Northwestern Europe', etc.	11	11	1	9	1	-
9. Miscellaneous	9	7	-	6	1	-

tion of differences between the two indices for countries in each regional group where both indices could be calculated as of cross-sectional census dates. The difference reaches ±2.0 or more in only seven countries (Austria 1961, +3.2; Puerto Rico 1960, +2.7; Jordan 1961, +2.4; Ireland 1961, +2.3; Ryukyu Islands 1960, +2.0; Tunisia 1966, +2.6; Central African Republic 1960, −5.5). The discrepancy in Central African Republic is due to gross error in the census data on age structure of the population. On the whole, ASI' tends to be biased upward as an estimate of ASI. This bias is most prevalent in the regional groups of Latin America, Spain, and Portugal and of northwestern Europe, northern America, and Oceania. An opposite bias prevails among the countries of Eastern Europe.

That the ratio between child and adult population is the most important feature of population structure relevant to the size of the labor force is indicated by the fact that in most cases, AI_c is much larger than the other partial indices. The largest positive and negative values of each partial index for cross-sectional census dates are in Table E.a. Extreme values of the indices are due in some cases to faults in the statistics of population by sex and age groups. Such faults explain the eccentric AI_m and AI_f for Central African Republic, AI_f for Guinea, and possibly AI_c for Togo, Dahomey, and Guinea.

Note that the values of ASI and the component indices do not depend only on the differences between the structure of the given country's population and the model, but also on the way in which these differences interact with the specific activity rates. With a given difference between $\dfrac{P_{10+}}{P}$ and the corresponding ratio in the

Appendix E

Table E.a

AI_c			
Austria, 1961	+6.4	Togo, 1958–60	−10.2
West Germany, 1961	+6.4	Dahomey, 1961	−9.2
Sweden, 1960	+6.1	Guinea, 1954/55	−6.3
AI_m			
Central African Rep., 1960	+1.5	Jordan, 1961	−2.4
Bulgaria, 1965	+1.3	Puerto Rico, 1960	−2.2
Switzerland, 1960	+1.3		
AI_f			
Central African Rep., 1960	+4.0	Austria, 1961	−2.5
Guinea, 1954/55	+2.0	West Germany, 1961	−2.1
		United Kingdom, 1961	−1.8
SI			
Pakistan, 1961	+1.7	Mozambique, 1950	−1.7
Singapore, 1957	+1.3	Portugal, 1960	−1.5
Libya, 1964	+1.2	East Germany, 1964	−1.2

model, values of AI_c will vary in proportion to the level of $Stand_t$. With given differences from the model as regards age structure of the population ten years and over of either sex, the values of AI_m and AI_f will vary both with the levels of $Stand_m$ and $Stand_f$ and with the forms of the age-curves of specific activity rates for each sex. In a population having the same activity rates for males or females in every age group from ten years up, AI_m or AI_f would be zero regardless of age structure. With a given difference from the model as regards the sex ratio in the population ten years and over, the value of SI will vary with the difference between $Stand_m$ and $Stand_f$. In a population in which $Stand_m$ and $Stand_f$ were equal, SI would be zero regardless of the sex ratio.

How the values of AI_m and AI_f are affected by the forms of age-curves of specific activity rates can be illustrated with the examples of females in Belgium (1961) and the United States (1960). These two countries have fairly similar age structures of adult population, both being "top-heavy" as compared with the model— that is, having larger proportions in the age groups above 35 or 45 years and smaller proportions in the younger groups, as shown by the comparison in Table E.2. Yet the values of AI_f are quite different: −1.65 for Belgium and −0.01 for the United States. The explanation is mainly in the fact that the activity rates of Belgian

Table E.2. Age structure of female population 10 years and over and female age-specific activity rates: Belgium (1961) and United States (1960)

Age (years)	Distribution of female population (percent)			Female activity rates	
	Model	Belgium 1961	U.S. 1960	Belgium 1961	U.S. 1960
10 years and over	100.0	100.0	100.0	23.5	31.3
10-14	14.3	8.7	11.5	2.4	1.8
15-19	12.9	7.5	9.2	40.6	27.6
20-24	11.5	6.9	7.7	52.2	44.8
25-29	10.3	7.6	7.7	36.5	35.1
30-34	9.1	8.2	8.5	31.2	35.5
35-39	8.1	8.4	8.9	30.0	40.2
40-44	7.1	6.7	8.2	30.0	45.3
45-49	6.2	7.1	7.7	28.4	47.4
50-54	5.4	7.8	6.8	25.3	45.8
55-59	4.5	7.7	6.0	20.1	39.6
60-64	3.7	7.1	5.2	9.4	29.5
65-69	2.9	5.9	4.6	5.4	16.6
70-74	2.0	4.5	3.6	3.5	9.6
75 and over	2.0	5.9	4.4	2.2	4.2

females are much higher in the younger than in the older groups, while the rates for the females in the United States are on a much more even plane in the age groups from 20 to 60 years.

Another way of measuring effects of population structure differences would be to select some sets of age-specific activity rates for males and females as a standard and see what the crude and refined activity rates of various countries would be, given their different population structures, if all had these same standard specific rates. This is what is done, in effect, when the population in a certain range of ages is taken to represent the "workers"— activity rates of 100 percent are assumed for these ages and rates of zero for younger and older groups. It would be more realistic to select for the standard some empirical model of activity rates according to sex and age.[2] But there will be little realism in the measures of population structure effects derived by such a method for countries where the actual activity rates are very different from the selected standard as regards their levels or forms of their age-curves.

[2] In United Nations, *The Aging of Populations and Its Economic and Social Implications* (New York, 1956), pp. 54ff., effects of varying age structures in model populations upon the relative size of the male labor force were explored with the use of two empirical models of male age-specific activity rates, typifying rates recorded in industrialized countries and in agricultural countries.

Appendix E

To illustrate with the data for Belgium and the United States: if the Belgian female age-specific activity rates are selected as the standard and applied to the female population structure of the United States, the resulting proportion of female labor force to female population ten years and over in the United States is 24.7 percent as compared with 23.5 percent for Belgium. The inference is that the age structure of the United States female population is slightly more favorable than that of Belgium to a large female labor force. But if the United States female age-specific rates are taken as the standard and applied to the Belgian age structure, the resulting proportion of female labor force to female population ten years and over in Belgium is 31.0 percent as compared with 31.3 percent for the United States, indicating almost no effect of the difference in age structure between the two countries.

In short, any method for measuring effects of population structure differences upon the relative sizes of the labor force in different populations is to some extent arbitrary. The method used for the present study has the advantage of taking into account the differences among countries in levels and age-curves of specific activity rates of the two sexes as well as the variations of population structure. While the selection of the model to serve as a standard for population structure is admittedly arbitrary, bias on this account is minimized by using a model that approximates the estimated structure of the world population instead of the structure of any particular country's population.[3]

[3] For further discussion of the problem of interactions in analysis of components of variations in labor force dimensions, see United Nations, *Methods of Analysing Census Data on Economic Activities of the Population* (New York, 1968), pp. 43–46.

Measures of Participation by Females in Agricultural and Nonagricultural Employment

The usual way of measuring participation by females (or males) in various occupation or industry sectors of employment is by occupation or industry-specific employment rates, which express the numbers employed in given sectors as percentages of the total female (or male) population of working ages. In the course of economic development, as the relative share of nonagricultural industries in total demand for labor expands, the participation by both females and males in the nonagricultural sector tends to increase and participation in agriculture to decrease. These trends are modified by sex-specific factors of labor demand and supply that affect the femininity of employment in each sector and thereby the trend of participation by females (and possibly also of males, to a lesser extent) in the labor force as a whole. To get a view of the influences of the latter factors, the percent shares of females in total agricultural and nonagricultural employment (FS_{ag} and FS_{nonag}) are used in this study as measures of sectoral participation by females.

In calculating these measures, the agricultural sector was identified with Division 0 of the International Standard Industrial Classification, including forestry, fishing, and hunting, as well as agriculture; and all other divisions of ISIC were allocated to the nonagricultural sector, including Division 9 (activities not adequately described). In the censuses of a few countries where the industry classifications deviated from the ISIC standard, mining was included in the agricultural sector or fishing and forestry in the nonagricultural sector, but these deviations would not substantially affect the measures. Industry classifications of employed workers were preferred as the basis for calculating female shares where they were available, but in some instances it was necessary to use classifications of the labor force including unemployed persons, who were allocated to the industries of their usual or most recent employment. In a few cases, occupational classifications were used as substitutes for industry classifications; the agricultural sector was then identified with the occupational group of "farmers, fisher-

235

men, hunters, loggers, and related workers" or similar rubrics in classifications provided by the census tabulations.

Female shares in both employment sectors are affected to some extent by the sex ratio in the population of working ages and the level of participation by males in the labor force, in addition to factors that pertain more directly to women's opportunities, propensities, and abilities to be employed. Table F.1 shows some

Table F.1. Examples of adjustment of female shares in agricultural and nonagricultural employment to eli effects of the sex ratio in the population 10 years of age and over and the refined activity of males

	FS_{ag}	FS_{nonag}	q_1	q_2	FS'_{ag}	FS'_{nonag}	FS''_{ag}	FS''_{nonag}	FS'''_{ag}	FS'''
U.S.S.R., 1959	54.0	44.2	.765	.840	41.3	33.8	45.4	37.1	34.7	28
Thailand, 1960	50.8	37.2	.998	.884	50.7	37.1	44.9	32.9	44.8	32
United States, 1960	9.3	33.6	.952	.772	8.9	32.0	7.2	25.9	6.9	24
Japan, 1960	51.8	33.0	.948	.811	49.1	31.3	42.0	26.8	39.8	25
Puerto Rico, 1960	1.7	31.3	.963	.618	1.6	30.1	1.1	19.3	1.0	18
Israel, 1961	18.9	26.5	1.026	.721	19.4	27.2	13.6	19.1	14.0	19
Singapore, 1957	34.5	16.3	1.144	.800	39.5	18.6	27.6	13.0	31.6	14
Singapore, 1966	24.1	21.5	1.023	.702	24.7	22.0	16.9	15.1	17.3	15

examples of the calculation of adjusted female shares that eliminate the influences of varying population sex ratios and male activity rates. FS'_{ag} and FS'_{nonag} represent the female shares that would obtain if, other factors being equal, the numbers of the two sexes in the population ten years of age and over were equal; these measures are derived by multiplying FS_{ag} and FS_{nonag} by the ratio of males to females in the population ten and over (q_1). FS''_{ag} and FS''_{nonag} represent the female shares that would obtain if, other factors being equal, 100 percent of the male population ten years of age and over were in the labor force; these are derived by multiplying FS_{ag} and FS_{nonag} by the factor, q_2, which is defined as follows:

$$q_2 = \frac{L_t}{P_{10+m} + L_f}$$

L_t denoting the labor force of both sexes, ten years and over; L_f the female labor force ten years and over; and P_{10+m} the male population ten years and over. Finally, FS'''_{ag} and FS'''_{nonag} represent the female shares that would obtain if, other factors being equal, the sex ratio in the population ten years and over were balanced, and at the same time all males ten years and over were in the labor force. These are derived by multiplying FS_{ag} and FS_{nonag} by the product of q_1 and q_2.[1]

The figures for the USSR (1959) provide an extreme example of the effect of an unbalanced sex ratio, due chiefly to the loss of lives of males in World War II. Comparing FS'_{ag} and FS'_{nonag} for the USSR with the corresponding measures for Thailand (1960), one sees that the difference in the population sex ratio is more than enough to account for FS_{ag} being 3.2 points higher and FS_{nonag} 7.0 points higher in the USSR than in Thailand.

The figures for Puerto Rico (1960) provide an extreme example of the effect of low participation by males in the labor force. Comparing FS''_{nonag} between Puerto Rico and Israel (1961), one can see that this factor is almost enough to account for FS_{nonag} being 4.8 points higher in Puerto Rico. Comparing the FS'''_{nonag} figures, one sees that Israel's FS_{nonag} would be a little higher than Puerto Rico's if the sex ratios were balanced and all males ten and over in both countries were in the labor force, other factors being equal. Likewise, in the comparison of FS'''_{nonag} between the United States (1960) and Japan (1960), one sees that with the effects of the differences in population sex ratio and male participation in the labor force eliminated, the female shares in nonagricultural employment would be a little higher in Japan than in the United States, whereas the opposite difference appears in the unadjusted figures.

The figures for Singapore provide an example of the effects of changes in the population sex ratio and the level of male participation in the labor force during the interval between two censuses. FS_{nonag} increased by 5.2 percentage points in Singapore between the 1957 and 1966 censuses, but the FS'''_{nonag} figures make it appear that this increase was due almost wholly to a decrease in the ratio of males to females in the population ten years and over, coupled with a decrease in the rate of participation by males in the labor force.

[1] Additional factors, which affect the levels of FS_{ag} and FS_{nonag}, but which are not taken into account in these calculations, include the employment rate of males (ratio of employed males to male labor force) for countries where the FS_{ag} and FS_{nonag} values are based on data for employed workers rather than total labor force; also the age limit of the tabulations of census data from which FS_{ag} and FS_{nonag} were derived, for countries where this limit was other than ten years.

Appendix F

The examples shown in Table F.1 are not typical; they were selected with a view to illustrating significant effects of variations in the population sex ratio and the level of participation by males in the labor force. On the whole, these factors do not play a primary role in shaping the patterns of international differences and time-trends of female shares in the two employment sectors.

Defects of Census Enumerations of Female Agricultural Workers and Unpaid Family Workers

G.1. *Examples of Underreporting of Female Workers in Agriculture*

The following examples are presented as illustrations of the tendency in the census returns of many countries to understate the numbers of females who take some part in agricultural work. This is by no means limited to the countries mentioned below.

North African countries. In the Algerian census of 1966,[1] only 23,315 females were returned as agricultural workers, but the census authorities estimated that about 1,200,000 additional females involved in farm work were not reported as economically active. A much larger number of female agricultural workers was returned in the 1954 census. Mainly on this account, the proportion of the total female population counted in the labor force was much higher in 1954: 25.2 percent as compared with 1.8 percent in 1966. If the estimate of unreported female agricultural workers in 1966 is added to the reported number, the percentage of the total female labor force to the total female population rises to 21.7. Other measures of labor force dimensions as of 1966 are affected as shown in Table G.a.

A similar anomaly appears in the statistics of Morocco, where the female refined activity rate (ten years and over) was 34.2 percent at the 1952 census and dropped to 9.2 percent at the 1960 census.[2] With reference to Tunisia, see the note in the next section on the effect upon measures of labor force dimensions as of the 1966 census due to omission of female unpaid family workers from the published labor force totals. In many other Arab countries and some non-Arab Moslem countries also, it appears likely that the statistics of recent censuses greatly under-

---

[1] Publications of the 1966 census of Algeria were not available to the author when the data for the present study were compiled. Data were taken from the I.L.O. *Yearbook of Labour Statistics* and Zdenek Vavra, "Demographic Patterns of Labour Force in Arab Countries" (Cairo Demographic Centre, Document SMP/71/P4, November 1971, mimeographed). See also Ahmed Bahri and B. Dellouci, "L'emploi en Algérie à travers le recensement de 1966," *Population* (Paris, numéro spécial, March 1971).

[2] Vavra, "Demographic Patterns," Table 1.

Table G.a

	As recorded	Including estimate of unreported female agricultural workers
Crude activity rate, both sexes	21.6	31.7
Female refined activity rate, ages		
10 and over	2.6	32.8
Female shares in employment:		
Agricultural sector (FS_{ag})	1.8	49.0
Nonagricultural sector (FS_{nonag})	7.7	7.7

state the numbers of females who take part, at least seasonally, in agricultural work. With reference to the Egyptian censuses, Nassef writes:

It is likely that underreporting of females in the labor force is an important factor in the low level of their recorded participation rate. In fact, any observer may see wives or daughters, particularly in rural areas, helping their husbands or fathers in various kinds of agricultural work such as picking cotton, watching cattle in the field, etc. That this work is not adequately reported may be due to the traditional line of thinking about women's role and/or to discounting of the importance of their part in the work of the farm.[3]

Latin American countries. In several countries in Latin America, where the most recent censuses show very few female workers in agriculture, much larger numbers were recorded in earlier censuses. The implication is that the questionnaires, definitions, and enumeration procedures in the recent censuses were framed in such a way as to minimize reporting of women's participation in the agricultural labor force.

In Peru, where the 1961 census showed 13.8 percent for the female share in agricultural employment, the ratio recorded in the 1940 census was 31.4 percent. The difference is scarcely credi-

[3] A. Nassef, *The Egyptian Labor Force: Its Dimensions and Changing Structure, 1907–1960* (University of Pennsylvania, Population Studies Center, Philadelphia, 1970), pp. 73–74. On underreporting of female workers in the census of Pakistan, especially in rural areas, see Ghazi M. Farooq, *Dimensions and Structure of Labor Force and Their Changes in the Process of Economic Development: A Case Study of Pakistan* (Ph.D. dissertation, University of Pennsylvania, 1970), pp. 47ff.

ble as a measure of change during the interval. The 1940 enumeration was based on a question about usual occupation, whereas a question about activity during a specified week was substituted at the 1961 census. It is possible that many females employed seasonally in agriculture may not have been employed during the 1961 census week.

In Colombia, FS_{ag} was less than 5 percent according to the censuses of 1964 and 1951, but 47 percent according to the 1938 census. Since the basis of enumeration in the Colombian censuses was usual occupation in 1938 and 1951, and activity during a specified week in 1964, a change in some other aspect of the definitions and procedures seems to have been responsible for the discrepancy between the 1938 and 1951 figures.[4]

In Honduras, where the census of 1961 (with a question on activity during a week) yielded FS_{ag} of 1.0 percent and a female standardized activity rate of 11.7, according to the 1950 census the refined rate was *58.3 (with a question about usual occupation). Although the 1950 census tabulations of Honduras did not give the classification of agricultural workers by sex, it is apparent that a large number of women must have been reported as active in agriculture. Because of the patent noncomparability of the 1950 and 1961 measures, the 1950 census data for Honduras were excluded from the compilation for this study.

Northwestern European countries. Female shares in agricultural employment recorded in recent censuses of several countries in northwestern Europe are listed in Table G.b.

In Sweden, an investigation of the 1960 census returns revealed that many farmers' wives who took part in farm work had not been reported as economically active. At the 1965 census, a special effort was made to improve enumeration of this segment of the labor force. The result is apparent in the jump of FS_{ag} to 2 1/2 times the 1960 level. There is little reason for believing that the true values of this ratio in Norway, Denmark, and the Netherlands are far below the Swedish level. The ratios recorded in Denmark

---

[4] Salazar and Reyes adjusted the 1938 Colombian census figures to conform with the definitions and classifications of the 1951 and 1964 enumerations. Their adjusted estimates indicate a female share of 11 percent in the primary sector of the labor force as of 1938. See Diego Salazar and Alvaro Reyes, "Análisis de la estructura y evolución de la fuerza de trabajo colombiana con base en los censos de población (1938–1964)," (Bogotá, Centro de Estudios sobre Desarollo Económico, Universidad de los Andes, 1969), p. 44.

Table G.b

		FS_{ag}
Sweden	1950	8.5
	1960	8.7
	1965	22.7
Norway	1950	7.5
	1960	4.6
Denmark	1950	23.4
	1960	9.4
Netherlands	1947	22.6
	1960	9.1

in 1950 and the Netherlands in 1947 were almost certainly nearer the truth than those indicated by the more recent censuses.[5]

Greece. FS_{ag} of 15.7 percent was recorded in Greece at the 1951 census. It jumped to 39.6 percent in 1961 as a result of improved enumeration. In this case, the effects on the levels of the female standardized activity rate and the crude activity rate were quite substantial. The 1951 census was omitted from the data compilation for this study in view of this discrepancy.

United States. A comparison between the returns of the 1960 U.S. census and estimates based on the Current Population Survey, in which the quality of reporting is superior, points to female workers in agriculture as one of the segments of the labor force that were least well enumerated in the census (Table G.c).[6] The female share in agricultural employment in the United States as calculated on the basis of the CPS data for April 1960 is 15.2 percent, instead of 10.0 percent as indicated by the census. Since April is not a high season for employment of women on farms, the annual average of FS_{ag} is higher: 18.3 for 1960, according to the CPS.

[5] The author is indebted to Dr. Ester Boserup for the information that a recent study of conditions of agriculture in Denmark (Danish Institute of Social Research, *The Social Consequences of Structural Changes in Danish Agriculture,* Copenhagen, 1970), showed the extent of women's participation in the agricultural labor force to be considerably greater than indicated by the 1960 census.

[6] Current Population Survey data from United States Bureau of Labor Statistics, Special Labor Force Report No. 14 (reprinted from *Monthly Labor Review,* April 1961), Table A–1. Census data from *United States Census of Population, 1960, United States Summary, Detailed Characteristics,* Table 210.

Table G.c

Employed civilians as of April 1960	Number according to census (Thousands)	Number according to CPS (Thousands)	Ratio, census/ CPS
Agriculture			
Males	3,973	4,575	.87
Females	442	819	.54
Other industries			
Males	41,713	39,574	1.05
Females	21,862	21,191	1.03

In April 1944, the current monthly sample survey of population and labor force in the United States was supplemented by a follow-up survey designed to verify the enumeration of female unpaid family workers in agriculture. The estimates obtained are shown in Table G.d.[7]

Table G.d

	Thousands of female unpaid family workers in agriculture, ages 14+
Enumerated in the regular current survey	860[a]
Enumerated in the follow-up survey	3,770
Missed by the regular survey	2,910
Worked 1–17 hours in the survey week	1,600
Worked 18 hours or more	1,310

[a] Including 200 thousand reported in the survey as nonagricultural workers.

General comment. Some understatement of female shares in the agricultural labor force may also occur in countries where the recorded shares are relatively large, but it is not easy to envisage deficiencies on the same proportionate scale as those indicated by the examples above occurring in countries such as Zaire, Ru-

[7] Louis J. Ducoff and Gertrude Bancroft, "Experiment in the Measurement of Unpaid Family Labor in Agriculture," *Journal of the American Statistical Association* 40 (1945), 205–13.

mania, and others, where females constitute a very large proportion of all workers enumerated in agriculture. It is hypothesized that underreporting in the censuses tends on the whole to be proportionately greater where women's actual contribution to agricultural labor supply is relatively minor than where it is major. Both the smallness of their actual contribution and the tendency to overlook what they do contribute may be viewed as expressions of low valuation of women's role as income producers compared with their role as homemakers and mothers. It is in the less developed countries, of course, where agriculture occupies a major share of the total labor force, that the errors and biases in enumeration of female agricultural workers have the greatest influence on the totals for the female labor force as a whole.

G.2. Correlation Between Recorded Female Shares in Agricultural and Nonagricultural Employment and the Sex Ratio of Rural-Urban Migration

If the examples in the preceding section make the reader wonder whether the census data on females in the agricultural labor force are at all related to reality, it is somewhat reassuring to note that there is a strong correlation between the relative levels of FS_{ag} and FS_{nonag} recorded in the censuses of different countries and the sex ratios of rural-urban migration, as might be expected if the measures were not wholly false. The hypothesis here is that higher FS_{nonag} than FS_{ag} implies greater opportunity for women's employment in urban than in rural areas, and consequently the female share in rural-urban migration should be relatively large.[8] Conversely, where FS_{nonag} is lower than FS_{ag}, the ratio of female to male migrants from rural to urban areas should be relatively low. The hypothesis is borne out by the comparison in Table G.1, where countries are cross-tabulated by directions of difference between FS_{ag} and FS_{nonag} and difference between the female shares in rural and urban population ten years of age and over (designated as FS_r and FS_u respectively). The latter measures serve reasonably well to indicate the sex ratios of net rural-urban migration. In more than three-fourths of all cases where both sets of data were ob-

---

[8] With reference to Chile, B. Herrick, *Urban Migration and Economic Development in Chile* (Cambridge, Mass., 1965) has suggested an explanation along this line for the preponderance of females among rural-urban migrants.

Appendix G

Table G.1. Differences between female shares in agricultural and nonagricultural employment (FS_{ag}, FS_{nonag}) and female shares in rural and urban population 10 years of age and over (FS_r, FS_u), in regional groups of countries, cross-sectional censuses

	Total	Region 1	Region 2	Region 3	Region 4	Region 5	Region 6	Region 7	Region 8	Region 9
Total number of countries	91	10	8	4	16	21	7	7	11	9
FS_{ag} exceeds FS_{nonag}:										
Total	36	5	1	2	14	1	7	4	-	3
FS_r exceeds FS_u	19	2	1	2	9	-	4	1	-	1
FS_u exceeds FS_r	5	-	-	-	1	-	3	1	-	-
FS_r, FS_u not available	12	3	-	-	4	1	-	2	-	2
FS_{nonag} exceeds FS_{ag}:										
Total	55	5	7	2	2	20	-	3	11	6
FS_u exceeds FS_r	40	-	1	-	1	19	-	3	11	5
FS_r exceeds FS_u	13	4	5	2	1	1	-	-	-	1
FS_r, FS_u not available	2	1	1	-	-	-	-	-	-	-
Total of parallel patterns	59	2	2	2	10	19	4	4	11	6
Total of opposite patterns	18	4	5	2	2	1	3	1	-	1
Total of FS_r, FS_u not available	14	4	1	-	4	1	-	2	-	2

tained, the directions of the differences are parallel, supporting the hypothesis stated above, and inspiring some confidence in the validity of the FS_{ag} and FS_{nonag} measures, at least as regards the directions of differences between them. It must be admitted, though, that agreement in directions of the differences is poor in Eastern European countries (region 6) and the Arab countries (region 2), and the data are not adequate to provide a good view of the pattern in tropical Africa and the non-Arab Moslem countries (regions 1 and 3).

Where the female share is greater in the rural than in the urban population but smaller in the agricultural than in the nonagricultural labor force, the possibility is suggested that the latter difference might be due to underreporting of female agricultural workers. Such a pattern is found in Namibia, Nigeria, Angola, Iraq, Jordan, and South Africa. Factors other than error in the labor force measures may, however, explain this kind of anomaly. Where the difference between female shares in agricultural and nonagricultural employment is small, as in Namibia, Angola, Iraq, and Jordan, according to the census returns, it can hardly be expected to have a very strong influence on the sex ratio among rural-urban migrants.

G.3. Enumeration of Female Unpaid Family Workers

It is especially the females who assist without pay in the work of family farms and other family-operated enterprises whose partici-

245

pation in the labor force goes to a large extent unreported in the censuses of many countries, while it is reported more fully in others. The numbers of female unpaid family workers shown by the census tabulations vary from less than 1 percent of the female population ten years of age and over in some countries to more than 50 percent in others. Table G.e shows some examples.

Table G.e

		Percentages of female population 10 years & over		
		Unpaid family workers	Others in labor force	Total in labor force
Guinea	1954/55	73.0	3.4	76.5
Liberia	1962	30.5	10.2	40.7
Ghana	1960	8.8	39.6	48.4
Botswana	1964	1.4	65.3	66.7
Sarawak	1960	42.6	8.2	50.8
Philippines	1960	7.9	16.5	24.4
Ceylon	1963	1.1	19.0	20.1
Bolivia	1950	40.0	19.0	59.0
Peru	1961	2.5	17.2	19.7
Ecuador	1962	1.1	14.7	15.8

The proportions of unpaid family workers should not be expected to be the same in all countries, since family enterprises play a much more important part in the economy in some countries than they do in others, and customs with regard to the participation of male and female family members in the work of such enterprises also vary. But the differences indicated by the census statistics are to a large extent unreal—artifacts of the definitions and enumeration procedures and of reporting biases rooted in the institutions and values of different cultures. While the variations occur chiefly in the reporting of women as unpaid family workers or housewives outside the labor force, practices vary also with regard to the classification by status of those counted in the labor force. For example in Botswana (1964), farmers' wives who took part in the farm work were apparently considered in most cases as partners in the farming enterprise and so were classified as self-employed rather than as unpaid family workers.

The reporting of female unpaid family workers may vary also between censuses in the same country. The figures for Czechoslovakia and Pakistan are remarkable examples (Table G.f). For Pakistan, these figures reinforce the suspicion that the sharp rise of the recorded activity rates of females between the 1951 and 1961 censuses was spurious. For Czechoslovakia, the figures suggest the possibility that women's participation in income-producing work may have increased between 1947 and 1961 even more than the census returns indicate.

Table G.f

| | | Percentages of female population 10 years & over | | |
		Unpaid family workers	Others in labor force	Total in labor force
Czechoslovakia	1947	17.3	22.0	39.3
	1961	0.5	45.0	45.5
Pakistan	1951	0.1	5.6	5.7
	1961	9.4	4.4	13.8

In Tunisia, about 250,000 female unpaid family workers enumerated in the 1966 census were not included in the labor force tabulations reproduced in the I.L.O. *Yearbooks of Labour Statistics.* The measures of activity rates calculated for the purposes of the present study have been adjusted to include these unpaid family workers. The effect is to raise the female refined activity rate from 4.5 to 22.1 percent and the crude activity rate of both sexes from 24.1 to 30.2. An industry classification of the unpaid family workers was, unfortunately, lacking, so it was not feasible to calculate adjusted measures of the female shares in agricultural and non-agricultural employment.

A device sometimes adopted for eliminating effects of spurious variations in the counts of unpaid family workers upon measures of labor force dimensions is to deduct unpaid family workers from the labor force totals. Appendix Table A.1 shows female standardized activity rates calculated on this basis (Stand$_f$ ex. UPFW) in addition to the rates calculated on the total labor force figures, for eighty-one countries for which the numbers of unpaid family workers were given. Excluding unpaid family workers, of course,

247

has the effect of lowering the mean level of the rates, and their variability as measured by the average deviation from the mean in the cross section is also diminished. The principal effect is to diminish the frequency of very high rates. Turkey's female refined activity rate (1960) drops from 62.7 including unpaid family workers to 8.0 excluding them; Guinea's rate (1954/55) drops from 76.5 to 3.6, and Thailand's (1960) from 75.3 to 13.8. Table G.g shows the frequency distributions of the female standardized rates with and without unpaid family workers.

Table G.g

	Including UPFW	Excluding UPFW
Under 10.0	7	14
10.0–19.9	19	30
20.0–29.9	20	19
30.0–39.9	14	14
40.0–49.9	10	2
50.0–59.9	5	1
60.0–69.9	3	1
70.0 & over	3	—
Total number	81	81

While excluding unpaid family workers eliminates much of the effect of error and noncomparability factors, it leaves a biased basis for comparisons of labor force dimensions. In comparing the United States and Turkey at the 1960 censuses, for example, while the female standardized activity rates including unpaid family workers (31.3 for the United States, 62.8 for Turkey) may exaggerate the relative contribution of women to the labor supply in Turkey, there is an opposite bias in the rates excluding unpaid family workers (30.6 for the United States, *8.0 for Turkey). There is a similar bias in time series of activity rates excluding unpaid family workers in a country undergoing industrialization. Since the relative share of family workers in the labor force typically decreases and the share of paid employees grows as industrialization advances, time series of such rates tend to exaggerate increases and minimize decreases in labor force participation.

Activity rates excluding unpaid family workers should not be considered as substitutes for total activity rates, therefore, but as supplementary measures, useful for testing the reliability of patterns of variations and focusing on a segment of the labor force that is measured more accurately and more consistently than the total. They can also be used to indicate an important aspect of the status of women, since unpaid family work does not afford the same independence that women may gain by employment for wages or self-employment.

Indicators of Economic Development

The index of relative development level of countries (RDL) used in this study is a composite of two economic indicators: energy consumption per head and percent share of the nonagricultural sector in total employment. These two indicators were compiled for each country as of the cross-sectional census year (or, for energy consumption, the nearest year in the time series published in the United Nations *Statistical Yearbooks*). The countries were ranked in ascending order of each of the two indicators, and the two rank numbers for each country were added together to derive the RDL index. Measures of energy consumption were lacking for three countries and of agricultural and nonagricultural employment for seven countries; in these cases, the missing indicator was estimated in view of the other indicator. The hundred countries were then grouped in quintiles of the RDL index, designated as Levels I, II, III, IV, and V. Table H.1 lists the countries in ascending rank order of the RDL within each quintile level, showing the values of the two indicators for each country.

   The RDL index, like other indicators of economic development, has its faults, but it seems to provide a more reliable ranking of countries by levels of development than is given by either of its components alone. While energy consumption and the nonagricultural share in employment are highly correlated, each deviates rather widely in some instances from the level typically corresponding to the given level of the other, as shown by the cross-tabulation in Table H.2. So the combination of the two in the RDL index helps to minimize erratic indications. Among countries where energy consumption appears to give an exaggerated indication of the development level are Bulgaria, Mexico, Poland, Rumania, Sarawak, South Africa, Trinidad and Tobago, and Venezuela. The nonagricultural share in employment is subject to a different bias, which is most plainly apparent in Hong Kong and Singapore, and can be seen also in other countries such as Jordan, Libya, Mauritius, Nigeria, Paraguay, Tunisia, and Uruguay. Underreporting of female workers in agriculture may be a part of the explanation in some of these cases. If the nonagricultural share were calculated with reference to male workers instead of the total of both sexes,

250

Table H.1. Ranking of countries by relative development level (RDL rank), energy consumption per head (Energy), and percent share of nonagricultural sector in total employment (Nonagricultural share): cross-sectional census years

RDL rank	Energy[a]	Nonagri-cultural share	RDL rank	Energy[a]	Nonagri-cultural share
RDL Level I					
1. Nepal, 1961	.004	6.2	11. Khmer Republic, 1962	.04	19.7
2. Portuguese Guinea, 1950		7.9	12. Thailand, 1960	.06	17.6
3. Botswana, 1964		9.2	13. Mozambique, 1950	.06	24.5
4. Haiti, 1950	.02	14.7	14. Sierra Leone, 1963	.07	22.7
5. Togo, 1958/60	.02		15. Pakistan, 1961	.07	24.4
6. Guinea, 1954/55	.03		16. Liberia, 1962	.12	19.1
7. Dahomey, 1961	.03		17. Sabah, 1960	.14	19.5
8. Sudan, 1956	.04	13.4	18. Bolivia, 1950	.09	27.9
9. Central African Rep., 1960	.04		19. Angola, 1960	.08	31.0
10. Zaire, 1955/57	.07	13.0	20. Nigeria, 1963	.03	43.2
RDL Level II					
21. Indonesia, 1961	.14	28.1	31. Dominican Republic, 1960	.16	38.6
22. India, 1961	.15	27.1	32. Paraguay, 1962	.10	45.3
23. Ghana, 1960	.10	38.2	33. South Korea, 1960	.26	34.1
24. Senegal, 1960/61	.10		34. Ceylon, 1963	.11	47.1
25. Morocco, 1960	.14	37.9	35. Sarawak, 1960	.71	18.6
26. El Salvador, 1961	.12	39.4	36. Ecuador, 1962	.17	44.4
27. Philippines, 1960	.15	35.0	37. Nicaragua, 1963	.27	40.4
28. Turkey, 1960	.25	25.1	38. Namibia, 1960		41.5
29. Honduras, 1961	.19	30.6	39. West Malaysia, 1957	.34	41.5
30. Guatemala, 1964	.18	34.6	40. United Arab Republic, 1960	.29	43.7
RDL Level III					
41. Algeria, 1966	.37	43.3	51. Ryukyu Islands, 1960	.27	57.3
42. Costa Rica, 1963	.25	50.7	52. Yugoslavia, 1961	.90	42.8
43. Syria, 1960	.26	49.8	53. Jordan, 1961	.25	62.2
44. Iraq, 1957	.35	45.0	54. Panama, 1960	.49	48.9
45. Taiwan, 1956	.39	44.4	55. Peru, 1961	.51	48.9
46. Tunisia, 1966	.24	57.4	56. Portugal, 1960	.38	56.8
47. Albania, 1960	.30		57. Iran, 1966	.40	53.8
48. Brazil, 1960	.34	48.4	58. Colombia, 1964	.49	52.7
49. Mauritius, 1962	.16	61.9	59. Libya, 1964	.32	61.0
50. Greece, 1961	.46	45.7	60. Mexico, 1960	.91	45.8
RDL Level IV					
61. Rumania, 1966	2.07	42.9	71. Finland, 1960	1.65	64.5
62. Jamaica, 1960	.52	59.1	72. Hungary, 1960	2.08	61.6
63. Cuba, 1953	.60	58.5	73. Uruguay, 1963	.79	81.7
64. Spain, 1960	.82	58.7	74. Italy, 1961	1.22	70.9
65. Guyana, 1960	.57	62.8	75. Ireland, 1961	2.06	64.0
66. Cyprus, 1960	.82	60.5	76. Puerto Rico, 1960	1.46	75.7
67. Bulgaria, 1965	2.56	55.7	77. Hong Kong, 1961	.51	92.6
68. Chile, 1960	.84	71.7	78. Argentina, 1960	1.09	82.0
69. Japan, 1960	1.17	67.4	79. Trinidad & Tobago, 1960	1.94	79.0
70. Poland, 1960	3.10	52.3	80. Singapore, 1957	.65	91.5
RDL Level V					
81. South Africa, 1960	2.38	68.2	91. Denmark, 1960	2.83	82.5
82. Venezuela, 1961	2.64	64.7	92. Sweden, 1960	3.49	86.2
83. Israel, 1961	1.39	86.4	93. Netherlands, 1960	2.69	89.3
84. Austria, 1961	2.18	77.2	94. West Germany, 1961	3.63	86.6
85. U.S.S.R., 1959	2.79	64.8	95. Australia, 1961	3.97	89.0
86. New Zealand, 1961	1.96	85.5	96. East Germany, 1964	5.58	
87. France, 1962	2.60	80.0	97. Canada, 1961	5.65	87.9
88. Switzerland, 1960	1.94	86.7	98. Belgium, 1961	4.14	92.6
89. Norway, 1960	2.74	80.5	99. United Kingdom, 1961	4.90	95.7
90. Czechoslovakia, 1961	5.09	75.1	100. United States, 1960	8.05	93.2

a
Equivalent of metric tons of coal consumed annually per head.

Appendix H

Table H.2. Cross-tabulation of frequency distributions of energy consumption per head and percent share of the nonagricultural sector in employment: cross-sectional census years

Nonagricultural share in employment (percent)	Energy consumption[a]								
	Total	Under .10	.10-.25	.25-.50	.50-1.00	1.00-2.00	2.00-3.00	3.00 & over	N.A.
Total	100	18	17	18	13	9	12	10	3
Under 20	11	6	2	-	1	-	-	-	2
20-30	7	4	3	-	-	-	-	-	-
30-40	9	2	6	1	-	-	-	-	-
40-50	19	2	2	10	3	-	1	-	1
50-60	11	-	1	5	3	-	1	1	-
60-70	12	-	2	1	2	2	5	-	-
70-80	7	-	-	-	1	3	2	1	-
80-90	12	-	-	-	1	4	3	4	-
90 and over	5	-	-	-	2	-	-	3	-
N.A.	7	4	1	1	-	-	-	1	-

[a] Equivalent of metric tons of coal consumed annually per head.

the levels of this indicator for most countries in Latin America would be lowered appreciably.

Two principal indicators of the speed of economic development of countries during intervals between postwar censuses are used in this study: the annual growth rate of gross domestic product per head ("GDP growth rate") and the annual increase in percent share of the nonagricultural sector in total employment ("increase of nonagricultural share"). Table H.3 shows the cross-tabulation

Table H.3. Cross-tabulation of frequency distributions of GDP growth rate and increase of nonagricultural share in employment, in countries where measures of intercensal changes in labor force dimensions were obtained

Increase of nonagricultural share[a]	GDP growth rate[b]							
	Total	Under 1.0	1.0-1.9	2.0-2.9	3.0-3.9	4.0-5.9	6.0 & over	N.A.
Total	58	5	11	12	8	7	8	7
Under .20	7	2	2	1	1	-	-	1
.20-.39	6	1	2	3	-	-	-	-
.40-.59	12	-	3	2	2	1	-	4
.60-.79	12	2	2	5	1	1	-	1
.80-.99	5	-	-	1	1	2	1	-
1.00 and over	13	-	1	-	2	3	6	1
N.A.	3	-	1	-	1	-	1	-

[a] Annual increase in percent share of nonagricultural sector in total of employed workers or labor force. Under .20 includes 2 countries where a decrease was recorded.

[b] Annual percent growth rate of gross domestic product per head during periods approximating the intercensal intervals. Under 1.0 includes 1 country where a negative rate was indicated.

252

of the two for the fifty-eight countries for which measures of inter-censal changes in male and female activity rates were obtained. The GDP growth rates were compiled from the United Nations *Yearbooks of National Accounts Statistics*, for periods correspond-ing as closely as the given time series would permit to the intervals between the censuses. For the socialist countries of Eastern Eu-rope, the growth rates are not strictly comparable with the mea-sures for other countries, but they have been used without adjust-ment for the analysis in this study.

The GDP growth rate and the increase of the nonagricultural share in employment are highly correlated, but there are con-siderable discrepancies between them in several cases, as Table H.3 shows. Notable instances of relatively low GDP growth rates associated with relatively high rates of increase in the nonagri-cultural share occur in Canada, Guyana, West Malaysia, and South Africa.

The rate of increase in the nonagricultural share in employment as calculated here has an inherent bias toward understatement of the speed of development in countries where the nonagricultural share is already very large. This bias would be even stronger if the rate were expressed in proportion to the initial level of the non-agricultural share, while an opposite bias would result from ex-pressing the rate in proportion to the initial level of the agricul-tural share. To illustrate, denote by p_1 and p_2, respectively, the percent shares of the nonagricultural sector in employment at the beginning and at the end of the intercensal period and by n, the number of years in the interval. Then the rate of shift from the agricultural to the nonagricultural sector as defined for the pur-pose of this study is:

$$r = \frac{p_2 - p_1}{n}$$

Alternative measures are:

$$r' = \frac{100\,r}{p_1}$$

$$r'' = \frac{100\,r}{100 - p_1}$$

Appendix H

The opposite biases of r and r' on the one hand and of r'' on the other are illustrated by the comparison in Table H.a.

Table H.a

Level of p_i	No. of countries	Median values of rates			GDP
		r	r'	r''	
Above 80.0	8	.42	.48	3.2	1.8
60.0–79.9	13	.76	.97	3.1	3.4
40.0–59.9	21	.69	1.30	1.4	3.0
20.0–39.9	12	.58	1.88	.8	2.4
Under 20.0	4	.30	1.93	.4	—

As an indicator of the speed of economic development, there seems to be little logical basis for preference among the three measures, r, r', and r''; but if the question of main interest is the influence of the agricultural-nonagricultural shift in employment structure upon the trends of participation in the labor force, it appears preferable to use r as the measure.

Index

Index

Cuba, 15, 35, 57, 163, 166, 172, 176, 180, 188, 196, 202, 251
Cyprus, 164, 167, 173, 177, 251
Czechoslovakia, 21, 51, 52, 163, 168, 172, 182, 190, 208, 247, 251

Dahomey, 16, 21, 31, 67, 162, 171, 231, 232, 251
Danish Institute of Social Research, 242
Davis, Lance E., 3
Dellouci, B., 239
Demeny, Paul, 224
Denmark, 90, 104, 164, 169, 173, 184, 192, 208, 213, 241, 242, 251
domestic service, 124–126
Dominican Republic, 16, 35, 163, 172, 180, 188, 251
Ducoff, Louis J., 243
Durand, John D., 5

Easterlin, Richard A., 110, 140
Ecuador, 21, 26, 32, 57, 163, 166, 168, 172, 176, 180, 196, 202, 246, 251
Egypt, see United Arab Republic
Elias, Andrew, 52, 215
El Salvador, 26, 135, 163, 166, 168, 170, 172, 176, 180, 188, 196, 202, 251
energy consumption, 250–252

factors influencing labor force dimensions and trends, 94–100, 123–128; level of development, 78–92, 101–113, 123–142, 147–157; speed of development, 114–117, 143, 155, 156; employment structure, 34, 51, 57, 69, 97, 98, 114–117, 124, 129–131, 136–138, 141–144, 151–155; urbanization, 26–28, 33, 108, 117–121, 141, 152, 155; wage and income levels, 98, 99, 128; labor demand, 19, 96–98, 127; marriage, fertility, and child mortality, 37–39, 59, 127, 128; cultural and institutional factors, 102, 127, 138, 154; substitution of sexes, 143–146; population structure, see age-sex index
Farooq, Ghazi, 93, 123, 210, 240
female shares in agricultural and nonagricultural employment, 33–36, 50–57, 60–63, 67–69, 72,

75, 76, 130–132, 135–146, 151–153, 156, 162–170, 218, 235–238, 244, 245
female shares in rural and urban population, 244, 245
Finegan, T. Aldrich, 19, 32, 100, 128
Finland, 60, 62, 164, 167, 169, 173, 176, 182, 190, 198, 204, 251
France, 60, 62, 123, 164, 169, 173, 182, 190, 209, 213, 251

Gambia, 70
Germany, East, 88, 164, 173, 208, 232, 251
Germany, West, 17, 35, 60, 62, 88, 90, 104, 164, 169, 173, 182, 190, 209, 214, 232, 251
Ghana, 38, 40, 67, 162, 166, 171, 178, 186, 194, 200, 246, 251
Greece, 60, 87, 164, 167, 173, 176, 182, 190, 198, 204, 212, 214, 242, 251
gross domestic product, growth rate, 114–117, 143, 144, 155, 156, 250–254
gross years of active life (GYAL), 178–207, 226, 227
Guatemala, 23, 26, 163, 166, 168, 170, 172, 176, 180, 188, 196, 202, 251
Guinea, 16, 31, 54, 162, 166, 171, 175, 178, 186, 194, 200, 221, 222, 226, 231, 232, 246, 248, 251
Guyana, 17, 68, 164, 167, 169, 170, 173, 177, 184, 192, 198, 206, 208, 251, 253

Haiti, 15, 17, 21, 26, 31, 35, 68, 87, 164, 174, 184, 192, 251
Herrick, B., 244
Honduras, 21, 26, 35, 163, 172, 180, 188, 211, 212, 241, 251
Hong Kong, 16, 17, 32, 90, 164, 169, 174, 184, 192, 250, 251
Hungary, 17, 32, 50–52, 60, 62, 90, 164, 168, 173, 182, 190, 251

India, 38, 40, 70, 123, 132, 162, 166, 171, 175, 178, 186, 194, 200, 210, 251
Indonesia, 54, 69, 162, 166, 171, 175, 178, 186, 194, 200, 251

256

Index

LIBRARY OF CONGRESS CATALOGING IN PUBLICATION DATA

Durand, John Dana.
  The labor force in economic development.

  Includes bibliographical references.
  1. Underdeveloped areas—Labor Supply.   I. Title.
HD5852.D87   331.1′1′091724   75-2988
ISBN 0-691-04207-1

CPSIA information can be obtained
at www.ICGtesting.com
Printed in the USA
LVHW022348270120
644934LV00010B/159